American Book Company

The Standards Experts

Passing the

Georgia End Of Course Test

9th Grade Literature & Composition

Written to the new 9th grade GPS Standards

Michael Kabel

Dr. Frank J. Pintozzi, Executive Editor

American Book Company
PO Box 2638
Woodstock, GA 30188-1383
Toll Free: 1 (888) 264-5877   Phone: (770) 928-2834
Fax: (770) 928-7483   Toll Free Fax: 1 (866) 827-3240
www.americanbookcompany.com

ACKNOWLEDGEMENTS

The author would like to gratefully acknowledge the formatting and technical contributions of Marsha Torrens.

Chapter Two includes an excerpt from the novel *Ask the Dust* by John Fante. Copyright Harper Collins Publishers, 2006.

This product/publication includes images from CorelDRAW 9 and 11 which are protected by the copyright laws of the United States, Canada, and elsewhere. Used under license.

Table of Contents

Chapter 3   Fiction, Nonfiction, Poetry & Drama   67

9RL1, 9RL3, 9RL4
9RC1, 9RC4

Chapter 4   Information Gathering & Research Skills   83

9W2, 9W3

Chapter 5   Planning & Drafting The Written Composition   99   9W1, 9W2, 9W3

Chapter 6   Revising the Written Composition   127   9W4

viii

Georgia 9th Grade Literature & Composition Preface

Passing The Georgia 9th Grade End of Course Test In Literature & Composition will help students who are learning or reviewing GPS standards for the Georgia 9th Grade End of Course Test in Literature and Composition. The materials in this book are based on the EOC test assessment standards as published by the Georgia Department of Education.

This book contains several sections:

1) General information about the book itself

2) A diagnostic pretest

3) An evaluation chart

4) Eight chapters that teach the concepts and skills needed for test readiness

5) Two practice tests

Standards are posted at the beginning of each chapter as well as in a correlation chart included in the answer manual.

<hr>

We welcome comments and suggestions about this book. Please contact us at

American Book Company
PO Box 2638
Woodstock, GA 30188-1383

Call Toll Free: (888) 264-5877
Phone: (770) 928-2834
Toll Free Fax: 1 (866) 827-3240

Or visit us online at
www.americanbookcompany.com

Michael Kabel was English & Language Arts Director for American Book Company. He received his Masters of Fine Arts in Writing from the University of New Orleans and has worked in media, public relations and publishing for fourteen years. His original fiction has appeared in numerous print and online publications, including *JMWW* and *The Baltimore Review.*

Dr. Frank J. Pintozzi is a former Profeesor of Education at Kennesaw (GA) State University. For over 28 years, he has taught English and reading at the high school and college levels as well as in teacher preparation courses in language arts and social studies. In addition to writing and editing state standard-specific texts for high school exit and end of course exams, he has edited and written numerous college textbooks.

INTRODUCTION TO THE GEORGIA 9TH GRADE EOCT IN LIT. AND COMP.

The **Georgia 9th Grade End of Course Test in Literature and Composition** is administered to all Georgia ninth-grade students as part of their course requirements for promotion to the tenth grade. This book offers complete preparation for that test and meets all GPS performance standards as described by the Georgia Department of Education.

In this book, you will prepare for the Georgia 9th Grade EOCT in Literature and Composition. First, you will take a pretest to determine your strengths and areas for improvement. In the chapters, you will learn and practice the skills and strategies important to preparing for the test. The last section contains two practice tests that will provide further preparation for the actual test.

FREQUENTLY ASKED QUESTIONS

Will this test be used to determine promotion for ninth graders?

Yes. The EOCT is the final exam in 9th Grade Literature and Composition classes and counts as fifteen percent of a student's final grade. All students must score at least a seventy percent to receive promotion to the tenth grade.

What is tested?

The reading test checks your literary comprehension, understanding of literary devices, skills at literary and factual analysis, grammar skills, and information discussion skills.

When do I take the test?

Students will take the test either in the fall/winter, spring, or summer of their ninth grade year, depending on their school district.

How much time do I have to take the exam?

The test is typically given in two sections of 45 – 60 minutes each. Individual school districts will determine either a one- or two-day test administration schedule.

When will I get the results?

School districts will determine how students will receive their test results.

How is the test scored?

The scores on the Georgia 9th Grade EOCT in Literature and Composition are reported between 200 and 700. A score of 400 is considered passing, while a score of 450 exceeds expectations. The scores are then translated to a 100-point scale for teachers to compute the student's final course grade. In this translation, a score of 400 converts to a score of 70 (passing), while a score of 450 converts to 90 (exceptional).

Where can I find additional test information?

The Web site of the Georgia Department of Education's Testing Program is http://public.doe.k12.ga.us/ci_testing.aspx.

Test-Taking Tips

1. Complete the chapters and practice tests in this book. This text will help you review the skills for the Georgia 9th Grade End of Course Test in Literature and Composition. The book also contains materials for reviewing skill standards established by the Georgia Department of Education.

2. Be prepared. Get a good night's sleep the day before your exam. Eat a well-balanced meal that contains plenty of proteins and carbohydrates.

3. Arrive early. Allow yourself at least 15 – 20 minutes to find your room and get settled before the test starts.

4. Keep your thoughts positive. Tell yourself you will do well on the exam.

5. Practice relaxation techniques. Talk to a close friend or see a counselor if you stress out before the test. They will suggest ways to deal with anxiety. Some other quick anxiety-relieving exercises include:

>   **1. Imagine yourself in your most favorite place.** Sit there and relax.
>
>   **2. Do a body scan.** Tense and relax each part of your body starting with your toes and ending with your forehead.
>
>   **3. Use the 3-12-6 method.** Inhale slowly for 3 seconds. Hold your breath for 12 seconds, and then exhale slowly for 6 seconds.

6. Read directions carefully. If you don't understand them, ask the proctor for further explanation before the exam starts.

7. Use your best approach for answering the questions. Some test-takers like to skim the questions and answers before reading the problem or passage. Others prefer to work the problem or read the passage before looking at the answers. Decide which approach works best for you.

8. Answer each question on the exam. Unless you are instructed not to, make sure you answer every question. If you are not sure of an answer, take an educated guess. Eliminate choices that are definitely wrong and then choose from the remaining answers.

9. Record your answers carefully. Make sure the number on your question matches the number on your answer sheet. If you need to change your answer, erase it completely. Smudges or stray marks may affect the grading of your exams, particularly if the tests are scored by a computer. If you take your test on a computer, be sure that you answer each question. Computers are now part of our daily lives, but test taking strategies vary only slightly over time.

10. Check your answers. Review your exam to make sure you have chosen the best responses. Change answers only if you are absolutely sure they are wrong.

Georgia 9th Grade Literature & Composition Diagnostic Pretest

The purpose of this diagnostic pretest is to measure your progress in reading comprehension, grammar, and critical thinking. This pretest is based on the **Georgia Performance Standards** and adheres to the sample question format provided by the Georgia Department of Education.

General Directions:

1. Read all directions carefully.

2 Read each question or sample. Then choose the best answer.

3 Choose only one answer for each question. If you change an answer, be sure to erase your original answer completely.

4 After taking the test, you or your instructor should score it using the answer key that accompanies this book. Then use the evaluation chart to review and practice for the reading comprehension and critical thinking skills tested on the End of Course Test.

Read this selection. Then answer the questions that follow it.

The Making of a Marine

1   The large, bulky bus slowed down as it turned onto a long, narrow bridge. The bridge led to an obscure island in the distance and was lined with dimly lit street lamps. The vibration, caused by the bus rolling over the planks of the bridge, startled me out of my listless sleep. I cupped my hands around my eyes and peered out of the dust-covered window. All that was visible, as far as I could see, was the somber water leisurely moving below the bridge. Little did I realize that this bridge was the beginning of my passage from boyhood to manhood in the Marines.

2   Suddenly, the interior bus lights flashed on. I had to blink several times to adjust my eyes to the unexpected flow of bright light. A husky, darkly tanned man stood up and faced the group of boys on the bus. He was immaculately dressed in a sharply pressed uniform, with rows of ribbons and badges over his left pocket. He looked like my grandfather, in the picture that had inspired me to join the military. The bus jerked to a stop, and the man who stood up introduced himself as the drill instructor. Then I and the rest of the boys on the bus were issued the first of many commands: "Recruits, get off the bus, NOW! Move, move, move!"

3   I joined the ranks of many other boys coming off the bus, and they all moved through the small door leading to the receiving barracks. Glancing at the sign above the door, I silently read to myself: "THROUGH THIS PORTAL PASS PROSPECTS FOR THE WORLD'S FINEST FIGHTING FORCE: THE UNITED STATES MARINE CORPS." This was it. The process of becoming a Marine was beginning for me, and I couldn't turn back now.

4   The first few weeks were the toughest. The drill instructors concentrated on breaking down the morale and hard-fast habits of all the recruits in our group. I had to learn to start living all over, I had to learn how to dress, eat, even go to the bathroom. I learned that every action of the day was limited to a certain time period. When it was time for chow, all of us recruits marched to the chow hall together. Inside the chow hall every recruit carried all of the trays, plates, and utensils the same way. We were taught how to fold our clothes, brush our teeth, and make a bed (known as a rack). There was even a specific form of vocabulary we were instructed to use. We were also introduced to the basics of military life which included marching, shining boots, and the use of a rifle (never called a gun).

5   The first phase examined the recruits' mental processes and was the hardest emotionally. The second phase began to test our physical abilities. Day after day was spent running in the scorching heat, with a ten-pound backpack on my back. I quickly learned that the purpose of running is more than just exercise: it is for the sake of staying alive. I and my group learned how to repel off seventy-five foot towers, crawl through live mine fields, run through obstacle courses, and tread water.

6   Boot camp became progressively harder as I moved from the second phase of training to the third phase of actually performing certain procedures. All of the recruits in my group had to fire their rifles and pistols, throw live grenades, and successfully complete their individual combat training courses. Several recruits began to drop out in the third phase due to the stress and difficulty of this stage. I began to see changes occurring in my life. I was becoming physically fit, more confident, and proficient in a leadership role.

7   The fourth, and final phase of training was graduation. As graduation approached, I found it difficult to sleep due to all the excitement. I quickly learned how to control my anxiety because there was still a great deal of work to prepare for in the final drill. The sun sparkled off of the neatly polished shoes of the recruits as we marched onto the parade deck. The feeling of pride in ourselves, our country, and our sense of accomplishment radiated from all the Marines in the group. I made a sharp right turn into the sunlight to face the crowd of onlookers. A smile turned up the corners of my mouth as I straightened my back to stand just a little taller.

8   I had made it through the process of becoming a Marine, an accomplishment not everyone can claim. I had also achieved a personal goal that changed me from a boy to an independent man. I had become a Marine!

1   Read this sentence from paragraph 1.   9RL5

> "All that was visible, as far as I could see, was the somber water leisurely moving below the bridge."

As used in the sentence, somber means

A   quiet.
B   dark.
C   flooded.
D   polluted.

2   Which of these contains a simile?   9RL1

A   Suddenly, the interior bus lights flashed on.
B   He looked like my grandfather, in the picture that had inspired me to join the military.
C   The drill instructors concentrated on breaking down the morale and hard-fast habits of all the recruits in our group.
D   I learn that every action of the day was limited to a certain time period.

3   Which of the following best explains the targeted audience of the passage?   9W2

A   people who have retired from the military
B   young people who may be thinking of joining the military
C   drill sergeants
D   people who have dropped out of basic training

4   Which of the following explains the author's point of view?   9RL1

A   first person
B   second person
C   third person limited
D   third person omniscient

5   The reader learns about the young man mainly through   9RL1

A   dialogue.
B   his own actions.
C   what others say about him.
D   his physical characteristics.

6   What is the correct punctuation for this sentence from paragraph 4?   9C2

A   I had to learn to start living all over: I had to learn how to dress, eat, even go to the bathroom.
B   I had to learn to start living all over I had to learn how to dress, eat, even go to the bathroom.
C   I had to learn to start living all over; I had to learn how to dress, eat, even go to the bathroom.
D   I had to learn to start living all over? I had to learn how to dress, eat, even go to the bathroom.

Read the following selection. Then answer the questions that follow it.

Mahalia Jackson Sang Pure Gospel

by Reginald Taylor
from *Turner Hill Times*, 20 September 2003

1   Her voice could be heard pouring out from many places: churches, symphonic halls, and even the Lincoln Memorial.

2   "Don't need any microphone," she said. "Just open the windows and the doors. And let the sound pour out."

3   Born in New Orleans in 1911, Mahalia Jackson grew up in the midst of urban poverty and the black exodus to the industrial cities of the North. In spite of this, Jackson was a happy person. She credits her happiness to her religious background which she was immersed in from a young age.

4   She first discovered her musical talent singing gospel hymns in the church. Others, including her husband, urged her to sing the secular music of the blues and jazz. However, she refused to change. "The blues are fine for listenin'," she said. "But I never would sing them. I was saved. Remember David in the Bible: Sing joyfully unto the Lord with a loud voice? I took his advice."

5   Jackson grew famous as record producers discovered her talent for singing gospel music. In 1958, she had the opportunity to collaborate with the great musical artist, Duke Ellington. In later years, Aretha Franklin would describe Jackson as her inspiration for singing.

6   But who were the influences in the life of Mahalia Jackson? Jackson heard the music of her muse as a teenager while working as a housekeeper. "When the old people weren't home and I'd be scrubbin' the floor, I'd turn on a Bessie Smith record to make the work go faster." Bessie Smith, it turned out, influenced Mahalia more than anyone else, even though Jackson never performed jazz.

7   Her passion for music took her north to Chicago, all the way out to New York, and eventually she even got to go to Europe. She also crossed over from a predominantly black audience at the beginning of her career to a predominantly white audience at her career's end.

8   Her dynamic spirit took on political tones as well when she sang before Martin Luther King, Jr.'s famous "I Have a Dream" speech. She also sang at his funeral following his assassination in 1968.

9   She died in 1972 at the age of 60, but she will always be remembered for her stirring voice, "I sing God's music because it makes me feel free. It gives me hope."

7   **Which of the following statements BEST summarizes this article?**   9W2

   A   Mahalia Jackson lived a long and happy life.

   B   Mahalia Jackson loved the blues but never sang them.

   C   The high point of Mahalia Jackson's life was singing for Martin Luther King Jr.'s. "I Have a Dream" speech.

   D   Mahalia Jackson was famous around the world for singing gospel music.

8   **Which of the following is an opinion in the article about Mahalia Jackson?**   9W1

   A   She was born in New Orleans in 1911.

   B   "The blues are for listenin."

   C   She sang at Martin Luther King, Jr.'s funeral.

   D   Her passion for music took her to Chicago.

9   **Which of the following statements BEST summarizes the author's bias and purpose?**   9W1

   A   The author seems to admire Jackson and presents positive information in order to influence the reader to have a positive view of Jackson and her music.

   B   The author presents only facts about Jackson and does not exhibit any bias either positive or negative or intended influence toward the audience.

   C   The author presents positive and negative information about Jackson with the apparent purpose of allowing readers to draw their own conclusions.

   D   The article does not provide any clues as to the author's bias or purpose.

10   **Read this sentence from paragraph 6.**   9RL5

> "Jackson heard the music of her muse as a teenager while working as a housekeeper."

Which dictionary definition of the word *muse* best applies to its use in this sentence?

   A   inspiration   **C**   idol

   B   friend   **D**   protégé

11 How would this sentence from paragraph 7 *best* be written to improve clarity and reduce repetition?

9W4

> Her passion for music took her north to Chicago, all the way out to New York, and eventually she even got to go to Europe.

A Her passion for music took her north to Chicago; New York; and eventually, to Europe.

B Her passion for music took her north to Chicago, New York, and eventually she went to Europe.

C Her passion for music took her north to Chicago, New York, and eventually, to Europe.

D Her passion for music took her north to Chicago, New York: and eventually, to Europe.

Read this essay written by a student. Then answer the questions that follow.

1   There is no reason why a person who is fifteen years old should not be allowed to get a driver's license. There is nothing magic about the number of years in a person's age. Teenagers can learn from having to maintain a vehicle. The real issue when considering whether a person should drive or not is their level of responsibility.

2   Driving a car puts you in a position of great opportunity and risk. Driving too fast, or recklessly, is dangerous. You can endanger your own life. You can also endanger the lives of everyone else on the road. Listening to the radio or talking to another passenger has caused many accidents on the road. But responsible drivers have the wide-open road in front of them and endless opportunities.

3   For a teenager who has already proven to be a responsible person, the ability to drive provides many benefits. For one, it encourages further development of responsibility. By rewarding a responsible teen with the freedom of driving, society teaches the teen that responsible behavior pays off in the long run. Whereas, if a responsible teen were denied the right to drive, he or she may think, what's the point of trying to be responsible? This lesson can carry over into school, work, and personal life. he parents of the teen will also benefit by not having to drive their teen around to work, school, and extracurricular activities.

4   Some people question whether fifteen-year-olds are old enough to drive. My answer is that some are. Some are not. The question is not the numerical age of the person, but how mature they are. If mature and responsible teens are given the opportunity to drive, then everyone benefits. Those who are not responsible should not be allowed to drive. But don't punish everyone just because of a few bad apples.

12 Which of these sentences is *least* important to the review and could be deleted?   9W3

    A Some people question whether fifteen-year-olds are old enough to drive.

    B The real issue when considering whether a person should drive or not is their level of responsibility.

    C This lesson can carry over into school, work, and personal life.

    D Teenagers can learn from having to maintain a vehicle.

13 Read this sentence from the essay: 9C1

> Whereas, if a responsible teen <u>were denied</u> the right to drive, he or she may think, what's the point of trying to be responsible?

What is the correct way to write the underlined verb in the sentence?

    A was denied   **C** is denied

    B has been denied   **D** no change

14 Which of these sentences from the essay *best* reveals the author's attitude about teenagers and driving?   9W1

    A "There is no reason why a person who is fifteen years old should not be allowed to get a driver's license."

    B "Driving a car puts you in a position of great opportunity and risk."

    C "You can endanger your own life."

    D "This lesson can carry over into school, work, and personal life."

15 These are some sources used in writing the essay: 9W3

    1. personal experience

    2. personal interviews with parents of teenagers

    3. accident reports

    4. personal interviews with teenagers

Which source probably gave the *best* information about teenagers and the age at which they feel they should be allowed to drive?

    A 1   **B** 2   **C** 3   **D** 4

16 Which of these sentences could be added to the review to explain how teenagers can gain the right to drive at an earlier age?   9W3

    A By writing to various local officials, teenagers can voice their opinions about the driving age.

    B Teenagers should encourage their parents to let them practice driving without a license.

    C Teenagers will probably not be allowed to drive at an earlier age.

    D Laws are made to be broken.

17 Read this sentence from paragraph 4 of the essay.   9C2

> "Some people question whether fifteen-year-olds are <u>old</u> enough to drive."

Which of these verbs would *best* replace the underlined part of the sentence?

    A able   **C** responsible

    B good   **D** dutiful

18 Which of the following is the *best* way to combine the following sentences from paragraph 4?   9W4

> My answer is that some are. Some are not.

    A My answer is that some are, and some are not.

    B My answer is that some are, but some are not.

    C My answer is that some are, or some are not.

    D My answer is that some are, for some are not.

Read the following student-written paragraph and answer the questions that follow:

animal sacrifices

Every year, the U. S. military sends shoppers to Europe. These shoppers are looking for a very special product: well-bred, intelligent German shepherds or other dogs, suitable for use by U.S. armed forces. These government procurement agents have a lot of money to spend: money that comes from the taxes each American citizen pays. They need a lot of money. They have to spend at least $3,000 for each Dog. And they buy more than 300 dogs. These canine prizes are shipped back to the United States. and trained in military camps for 100 days. After they graduate, they take on some of the most dangerous and risky work any soldier can do. Often they are in the line of fire, along with their trainers.

Many dogs suffer terribly and die. In Vietnam alone, hundreds of dogs were killed in battle. Most military dogs brought to Vietnam never returned. Here at home, you would not want your pet to be put in harm's way on purpose. . We have animal protection laws to prevent that; however, these laws don't seem to apply to all dogs.

19 Which of the following is the correct way to capitalize the title? 9C2

A   Animal sacrifices
B   animal Sacrifices
C   Animal Sacrifices
D   ANIMAL SACRIFICES

20 What change should be made to correct the following sentence? 9C2

They have to spend at least $3,000 for each Dog.

A   change *they* to *we*
B   change *have to spend* to *had to spend*
C   change *$3000* to *three thousand*
D   change *Dog* to *dog*

21 What is the best way to combine the following sentences? 9W4

These canine prizes are shipped back to the United States. and trained in military camps for 100 days.

A   These canine prizes are shipped back to the United States. and trained in military camps for 100 days.
B   These canine prizes are shipped back to the United States: and trained in military camps for 100 days.
C   These canine prizes are shipped back to the United States and trained in military camps for 100 days.
D   These canine prizes are shipped back to the United States, and they are trained in military camps for 100 days.

22 The word *procurement* in the following sentence most likely means 9RL5

The government procurement agents have a lot of money to spend: money that comes from the taxes each American citizen pays.

A   animal welfare.   C   intelligence.
B   purchasing.   D   watchdog.

23 Which of the following sentences states an opinion? 9W1

A   Every year, the U. S. military sends shoppers to Europe.
B   And they buy more than 300 dogs.
C   These canine prizes are shipped back to the United States.
D   After they graduate, they take on some of the most dangerous and risky work any soldier can do.

24 To reduce wordiness, which is the *best* revision of the following sentence? 9W4

> These shoppers are looking for a very special product: well-bred, intelligent German shepherds or other dogs, suitable for use by U.S. armed forces.

A   These shoppers are looking for a very special product: well-bred, intelligent German shepherds or other dogs, suitable for use by U.S. armed forces.

B   These shoppers are looking for well-bred, intelligent dogs suitable for the American military.

C   These shoppers are looking for a very special product: well-bred German shepherds or other dogs, suitable for use by U.S. armed forces.

D   They look for intelligent German shepherds or other dogs, suitable for use by U.S. armed forces.

25 In the last sentence, the author makes a comparison in order to 9W1

A   encourage the audience to make a personal connection with his argument.

B   show how many people lose their pets to the military.

C   worry too much about German shepherds and other European dogs.

D   fulfill the minimum word count for the assignment.

Read the following passage and answer the questions that follow:

Rescuing Others a Way of Life for Upper Sierra Woman

Upper Sierra resident Brenda Harrison, along with her dog, her son and her friend were on vacation last week when she was summoned to find two boys lost in the woods.

They were all staying at Joan Heintzelmann's summer home in Mountain Pass, Torro County, when Brenda received a call that two boys were lost in Mount Eden State Forest.

Harrison, along with her dog, Hunter, is a member of the United States Volunteer Wilderness Team. "We're on the State Task Force One, part of the state police office of emergency management," she said. "It's a state disaster team. What we do is train for wilderness and river areas."

Brenda is qualified to go out as a ground team member and is in the process of training Hunter, a German shepherd that weighs almost 100 pounds.

"We packed up and left after I got paged about 10:45 p.m.," she said. "Actually, the park is on Route 42 so it was on our way home. We got there around midnight, talked to the police and asked what they had done so far."

Harrison was told that searchers had driven around and taken tracking dogs into the woods to look for the 9- and 12-year-old boys who had been playing a modern day hide-and-seek game. They were reported missing around 7:30 p.m., she said.

Before going into the woods, the team of three, plus Hunter, picked up another member, a local man who knew his way around the woods.

"When you're out in the middle of the woods, you want to know that everyone on your team has training. Joan and I trust each other, and I trust my son's knowledge," she said.

Steven, 14, a Murdock High School freshman, went to ground search rescue school at Fort Irwin last spring, a program run by the Civil Air Patrol. "It's a great organization for kids," she said.

"Steven knows how to use a compass and a map," Harrison said. "He was my communication person. He was talking to the state police the whole time. He also helped carry the 9-year-old boy out of the woods."

"Before going in, we studied a map of the park, Steven said. "We were walking through massive briars and trees. It was 35 degrees that night. We found them about 1:30 a.m. They weren't dressed for such a drop in temperature, but they were fine, just very cold," she said. "I don't think they will go that deep in the woods any more."

Harrison is modest about the rescues she has been involved in. "It's just what I do," she said. "The next day I go back to my normal life. It's a way of putting my talent to good use."

Her normal life is a full one. Besides Steven, she has two daughters and is a full-time student studying for a dual degree in education and special education.

She takes her dogs to class with her. "A lot of time I train my dogs after class," she said. "We train all over Nevada. Training has to be continuous in order to reinforce what they've been taught. Hunter thinks it's a game. He loves to go to work."

She and her husband are both members of the Upper Sierra First Aid Squad, which sometimes calls her to aid them with her dogs. She said she and her team members are going back to Mount Eden State Forest to look around. "I need to see it during the daytime. I remember how massive the woods looked."

26 **According to the information in the article, why would the search and rescue volunteers work in teams?**   9RL2

    A so the dogs don't fight with each other

    B because each individual has special knowledge to contribute to the team

    C to keep the dogs calm and focused on the rescue

    D to fulfill the safety requirements of the police who are involved

27 **In this article, the writer's main focus is to**   9W1

    A explain the importance of first aid.

    B analyze the special skills that a rescue dog provides.

    C describe the emotional response to finding missing children.

    D profile a member of the Wilderness Rescue Team.

28 **Read the following excerpt from the passage:**   9RL1

> "… a local man who knew his way around the woods."

By reading this excerpt, we learn about the man's character through

    A action.   **C** description.

    B dialogue.   **D** narration.

29 **Which statement is *best* supported by the information in the article?**   9W1

    A Trained dogs are skilled at search and rescue.

    B Trust and teamwork are important in search and rescues.

    C Children need survival skills before venturing into the forest.

    D Mount Eden State Park is a dangerous place.

30 **Which of the following lines from the article *best* describes Brenda Harrison's personality?**   9RL1

    A Her normal life is a full one.

    B She takes her dogs to class with her.

    C She is modest about the rescues she has been involved in.

    D She and her dog, Hunter, are members of the United States Wilderness Team.

Read the following excerpt from Sophocles' "Oedipus the King" and answer the questions that follow:

Introduction: "Oedipus the King" is famous for its tragic ending. Oedipus, king of Thebes, is determined to find the truth of his birth, at all costs. He believes that finding truth can only be a right action. He discovers he has lived the fate he tried all of his life to escape: to murder his father and marry his mother. He has done these acts unknowingly since he was switched at birth. The truth destroys Oedipus and his family. The following scene is a conversation between Oedipus and his wife/mother about the truth of his birth.

Characters:
OEDIPUS the king.
JOCASTA mother/wife of Oedipus.
MESSENGER to the king.
LEADER of chorus.

TIME AND SCENE: *The royal house of Thebes. Double doors dominate the facade; a stone altar stands at the center of the stage. In the courtyard of the palace, a messenger has come from Corinth with news of the death of the man who Oedipus thought was his father and reveals how Oedipus was switched at birth.*

OEDIPUS. What? You took me from someone else? You didn't find me yourself?

MESSENGER. No sir, another shepherd passed you on to me.

OEDIPUS. Who? Do you know? Describe him.

MESSENGER. He called himself a servant of... if I remember rightly — Laius.

[JOCASTA *turns sharply.*]

OEDIPUS. The king of the land who ruled here long ago?

MESSENGER. That's the one. That herdsman was *his* man.

OEDIPUS. Is he still alive? Can I see him?

MESSENGER. They'd know best, the people of these parts.

[OEDIPUS *and the* MESSENGER *turn to the* CHORUS.]

OEDIPUS. Does anyone know that herdsman, the one he mentioned? Anyone seen him in the fields, here in the city? Out with it! The time has come to reveal this once for all.

LEADER. I think he's the very shepherd you wanted to see, a moment ago. But the queen, Jocasta, she's the one to say.

OEDIPUS. Jocasta, you remember the man we just sent for? Is *that* the one he means?

JOCASTA. That man... why ask? Old shepherd, talk, empty nonsense, don't give it another thought, don't even think —

OEDIPUS. What — give up now, with a clue like this? Fail to solve the mystery of my birth? Not for all the world!

JOCASTA. Stop — in the name of god, if you love your own life, call off this search! My suffering is enough.

OEDIPUS. Courage! Even if my mother turns out to be a slave, and I a slave, three generations back, *you* would not seem common.

JOCASTA. Oh no. Listen to me, I beg you. Don't do this.

OEDIPUS. Listen to you? No more. I must know it all, must see the truth at last.

JOCASTA. No, please — for your sake — I want the best for you!

OEDIPUS.   Your best is more than I can bear.

JOCASTA. You're doomed — may you never fathom who you are! [*To a servant.*]

OEDIPUS.   Hurry, fetch me the herdsman, now! Leave her to glory in her royal birth.

JOCASTA. Aieeeeeeee — man of agony — that is the only name I have for you, that, no other — ever, ever, ever!

[*Flinging through the palace doors, A long tense silence follows.*]

LEADER.   Where's she gone, Oedipus? Rushing off, such wild grief... I'm afraid that from this silence something monstrous may come bursting forth.

OEDIPUS.   Let it burst!   Whatever will, whatever must!   I must know my birth, no matter how common it may be — I must see my origins face-to-face....

31   What is the main idea of this dialogue?   9RL1

A   It is important to know one's heritage.

B   Some secrets are best kept.

C   It is acceptable to lie to protect a person's feelings

D   Never trust what a stranger tells you.

32   Which of these quotes from Oedipus   9RL1
best reveals what he assumes about his birth?

A   "Courage! Even if my mother turns out to be a slave, for three generations back, *you* would not seem common."

B   "Listen to you? No more. I must know it all, must see the truth at last."

C   "Your best is more than I can bear."

D   "Hurry, fetch me the herdsman, now! Leave her to glory in her royal birth."

33   Why is Oedipus' situation ironic?   9RL1

A   He knows the truth of his birth but is in denial.

B   The messenger he spoke to is his father.

C   He tries to do what he believes is best, and it destroys his life.

D   He is destined to become a slave.

34   Read this sentence from the dialogue:

JOCASTA. "Stop — in the name of god, if you love your own life, call off this search! My suffering is enough."

Which sentence would *most* strengthen   9W1
Jocasta's argument that Oedipus should not seek the truth?

A   The only way to preserve your sanity is to cease searching for the truth.

B   You already know too much.

C   Questions can be harmful, and I fear that you will harm yourself.

D   If you knew what I do, you would not be happy.

35   Which of the following *best* explains   9RL3
the cause of Oedipus' disaster?

A   his insistence on knowing the truth

B   his wife

C   his parents

D   the messenger

36   Read this sentence from the dialogue: 9RL5

JOCASTA. You're doomed — may you never fathom who you are!

Doomed is to _____ as *hurry* is to *rush*.

A   lucky   C   cursed

B   quiet   D   stifled

37   Which of the following *best* explains   9RL1
the author's purpose?

A   to entertain   C   to persuade

B   to inform   D   to instruct

Read the following passage and answer the questions that follow:

Gangsters & Cowboys: American Films Reflect Their Times

By the height of the Great Depression in 1933, more Americans were flocking to movies than ever before, eager to escape the crushing poverty and pervading sense of hopelessness that massive unemployment and growing debt brought on a seemingly daily basis. Because tickets cost only pennies and offered hours of diversion, they existed for millions of Americans as a cheap way to fill the hours of the day. Moreover, movies had yet to escape the public perception as a "working class" medium — fit not for the cultured, educated elite but for the lower, blue collar citizen and people of little, if any, secondary or high school education. Hollywood responded by making films that both appealed to peoples' yearnings for release from economic want and attacked the government and social systems many people held at least partly responsible for the Depression.

A great example of the films that both exploited and glamorized wealth were the hugely popular "Thin Man" series, starring William Powell and Myrna Loy. The two played Nick and Nora Charles, rich socialites who solved murders among New York's elite society. Set in luxurious wardrooms and expensive nightclubs, the murders always involved the idle rich and were motivated by petty emotions of greed and vanity. Powell's Nick, a former working class gumshoe, uses a common sense logic and "from the streets" attitude to see through the pomp and snobbery of the wealthy. In every example, his unpretentious common sense won out over the idle rich's treachery, prevailing for justice regardless of economic station.

imilarly, the gangster films that first became prominent during this period showed audiences the modern-day outlaws of that era, individuals who defied the systems responsible for the Depression and made their own way in an uncaring environment. Films such as *The Roaring 20's* and *Angels with Dirty Faces* showed working-class men and women clawing their way into riches despite the police and courts who stood in their way. Such social institutions were, to many people, symbolic of the same economic and social systems at fault for the Depression. That the criminals often died violently was almost beside the point to audiences who devoured these films. The outlaw heroes won out, even in death.

James Cagney

By the 1970s, anxiety regarding the nation's direction and sense of identity became reflected in popular entertainment, as a new generation of writers and directors — products of the social conscience of the previous decade — exerted their influence on the entertainment mainstream. In the aftermath of the Vietnam War and the growing Watergate scandal, American film audiences entered into a new romance with the Western genre, albeit a new strain that served as social allegory. In these "New Westerns," the heroes were frequently lawbreakers and outcasts who rejected social convention and morality in order to make a life for themselves on the American frontier. Films such as *Butch Cassidy and the Sundance Kid* and *Jeremiah Johnson* (both starring Robert Redford) resonated deeply with audiences worried about confining government and technological structures; *The Outlaw Josie Wales*, about a Confederate solider (Clint Eastwood) looking to lead a productive life in the West, spoke to the post-Vietnam yearning for individual redemption. Similarly, the brutal violence of vigilante films such as *Dirty Harry* (also with Eastwood) and *Taxi Driver* enthralled audiences troubled by skyrocketing crime rates and a weakened justice system. In both types of films, the recurring theme is; "don't trust governments or economies; you're on your own."

The theme of the individual against crushing social pressure continued throughout the decade, spiraling into urban political drama (*Serpico*), science fiction (*The Omega Man*), and even romance (*Love Story*). While by the beginnings of the '80s the pessimism had thawed somewhat, the '70s spirit of individualism influenced the next generation of filmmakers who came of age in the 1990s. Directors such as P.T. Anderson, Steven Soderbergh and The Wachowski brothers adapted the outlaw filmmaker creed, crafting anti-establishment works such as *Magnolia*, *Traffic* and *The Matrix* trilogy.

38 **What is the main point the author makes about films in this article?** 9RL1

  A Film studios only make films that will earn money.

  B Movies reflect the fears and desires of society at any given time.

  C Only movies with big stars are popular with audiences.

  D People can learn a great deal of history from the movies.

39 **How does the author build an argument in this passage?** 9W1

  A by using an emotional appeal to influence readers

  B by including vivid description to illustrate main points

  C by using clear organization and detailed supporting facts

  D by offering contrasting views to point out the best choice

40 **The author says that, in the 1970s, audiences were "stressed by skyrocketing crime and a *destabilized* justice system." As used in the sentence, *destabilized* means** 9RL5

  A helpless.

  B uneven.

  C weakened.

  D excessive.

41 **According to the passage, what kind of movie hero became popular in the 1970s?** 9RL1

  A lawbreakers and outcasts

  B cops and robbers

  C politicians and newsmakers

  D cowboys and Indians

42 **What is the main reason the author gives for booming movie attendance during the Depression?** 9RL3

  A So many great films were being made that people wanted to see them.

  B The blue-collar class had no other entertainment available to attend.

  C Many new film stars were rising and capturing people's attention.

  D Movies offered an escape from day-to-day poverty and unemployment.

43 **According to this passage, the writers and directors who became important in the 1970s were influenced by what event(s)?** 9RL3

  A the hardship of the Great Depression

  B the Vietnam War and the Watergate scandal

  C government control and new technology

  D gangster violence and vigilantes acting out

44 What is the correct way to punctuate the following sentence from the passage? 9C2

In both types of films, the recurring theme is; "don't trust governments or economies; you're on your own."

  A In both types of films, the recurring theme is: "Don't trust governments or economies; you're on your own."

  B In both types of films, the recurring theme is; Don't trust governments or economies; you're on your own.

  C In both types of films, the recurring theme is; "Don't trust governments or economies, you're on your own."

  D In both types of films; the recurring theme is; "Don't trust governments or economies; you're on your own."

SECTION II

Read the following poem and answer the questions which follow:

The New Colossus
by Emma Lazarus

Not like the brazen giant of Greek fame
With conquering limbs astride from land to land;
Here at our sea-washed, sunset gates shall stand
A mighty woman with a torch, whose flame
5 Is the imprisoned lightning, and her name
Mother of Exiles. From her beacon-hand
Glows world-wide welcome; her mild eyes command
The air-bridged harbor that twin cities frame,
"Keep, ancient lands, your storied pomp!" cries she
10 With silent lips. "Give me your tired, your poor,
Your huddled masses yearning to breathe free,
The wretched refuse of your teeming shore,
Send these, the homeless, tempest-tossed to me,
I lift my lamp beside the golden door!"

45 This poem is a(n)   9RL1

A epic.   C lyric.
B sonnet.   D ballad.

46 Lines 9 – 11 suggest that   9RL3

A the ancient world should keep their traditions favoring the rich.
B the ancient world is rich with ceremony and art.
C the statue welcomes the less fortunate people.
D the ancient world is more courteous and ceremonial than the United States.

47 Read the following phrase from the poem:

> "the wretched refuse of your teeming shore"

The phrase means   9RL1

A the garbage from your beaches.
B people who desperately search for a better life.
C the excess seafood that is spoiled and left on the beach.
D the toxic waste that flows from the rivers into the sea.

48 The mood of the poem is *best* described as   9RL1

A sad.   C gloomy.
B hopeful.   D mysterious.

49 Based on context clues, the word *astride* in line 2 means   9RL5

A on top of.
B close to.
C on both sides of.
D near.

Read the following excerpt from Washington Irving's "The Devil and Tom Walker" and answer the questions that follow:

About the year 1727, just at the time when earthquakes were prevalent in New England, and shook many tall sinners down upon their knees, there lived near this place a meager miserly fellow of the name of Tom Walker. He had a wife as miserly as himself; they were so miserly that they even conspired to cheat each other. Whatever the woman could lay hands on she hid away: a hen could not cackle but she was on the alert to secure the new-laid egg. Her husband was continually prying about to detect her secret hoards, and many and fierce were the conflicts that took place about what ought to have been common property. They lived in a forlorn looking house that stood alone and had an air of starvation. A few straggling spavin trees, emblems of sterility, grew near it; no smoke ever curled from its chimney; no traveler stopped at its door. A miserable horse, whose ribs were as articulate as the bars of a gridiron, stalked about a field where a thin carpet of moss, scarcely covering the ragged beds of pudding stone, tantalized and balked his hunger; and sometimes he would lean his head over the fence, look piteously at the passer by, and seem to petition deliverance from this land of famine. The house and its inmates had altogether a bad name. Tom's wife was a tall **termagant**, fierce of temper, loud of tongue, and strong of arm. Her voice was often heard in wordy warfare with her husband; and his face sometimes showed signs that their conflicts were not confined to words. No one ventured, however, to interfere between them; the lonely wayfarer shrunk within himself at the horrid clamor and clapper clawing; eyed the den of discord askance, and hurried on his way, rejoicing, if a bachelor, in his celibacy.

50 The tone of the passage is *best* described as   9RL1

A upbeat and nostalgic.
B sad and critical.
C amused and content.
D indifferent and innocent.

51 The mood of the passage is *best* described as   9RL1

A depressed.   C anxious.
B tranquil.   D angry.

52 Which of the following sentences shows conflict in the passage?   9RL1

A The house and its inmates had altogether a bad name.
B They lived in a forlorn looking house that stood alone and had an air of starvation.
C Whatever the woman could lay hands on she hid away: a hen could not cackle but she was on the alert to secure the new-laid egg.
D He had a wife as miserly as himself; they were so miserly that they even conspired to cheat each other.

53 The story is told in the _____ person.   9RL1

A first   C third limited
B second   D third omniscient

54 Which of the following is not used to convey setting?   9RL1

A dialogue   C imagery
B description   D style

55 Read the following sentence from the passage: 9RL5

> Tom's wife was a tall termagant, fierce of temper, loud of tongue, and strong of arm.

As used in the sentence, *termagant* most likely means

A a happy, compassionate woman
B someone suffering from depression
C a spiteful, scornful wife
D a young maiden

56 What statement best explains why the author includes the following sentence?   9W1

> They lived in a forlorn looking house that stood alone and had an air of starvation.

A to describe how the characters' setting relates to their personalities
B to show how setting often contrasts with character
C to depict typical conditions in the 18th century
D using words like "forlorn" and "starvation" makes the author feel smarter

Read the following letter and answer the questions that follow:

A Letter Home

Platte River, June 3rd, 1836

Dear Sister Harriet and Brother Edward:

1   Friday eve, six o'clock. We have just encamped for the night near the bluffs over against the river. The bottoms are a soft, wet plain, and we were obliged to leave the river yesterday for the bluffs. The face of the country yesterday afternoon and today has been rolling sand bluffs, mostly barren, quite unlike what our eyes have been satiated with for weeks past. No timber nearer than the Platte, and the water tonight is very bad — got from a small ravine. We have usually had good water previous to this.

2   Our fuel for cooking since we left timber (no timber except on rivers) has been dried buffalo dung; we now find plenty of it, and it answers a very good purpose, similar to the kind of coal used in Pennsylvania (I suppose now Harriet will make up a face at this, but if she was here she would be glad to have her supper cooked at any rate in this scarce timber country). The present time in our journey is a very important one. The hunter brought us buffalo meat yesterday for the first time. Buffalo were seen today, but none have been taken. We have some for supper tonight. Husband is cooking it — no one of the company professes the art but himself. I expect it will be very good. I have so much to say to the children that I do not know in what part of my story to begin. I have very little time to write. I will first tell you what our company consists of. We are ten in number; five missionaries, three Indian boys and two young men employed to assist in packing animals.

Farewell to all,

Narcissa Prentiss

57 By reading the passage, we know that   9RL2
its author

A   absolutely cannot stand the Old West.

B   is on a journey across the Great Plains.

C   is terrified of Indians.

D   probably won't live to see the journey's conclusion.

58 This selection could *best* be described   9RL1
as which literary genre?

A   nonfiction   C   poetry

B   fiction   D   drama

59 Which of the following might be a   9W1
better title for the passage?

A   Buffalo Is Some Good Eatin', Lemme Tell Ya

B   Across the Great Plains

C   I'm So Darn Homesick

D   Almost Home

60 The author most likely makes a   9W1
comparison between buffalo dung and
Pennsylvania coal in order to

A   make a sarcastic comment about Pennsylvania coal.

B   help her audience visualize the shape and properties of their current fuel.

C   show why they are starving.

D   relate something funny that happened on their trip.

61 In paragraph 1, the *face of the country*   9RL4
most likely means

A   the features of the people that live there.

B   a broad, uneven map of their surroundings.

C   the contour and shape of the surrounding terrain.

D   the current cultural mood.

62 The tone of the piece can best be   9RL1
described as

A   upbeat.   C   depressed.

B   determined.   D   angry.

63 Which of the following is a fragment?   9C2

A   Friday eve, six o'clock.

B   We have just encamped for the night near the bluffs over against the river.

C   The bottoms are a soft, wet plain, and we were obliged to leave the river yesterday for the bluffs.

D   all of the above.

Read the following essay and answer the questions that follow:

What Is Ethics, Anyway?

Ethics is a concept we often hear about, but few people today stop to think what it really means. However, philosophers and statesmen since the time of Plato have contemplated the definition and details of ethics, which is sometimes difficult to state. Clearly, ethics is not something invented by one person or even a society, but has some well-founded standards on which it is based.

Some people equate ethics with feelings being ethical is not simply following one's feelings. A criminal may "feel" robbing a person is okay, when really it is wrong and unethical to steal. Many people may identify ethics with religion, and it is true that most religions include high ethical standards and strong motivation for people to behave morally. But ethics cannot be confined only to religion, or only religious people could be ethical. There are even cases in which religious teaching and ethics clash: for example, some religions inhibit the rights of women, which opposes the ethical standard of basic justice.

Ethics also is not simply following laws or what is accepted by a society. To make a long story short, the laws of civilized nations often embody ethical standards. However, unethical laws can exist. For example, laws have allowed slavery, which is unethical behavior as it takes the freedom of another human being. Therefore, laws and other conventions accepted by a society cannot be the measure for what is ethical. Doing "whatever society accepts" may be far outside the realm of ethics — Nazi Germany is an example of an ethically debased society.

What ethics really refers to is a system of people's moral standards and values. It's like a road map of qualities that people want to have to be "decent human beings." It is also the formal study of the standards of human behavior. Ethics relies on well-based standards of "right" (like honesty, compassion, and loyalty) and "wrong" (like stealing, murder, and fraud). Above all, ethical standards encompass ideas such as respect for others, honesty, justice, doing good and preventing harm.

64 The tone of the piece can *best* be described as   9RL1

A   objective.

B   biased.

C   hostile.

D   indifferent.

65 By reading the passage, we can determine that ethics   9W1

A   exists outside of the rules of church, government, and culture.

B   is rarely practiced.

C   has been around a relatively short amount of time.

D   is of concern only to philosophers.

66 Read the following sentence from the passage: 9RL5

> Nazi Germany is an example of an ethically debased society.

As used in the last sentence of paragraph three, *debased* means

  A virtuous.   **C** corrupted.

  B serene.   **D** destroyed.

67 Which of the following sentences is a *fact*?   9W2

  A But ethics cannot be confined only to religion, or only religious people could be ethical.

  B Therefore, laws and other conventions accepted by a society cannot be the measure for what is ethical.

  C Ethics is a concept we hear about, but few people today stop to think what it really means.

  D Ethics relies on well-based standards of "right" (like honesty, compassion, and loyalty) and "wrong" (like stealing, murder, and fraud).

68 Read the following sentence taken from the passage: 9W1

> Ethics is a concept we often hear about, but few people today stop to think what it really means.

The author is guilty of _____ in making his point.

  A fallacies

  B facts

  C generalizations

  D informal language

69 Which of the following sentences contains a transitional word or phrase?   9W1

  A What ethics really refers to is a system of people's moral standards and values.

  B Ethics also is not simply following laws or what is accepted by a society.

  C But ethics cannot be confined only to religion, or only religious people could be ethical.

  D Therefore, laws and other conventions accepted by a society cannot be the measure for what is ethical.

70 Which of the following is a run-on sentence taken from the passage?   9C2

  A What ethics really refers to is a system of people's moral standards and values.

  B Some people equate ethics with feelings being ethical is not simply following one's feelings.

  C Therefore, laws and other conventions accepted by a society cannot be the measure for what is ethical.

  D However, unethical laws can exist.

71 By reading the passage, we know that the author   9RL2

  A cares little for modern interpretations of ethics.

  B only knows what he reads in books.

  C does not really care about examples of ethics in history.

  D believes ethics to be a vitally important part of a society's well-being.

72 Which of the following examples, taken from the passage, contains a cliche?   9W4

  A To make a long story short, the laws of civilized nations often embody ethical standards.

  B A criminal may "feel" robbing a person is okay, when really it is wrong and unethical to steal.

  C However, unethical laws can exist.

  D Therefore, laws and other conventions accepted by a society cannot be the measure for what is ethical.

Read the following poem. Then, answer the questions that follow:

Some glory in their birth, some in their skill,

Some in their wealth, some in their body's force,

Some in their garments though new-fangled ill;

Some in their hawks and hounds, some in their horse;

And every humour hath his adjunct pleasure,

Wherein it finds a joy above the rest:

But these particulars are not my measure,

All these I better in one general best.

Thy love is better than high birth to me,

Richer than wealth, prouder than garments' costs,

Of more delight than hawks and horses be;

And having thee, of all men's pride I boast:

Wretched in this alone, that thou mayst take

All this away, and me most wretchcd make.

–William Shakespeare

73 The passage is an example of a(n)   9RL1

A epic.   **C** ballad.

B sonnet.   **D** haiku.

74 **An example of alliteration in the poem**   RL1
is

A "hawks and hounds."

B rhyming force and horse.

C "and having thee."

D repeated use of "Some" in lines 1 – 4.

75 **How is the poet's attitude towards**   9W1
hawks and hounds similar?

A He cares for neither.

B He wants them for his love.

C He hopes to impress a woman with them.

D He has given them up for his love.

Read the following passage. Then answer the questions that follow:

"The place has a reputation — a bad one." [said Whitney.]

"Cannibals?" suggested Rainsford.

"Hardly. Even cannibals wouldn't live in such a God-forsaken place. But it's gotten into sailor lore, somehow. Didn't you notice that the crew's nerves seemed a bit jumpy today?"

"They were a bit strange, now you mention it. Even Captain Nielsen —"

"Yes, even that tough-minded old Swede, who'd go up to the devil himself and ask him for a light. Those fishy blue eyes held a look I never saw there before. All I could get out of him was 'This place has an evil name among seafaring men, sir.' Then he said to me, very gravely, 'Don't you feel anything?'— as if the air about us was actually poisonous. Now, you mustn't laugh when I tell you this — I did feel something like a sudden chill.

"There was no breeze. The sea was as flat as a plate-glass window. We were drawing near the island then. What I felt was a — a mental chill; a sort of sudden dread."

"Pure imagination," said Rainsford. "One superstitious sailor can taint the whole ship's company with his fear."

"Maybe. But sometimes I think sailors have an extra sense that tells them when they are in danger. Sometimes I think evil is a tangible thing — with wavelengths, just as sound and light have. An evil place can, so to speak, broadcast vibrations of evil. Anyhow, I'm glad we're getting out of this zone. Well, I think I'll turn in now, Rainsford."

– excerpted from "The Most Dangerous Game," by Richard Connel

76 The tone of the passage can best be described as   9RL1

   A sentimental.   **C** suspenseful.

   B indifferent.   **D** hopeful.

77 How does the author characterize sailors in the passage?   9RL1

   A Sailors are skilled at navigating.

   B Sailors are superstitious.

   C Sailors like to tell stories.

   D Sailors are evil.

78 In the last paragraph, what is Whitney, the speaker, saying about evil?   9W1

   A Evil is all around us.

   B Evil is within each of us.

   C Evil is created by imagination.

   D Evil will never win over good.

79 What conclusion has Rainsford come to when he says, "Pure imagination?"   9RL1

   A The sailors are imaginary.

   B Imagination is pure entertainment.

   C The island is imaginary.

   D There is nothing to fear on the island.

80 Based on the theme of the passage, we know that there is   9RL2

   A only something in Whitney's imagination.

   B nothing to fear on the island.

   C something to fear on the island.

   D tangible evil lurking over the characters' shoulders.

Georgia English I End of Course Test Diagnostic Pretest

EVALUATION CHART

Directions: On the following chart, circle the question numbers that you answered incorrectly and evaluate the results. Then turn to the appropriate topics (organized by chapters), read the explanations, and complete the exercises. Review other chapters as necessary. Finally, complete the **two practice tests** to further prepare yourself for the Georgia English I EOCT.

Chapter	Performance Standards	Questions
Chapter 1: Strategies to Improve Understanding	ELA9RL1, ELA9RL3, ELA9RL5, ELA9RC3	1, 7, 10, 14, 22, 27, 31, 32, 36, 37, 38, 40, 41, 42, 46, 49, 55, 58, 59, 62, 64, 66, 79, 80
Chapter 2: Literary Elements & Devices	ELA9RL1, ELA9RL2, ELA9RC2	4, 5, 26, 28, 30, 31, 33, 35, 41, 48, 50, 51, 52, 53, 54, 56, 57, 62, 64, 71, 73, 74, 77, 78, 80
Chapter 3: Fiction, Nonfiction, Poetry & Drama	ELA9RL1, ELA9RL3, ELA9RL4, ELA9RC1, ELA9RC4	2, 4, 5, 14, 31, 32, 33, 37, 41, 42, 43, 45, 46, 47, 50, 51, 52, 53, 54, 58, 61, 62, 64, 73, 74, 75, 76, 80
Chapter 4: Information Gathering & Research Skills	ELA9W2, ELA9W3	3, 8, 9, 12, 15, 16, 18, 21, 24, 42, 67, 69, 72, 79
Chapter 5: Planning & Drafting the Written Composition	ELA9W1, ELA9W2, ELA9W3	3, 8, 9, 11, 12, 14, 15, 16, 21, 23, 24, 25, 27, 29, 34, 38, 39, 41, 42, 56, 59, 60, 65, 67, 68, 69, 78
Chapter 6: Revising the Written Composition	ELAW3, ELA9W4	11, 12, 16, 17, 18, 21, 24, 29, 59, 69, 72
Chapter 7: Grammar & Conventions	ELA9C1, ELA9C2	6, 13, 17, 19, 20, 44, 63, 70
Chapter 8: Speaking, Listening & Viewing	ELA9LSV1, ELA9LSV2	General review of chapter is helpful.

Chapter 1
Strategies to Improve Understanding

This chapter addresses the following performance standards:

Standards	ELA9RL1, ELA9RL3, ELA9RL5, ELA9RC3, ELA9W2

As you come to the end of your first year of high school, ask yourself this question: Do I truly understand what I'm reading, or are my eyes just soaking words off the page?

To say someone "learns to read" while still a child in elementary school is misleading. The skill of reading develops as we grow older, so that reading a work at age ten has a different effect on us than when we reread it at 15. Reading draws the reader in mentally, and as we understand a book more, our enjoyment grows deeper. One effect of this changing relationship is that the books that fascinate us as children bore us as teenagers, and vice versa. Yet the act of reading to understand remains constant, despite often vast differences in age and reading ability.

The **Georgia 9th Grade Literature and Composition End of Course Test** will require you to show a solid understanding of literature, to be familiar with the basis of arguments, and to demonstrate a strong mastery of grammar. You will be required to discuss fiction in its different types, to distinguish between nonfiction and opinion, and to tell one type of work from another. While the *techniques* used to reach your conclusions may be shared by everyone, the conclusions themselves will be your own.

Chapter One contains strategies to sharpen your understanding for reading texts, and addresses the following elements to that end:

1. Improving understanding of *diction*
2. Identifying *the main idea* of a passage
3. Using *context clues* to decipher unfamiliar words
4. Understanding word *derivation*
5. Using *literary criticism* when evaluating a text
6. Learning how to summarize

If these relationships seem complicated, don't worry. In learning to recognize the basic structure of written works, your ability to read will grow more powerful and your understanding more *intuitive* (automatic). We begin by looking at **diction**, the author's use of language when writing a work or passage.

DICTION

Diction is the first step in gathering clues to an author's reasons for writing text. When discussing how a person speaks, *diction* sometimes refers to his way of pronouncing words — his accents and inflections when speaking. In writing, however, diction refers to an author's choice of words, especially in regard to clearness and effectiveness.

Diction as it applies to the Georgia Ninth Grade EOCT refers to:

- the author's purpose
- the audience
- the author's voice & style
- the author's language & **tone**, or attitude

AUTHOR'S PURPOSE

You can determine the **author's purpose** from the way he writes. For example, imagine one reporter writes a required article about laws for conserving water. Another reporter writes an opinion-based article to persuade others to conserve water. The first reporter aims to inform, while the second reporter is motivated to persuade others to agree with his personal belief in civic duty.

The ability to determine the author's purpose in writing a specific text can greatly enhance your reading comprehension. Listed below are some reasons, meanings and examples of ways that authors can express a purpose in a passage:

Author's Purpose		
Purpose	**Definition**	**Sample Titles**
to inform	to present facts and details	"Ocean Fishes"
to entertain	to amuse or offer enjoyment	"Time I Slipped in the Mud"
to persuade	to urge action on an issue	"Raise Penalties for Polluters"
to instruct	to teach concepts and facts	"Tips for Healthy Living"
to create suspense	to convey uncertainty	"Will Tom Win the Race?"
to motivate	to encourage to act	"You Can Survive!"
to cause doubt	to be skeptical	"Are Adults Responsible?"
to describe an event	to narrate	"9-11: USA Under Fire!"
to teach a lesson	to furnish knowledge	"Mastering Exponents"
to introduce a character	to describe a person's traits	"First Look at Captain Nemo"
to create a mood	to establish atmosphere	"Gloom in the House of Usher"
to relate an adventure	to tell an exciting story	"Lost in a Cave"
to share a personal experience	to tell about an event in your life	"The Time I Learned to Share"
to describe feelings	to communicate emotions through words	"When My Dog Died"

Practice 1: Author's Purpose

Identify the author's purpose for each of the following passages:

1. The fire crackled musically. From it swelled light smoke. Overhead the foliage moved softly. The leaves, with their faces turned toward the blaze, were colored shifting hues of silver, often edged with red. Far off to the right, through a window in the forest, could be seen a handful of stars lying, like glittering pebbles, on the black level of the night.

   – excerpted from *The Red Badge of Courage*, by Stephen Crane

   A.   To describe an event during the war.
   B.   To create a mood of momentary peace.
   C.   To persuade that war is destructive.
   D.   To teach a lesson about nature.

2. Columbus' own successful voyage in 1492 prompted a papal bull* dividing the globe between rivals Spain and Portugal. However, the Portuguese protested that the pope's line left them too little Atlantic sea room for their voyages to India. The line was shifted 270 leagues westward in 1494 by the Treaty of Tordesillas. Thus, by circumstance rather than design, the Portuguese gained Brazil and gave their language to more than half the people of South America.

*formal declaration

   A.   To describe the creation of maps.
   B.   To describe feelings about different papal bulls.
   C.   To relate an adventure off the Atlantic coasts of South America.
   D.   To inform readers about one effect of Columbus's voyage.

AUDIENCE

Once authors are clear about their purpose for writing, they must consider their **audience** — the person(s) for whom they will write. An audience might consist of one particular person, a specific group, or a larger unknown mass of people.

Knowing the audience gives authors information that is important to consider when making decisions about how they will write. For instance, if an author is writing about the planets, it is important to know if the audience is elementary school children or college astronomy majors.

Some factors an author will consider in addressing an audience include the following:

the audience's interest	what topics or information are of interest to the audience
the audience's prior knowledge	what the audience already knows about the topic
the audience's vocabulary	language that the audience will understand
what the audience needs and wants to know	predicting the information or explanations that the audience expects

In persuasive writing such as editorials, arguments, and opinion articles, the author needs to consider the position the audience is likely to be currently supporting. Imagine if you were trying to persuade your friends to go to a new amusement park. You would probably mention the great rides and entertainment. You might want to remind them that the price for everything is included in the admission. However, if you were trying to persuade your parents to take your entire family, you might focus on the fact that it is very safe for your younger brothers and sisters and that your parents deserve to have a day of recreation, as well.

Practice 2:   Determining Audience

Read the following two paragraphs, written by the same person. Try to develop a picture of the audience the writer had in mind. How would you describe the intended audience of each paragraph? What evidence is there for your description?

Paragraph One

Since you're in the market for a new car, I wanted to tell you about mine. My new car is the best one I've owned. It's a 2004 Puma. It's got a 5.0 L overhead cam engine with multi-port fuel injection. It can do 0 – 60 mph in 5 seconds. With that much engine, passing cars on the highway is a breeze, but handling corners on back roads is a little trickier than with my old truck. I love the rush I get when I'm cruising around with my new wheels. You should consider buying one, too.

Paragraph Two

Since you're in the market for a new car, I wanted to tell you about mine. My new car is the best one I've owned. It's a 2004 Puma. This sporty two-door is canary yellow with electric blue racing stripes and silver mag wheels. It has Cordovan leather seats and a concert hall-quality sound system. The sunroof is the perfect finishing touch. You should see the looks I get when I'm cruising around with my new wheels. You should consider buying one, too.

A more detailed explanation of audience awareness is given in Chapter Five.

VOICE, CLARITY & STYLE

Writers write for different purposes: to amuse, entertain, move to action, anger, and so on. For every human experience, there is probably something written that both encourages or discourages it. But the language used in writing varies according to its subject matter, and as readers, we need to be adept at detecting faulty or imperfect language.

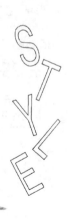

A writer's unique way of conveying the point he wants to express is called his **style**. The extent to which he can shape that style to be understood and appreciated by his audience determines the **clarity** of his writing **voice**. All writers have a style and voice, from the giants of literature to the most inexperienced writing student. You have a voice yourself, and though you are just beginning to develop it, it is your own.

In most nonfiction, a **neutral** voice is used in the presentation of facts. The writer is careful not to let emotions cloud the presentation of events and facts. In persuasive writing such as commentaries and editorials, the author sometimes adopts a **tone** (or attitude towards his subject) of heated anger, cool aloofness, or even detached amusement.

When you read, pay careful attention to the voice being used. If the wording and phrasing seems inappropriate, the work is probably much harder to take seriously.

THE MAIN IDEA

> "The **main idea** or central point of any passage can be found in two different ways."

The sentence above is a good example of a main idea topic sentence — it says in a broad statement what its paragraph will be about. A sentence's **topic** is another word for its *subject*.

Main ideas are **broad statements about the subject of a passage**. Statements of details alone cannot be main ideas.

Rule 1.   Main ideas may be directly stated in a topic sentence. Topic sentences can be found in the title, the introduction, or even the beginning or ending sentence of a paragraph.

Rule 2.   Authors may also show the main idea by implying, hinting, or suggesting it through details and facts, not by directly stating it. This is called an **implied main idea**.

THE DIRECTLY STATED MAIN IDEA

In a **directly stated main idea**, the basic thought to be communicated is usually found either in the beginning sentence or among the ending sentences. An author usually reinforces her ideas with **details**. Details are items of information that answer the 5 Ws and H of journalism: *who?, what?, where?, when?, why?, and how?* They both fill in information and explain the main idea.

The example below shows a directly stated main idea in the first sentence:

Mockingbirds are common and popular birds in the eastern and southern regions of the United States. The mockingbird is the state bird for Arkansas, Florida, Mississippi, Tennessee, and Texas. "Mockers," as they are affectionately called, are known for their ability to mimic other birds, mammals, and insects with song and sounds. Mockingbirds often live close to human homes, nesting in ornamental hedges.

After reading the first sentence, we know that the passage is about mockingbirds. The rest of the paragraph gives details about how the mockingbird is common and why it is popular.

Finding a Stated Main Idea
1. Read the title. The main topic of a paragraph or passage is often mentioned in its title.
2. Read the first and last sentence of each paragraph. Most of the key words and ideas are stated at the beginning and ending of their texts.
3. Choose the answer that is the best statement or restatement of the passage's main idea. Your choice should contain the key words mentioned in the title and the first and/or last sentence.
4. Always read the entire passage.

THE IMPLIED MAIN IDEA

An author can also give information without directly stating it, by subtly giving clues and suggestions and using details contained within the passage. Read the passage below, and see if you can determine the season of the year described:

> Sam's favorite part of the hike was watching the colorful leaves falling through the cold, clear air.

The season isn't directly stated, but a reader can conclude the season is autumn because of the hints given. Because the season is described with details, but without using the word "autumn," the season is *implied*.

An **implied main idea** can be found by reading more than one sentence and looking for clues. Look for the implied main idea in the following passage:

Traveling the Speed of Light

In 1905, a scientist named Albert Einstein published his most famous theory: the Special Theory of Relativity. The theory states the faster an object travels, the heavier it becomes. Therefore, an object traveling at 300,000 kilometers per second, or the speed of light, would be extremely heavy. The theory also connects the speed of light with the passage of time. Einstein believed everything in the universe is connected and that traveling the speed of light would slow time down. Light is the fastest thing known to science. If scientists can figure out a way to travel the speed of light, they would be able to discover whether the theory is true or false. Most scientists consider Albert Einstein a genius.

What is the implied main idea of the paragraph?

A. Albert Einstein may be the smartest man who ever lived.

B. The speed of light is still an important and puzzling concept for scientists.

C. The speed of light is the fastest thing known to man.

D. A rocket ship might weigh a lot more if it traveled the speed of light.

The title suggests the subject of the passage is the speed of light but does not give the reader enough information to identify the main idea. It is only after we read the entire paragraph that we understand the implied main idea, as correctly expressed in choice *B*.

Determining An Implied Main Idea
1. Read the title and first sentence. Both will help you identify the topic of the selection.
2. Read the entire paragraph or passage to get a general understanding of the material.
3. Note the facts and details in each paragraph. Think of overall ideas they have in common.
4. Choose the answer that summarizes all of the passage's facts and ideas. Confirm your choice by going back over the passage to recheck your evidence.

Practice 3: Main Idea in a Paragraph

Read each of the following paragraphs. Decide whether the main idea is stated or implied. If the main idea is *stated*, underline it. If the main idea is *implied*, write it in your own words on a separate sheet of paper. Discuss your answers with your classmates and teacher.

A Visit to Germany

In Germany, lunch is the main meal for most families. Supper is a cold meal which resembles a light American lunch. Potatoes are a favorite dish. They are cooked in many ways and with different spices. Germans also like to eat sausage, or "wurst." Fresh bread rolls are stuffed with wurst for a snack. Some kinds of food, like seafood, may be difficult to find in most restaurants in Germany, but the hundreds of varieties of wursts make meals interesting and tasty.

A Golden Seal

In 1922, the Newbery Award became the first children's book award in the world. The award is named after an eighteenth-century English bookseller, John Newbery. In the library or media center, you can find the books that have won this important award. A bright gold seal is printed on the cover of all winning books. It is the best known and most discussed children's book award in the country.

Practice 4: Media Search for Main Ideas

A. Idea Exchange. On your own or in a group, look for paragraphs and passages on different subjects in newspapers, magazines, books, or the Internet. Write out the stated or implied main ideas you find on a separate sheet of paper. Bring the articles to class. Exchange only the articles with another student or group members. See if they identify the same main ideas that you did. Then share the results of your efforts with your instructor.

B. Photo Titles. Share photos or pictures with a partner. Then think of titles or main ideas to go with them.

C. **News Story Headlines.** Bring news stories to class. Cut out the headlines, and keep them separate. Exchange only the articles, and write your own headlines. Compare your own headlines with the original headlines.

SUBORDINATE IDEAS

In addition to the main idea, a passage may contain **subordinate ideas,** which are ideas less significant than the main idea. The subordinate ideas are the topics or main ideas of paragraphs in a longer passage, while the main idea is the overall controlling idea of the entire passage. These subordinate ideas are really the building blocks to the main idea. In the paragraph above about the speed of light, the details about how fast light travels and scientists' efforts to prove its speed are subordinate ideas.

CONTEXT AND CONTEXT CLUES

We give names to ideas, events, objects and emotions. Often, however, there is no way to tell a word's meaning by the word alone. Consider the word "globe." There is nothing about the combination of the letters G-L-O-B-E to suggest the entire earth, yet everyone knows "the globe" refers to a model of the land and sea features on the planet.

Learning new words in a language requires knowing how to decode the word's meaning. Maybe the simplest approach involves understanding how a word is used within a sentence and extracting the meaning from its use.

Words and ideas surrounding a word are called the **context.** Using **context clues** means to look at the way words are used in combination with other words in their setting. To use context clues, look at the words *around* an unknown word. Think about the meaning of these words and the idea of the whole sentence. Then match the meaning of the unknown word to the meaning of the known text surrounding it.

In the following statements, choose the word which best reflects the meaning of the underlined word.

1. Ted seemed absolutely honest, but something told me he was **prevaricating** anyway.

    A.   crying   B.   hoping   C.   speaking   D.   lying

By paying attention to context clues, we can determine that the act of prevaricating is not like being honest. The word "but" signals a contrast, that the speaker feels the Ted of the sentence seems honest, but probably is not. That contrast points us to the correct answer, *D.* Prevaricating is another word for lying.

Context clues help us determine the meaning of words from the way they are used in a sentence. The idea or message of the whole text becomes clearer if we use the correct meaning. By looking at and analyzing the phrases and **signal words** that come before or after a particular word, you can often figure out its meaning.

Context Clues	Signal Words
Comparison	*also, like, resembling, too, both, than* Look for clues that show an unfamiliar word is similar to a familiar word or phrase. **Example:** The accident *felled* the utility pole like tree for timber.
Contrast	*but, however, while, instead of, yet, unlike* Look for clues that indicate an unfamiliar word is the opposite of a familiar word or phrase. **Example:** Stephanie is usually in a state of *composure,* while her sister is mostly boisterous.
Definition or Restatement	*is, or, that is, in other words, which* Look for words that define the term or restate it in other words. **Example:** The principle's idea is to *circuit* — or move around — the campus weekly to make sure everything is secure.
Example	*or example, for instance, such as* Look for examples used in context that reveal the meaning of an unfamiliar word. **Example:** People use all sorts of *vehicles* such as cars, bicycles, rickshaws, airplanes, boats, and motorcycles.

Practice 5: Using Context Clues

Above each bolded word, write its meaning. Use context clues to help you.

1. Those who cannot afford **bail** cannot be freed on pre-trial release.

2. Hank said the ocean was very **tranquil;** I also thought the ocean was peaceful.

3. Sometimes strong **herbicides** are needed to eliminate weeds from the garden.

4. As the snow **accumulates**, traveling the roads becomes more dangerous.

5. At the sound of Silver's **clattering** footsteps, the stable boy turned with a start.

6. **Residues** such as ammonia even show up in grain sprayed with **pesticides**.

7. While Greenland is an island, Antarctica's larger size makes it a **continent**.

8. You could smell the freshly caught catfish **sizzling** over the fire.

9. **Mulch**, which is composed of grass clippings and leaves, keeps soil moist around trees and shrubs.

10. Instead of **incarcerating** youthful offenders, let's educate them so that they can hold well-paying jobs in the workplace.

Practice 6: More Passage Practice With Context Clues

Read the following article. Then answer the questions that follow.

Do You Want Your Camel Rare or Well-done (in)?

Just imagine it, a rare camel, newly discovered by scientists but well-known by hunters, is being done in by the **appetites** of desert dwellers.

Scientists had noted a difference in the wild camels of the Gobi desert region and the domesticated camels of the same region. These wild camels have a healthier growth of hair on their knee caps and a wider space between their humps than their **domesticated** cousins. The scientists, looking closer compared not just the **appearance** of the camels, but their genetic material as well. They found great differences in the genetic codes of the camels. This discovery led scientists to theorize that the wild camel is a new **species**.

That may explain why, apart from other land mammals, this wild creature can thrive on the salty water found in its desert home. The extreme amount of salt in the water results from its origins. The water boils up from under the desert floor, creating desert springs. The wild camels have no **competition** for the salt water at these springs, and so they visit the springs to drink the salt water with no fear.

Unfortunately for the camel, this may be its undoing. Does drinking salty water season the camels' flesh, making it enjoyable to humans, or is it the only "game" in town? The hunters don't care and aren't picky eaters. They have been laying mines around the springs where the unwary camels come to drink. After blowing the camels up, the hunters harvest their meat. We can only imagine that scene: "Who wants a leg?"

So, will scientists next decide that these hunters, blowing up innocent animals for food, are a new species of humans, or are we all capable of such carnage? What? Did you say, "Pass the pepper?"

1. Which dictionary meaning of the word **appetites** best applies to its use in the passage?

   A. eating   B. hungers   C. stomach   D. will

2. In the context of this passage, what does the word **domesticated** mean?

   A. tamed   B. ignorant   C. bald   D. cooked

3. Which dictionary meaning of the word **appearance** best applies to its use in the passage?

   A. apparition   B. manifestations   C. appearing   D. outward features

4. In the context of this passage, which of the following is closest in meaning to **species**?

   A. type   B. biological   C. seasoning   D. life

5. In this passage, which of the following is closest in meaning to the word **competition**?

   A. teams   B. fish   C. taste   D. rivals

WORD DERIVATIONS AND ANALYSIS

Just as context points to the meaning of a word by using the word around it, **word analysis** involves determining word meaning based on smaller components, called **roots** (the main part of the words), **prefixes** (the beginning of words), and **suffixes** (the ending of words). The process of building words from their components is called **derivation**.

Many of the words used in modern English can trace their origins back more than 2600 years, to the civilizations of ancient Greece and Rome. For example, the word **extraterrestrial**, "extra-" is a prefix (one or more letters or syllables added to the beginning of the word) that means outside or beyond, and the root "terra" comes from the Latin word for earth; "-ial" is a suffix (one or more letters or syllables added to the end of the word) which means act of, like, or as. By dividing *extraterrestrial* into its word parts, you discover that it means "not of this earth."

You can use the same process for other words. The root "dor" found in *dormant* and *dormitory* comes from the Latin word for "to sleep." Such words that share common roots are called **cognates**.

Some common prefixes, roots, and suffixes are listed below:.

Prefixes					
Prefix	**Meaning**	**Example**	**Prefix**	**Meaning**	**Example**
ab-	away from	absent	inter-	between	interstate
ad-	near, at	adhere	intra-	within	intramural
anti-	against	antigravity	mis-	incorrect	mistaken
bi-	twice, two	bi-monthly	non-	negative	nonathletic
com-	with	community	post-	after	postnatal
de-	reverse remove	deregulate	pre-	before, in front of in	premix
dis-	to cause to be	dishonest	pro-	support of	proclaim
en-	out, not	endear	re-	again	review
ex-	not	extinguish	semi-	partial, somewhat	semicircle
il-	not	illegal	sub-	under, beneath	submarine
in-		insecure	un-	not	unknown

Roots					
Root	**Meaning**	**Example**	**Root**	**Meaning**	**Example**
ann	year	annual	micro	small	microscope
aqua	water	aquarium	multi	many	multiply
aud	hear	auditorium	ped	foot	pedestrian
biblio	book	bibliography	path	feeling	sympathy
bio	life	biography	phon	sound	telephone
cent	hundred	century	port	convey	transport
chrono	time	chronological	rad	light	radiation
dic	to speak	diction	scope	see	microscope
gen	race, kind	genetic	scribe	to write	scripture
ject	put	injection	tele	distance	television
magni	large, great	magnify	ven	to come,	convene
med	middle	medium	viv, vit	life	vital

Suffixes					
Suffix	**Meaning**	**Example**	**Suffix**	**Meaning**	**Example**
-able	capable of being	lovable	-itive	having the nature of	talkative
-age	related to	marriage			easily, quietly
-al, -ial	act of, of, like	industrial	-ly	in a like manner	thoughtless
-ance	state or quality of	acceptance	-less	without	biology
-dom	general condition	freedom	-logy	study of	contentment
-en	made of,	wooden,	-ment	condition of	neatness
	to become	redden	-ness	quality, degree	nervous
-er, -or	one who	employer,	-ous	condition	relationship
		actor	-ship	full of	construction
-ful	full of	cheerful	-tion	action, process	venture
-hood	state of	childhood	-ure	state of being	forward,
-ify	to make	magnify	-ward	to a given	homeward
-ish	having quality of	foolish,		destination	
		childish			
-itis	inflammation	arthritis			

USING ROOT WORDS TO DETERMINE WORD MEANINGS

By using your knowledge of **root words**, you can often determine the meaning of words with which you are not familiar. Even if you don't know the specific root word used, if you know some similar words, you can figure out the new word. For example, in deriving the word *marigraph*, and you are not certain of the meaning, you can think of some words with similar construction such as *marine, marina, mariner,* and *maritime.* What do those words have in common? They all are related to the ocean or sea.

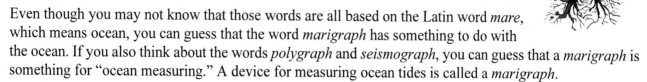

Even though you may not know that those words are all based on the Latin word *mare*, which means ocean, you can guess that the word *marigraph* has something to do with the ocean. If you also think about the words *polygraph* and *seismograph*, you can guess that a *marigraph* is something for "ocean measuring." A device for measuring ocean tides is called a *marigraph.*

Practice 7: Derivation and Word Analysis

A. On your own paper, divide each of the following words into prefixes, suffixes, and roots (when possible), and explain how these parts make up the meaning of the word. If you need help, consult a dictionary

> **Example:** 1. illegible: il (not) + leg(ere) (to read) + able (capable of being) = not capable of being read

1. argument

2. unqualified

3. illiterate

4. expel

5. bilateral

B. Select a page from your literature book or from a novel you've read. Find ten words with three or more **syllables (sounds)**. List these words, and next to each one, define any prefixes, suffixes and roots in each word. If you need help, use a dictionary. Explain the meaning of each word.

IDIOMS AND LITERAL AND FIGURATIVE MEANING

Idioms are expressions whose literal meanings are not signified by what their words suggest. For example, "to let the cat of the bag" means to reveal a secret or an unpleasant truth. It does not mean to actually release a cat from a cloth container. The **figurative meaning**, which is to say, what is *meant* by the expression, is to divulge information; the **literal meaning** is to free a kitty.

Idioms date back centuries, and gain and lose popularity with changing fashion. Many, such as the example above, have their roots in medieval custom or fashion, while some arise from movies and literature. Others come into use through a reflection of current events or popular culture. Idioms can be tricky taken at face value, and should be regarded with skepticism by the careful reader.

Practice 8: Idioms And Literal Meanings

Make a chart of ten idioms used in everyday life, using friends and family members to assist you. Write both the figurative and literal meanings of each expression in different columns, and share your results with a classmate, teacher, or mentor.

LITERARY CRITICISM

The word "criticism" in modern speech has almost a negative connotation, though in truth its meaning is much more objective:

> **crit·i·cism** *n* the practice of analyzing, interpreting, critiquing, or evaluating a creative work; a critical essay or article; a critique.

To say we *criticize* literature means to hold it up to inspection, to peel apart its different layers and components and judge its worth both as a whole and as the sum of its parts. Criticizing literature allows us to be detectives as well, understanding the basics from which a book or film works.

There are three basic approaches, or *techniques*, to criticizing literature: **historical context, cultural relevance,** and **autobiographical perspective**.

HISTORICAL CONTEXT

Historical criticism involves looking at the time period in which the author lived and considering the politics, economics, and culture of his time and place. Because writers live in the world and create art about what they experience, by extension it is almost impossible for any kind of work not to have a historical **context**, or perspective.

Historical context differs from other forms of literary criticism in that it focuses on the "big picture," the world as it existed in a given time and place. It works best with large, sprawling works such as historical dramas and epic romances.

For example, George Orwell wrote *1984*, about a futuristic police state that oppresses the individual, in Scotland during the late 1940s. At that time, the Soviet Union was expanding its holdings ever closer to democratic Western Europe, replacing whole nations with a series of *totalitarian* (all-powerful government) regimes. Orwell was concerned that *socialism* — the political philosophy of Soviet countries — placed too much emphasis on groups and minimalized the importance of the individual. In *1984*, he created a war-torn, paranoid nation-state where everyone spies on everyone else and personal freedoms are sacrificed for the sake of "the movement." Ultimately, the book became a tremendous rallying point against socialism and government abbreviation of personal rights. Its evil, all-seeing authority figure, Big Brother, has become synonymous with government spying on citizens.

An example of looking for historical detail in a work can also be found in non-fiction writings. If an author is writing about the sinking of the HMS *Titanic*, the details should describe and show an understanding of the time in which the *Titanic* sailed. If the author wrote that part of the panic was caused by difficulty in putting on life jackets, after reading it the reader must understand *why* it was difficult.

Titanic

The author's responsibility would be to describe the large group of third-class passengers who could not understand English, and that many of these passengers had never been on a ship before. Thus, they had never put on life jackets. The language barrier, combined with the heavy, awkward life jackets and newness of the situation, made the deaths of the passengers understandable (though not excusable).

Practice 9: Historical Context

Read the following passage. Then answer the questions that follow.

The Wonder of Pelé

Soccer, or *futebol*, has produced more controversy than peace throughout the world. The world expects hard knocks and national loyalty from soccer teams and gets it in abundance. In contrast, the United States expects high scores and easily recognizable heroes from every sport and finds very little of either in soccer. There was a time, however, when the world and the United States had all their expectations met by one man. This man was named Pelé.

Pelé

Pelé was born in 1940 in Tres Coracoes, a poor town in Brazil. His ancestors were African slaves. Pelé began playing soccer professionally at the age of fifteen in 1955 and became a star in the world of soccer by 1958. It was in this year that he played in the World Cup finals, scoring two goals for Brazil against Sweden. Pelé was a great athlete, holding the record for the most goals per game scored in a career. He is also the only person to have scored goals in three winning World Cup games.

Pelé's triumphs on the field, however, pale against his record for promoting peace and soccer throughout the world. He spoke with crowds in America in the 1960s, signing autographs for adoring fans despite high tensions between black and white people over the Civil Rights Movement. In 1977, Pelé met with boxer Mohammed Ali, who, as a black athlete, had not been wholly accepted by American society during the previous two decades. Though popular around the world, including the United States, Pelé stayed loyal to his home country of Brazil until his career ended, refusing offers of millions of dollars from other teams. In his last exhibition game, he played for both teams: one in the first half, the other in the second half. In order to promote soccer in the United States, Pelé signed to play with the New York Cosmos after he retired from the Brazilian team at age 34. His fame, personality, and ability won millions of United States fans for the sport of soccer.

Pelé is now a wealthy man. He still feels the pull of his fans and of the great need for peace around the world. He says that more than wanting children to follow his example on the soccer field, he would like them to follow his example of sportsmanship off the field in the wider world. As a great athlete, Pelé has demonstrated good will and dignity to his legion of fans. That is the wonder of Pelé.

1. What conclusion can be drawn about the game of soccer during the time of Pelé's youth?

    A. Soccer was known to fans only as futebol.

    B. The game was wildly popular in almost every country around the world.

    C. The game was not very interesting to anyone because of low scores.

    D. Soccer was not very well-known nor popular in the United States.

2. What is most unusual about Pelé's acceptance in the United States in the '60s and '70s?

    A. Americans did not understand soccer or the Brazilian language.

    B. At that time, the United States was still a largely segregated society, with many racial tensions.

    C. Americans were busy trying to beat Russia in the Cold War.

    D. People in the United States thought Pelé was too young to have received the fame he had.

3. What can you infer about Pele's place in soccer history?

    A. Today's young athletes, like Tiger Woods, will replace Pelé in the minds and hearts of soccer fans.

    B. Pelé will be remembered as the athlete who could never win the "big game."

    C. Pelé's records have stood for decades, but he will also be remembered as a good person.

    D. The modern inventions of instant replay and computer scoring make Pelé's accomplishments seem small.

CULTURAL RELEVANCE

Besides history, **culture** also has a deep and inescapable impact on a creative work. There is an old saying that "art does not exist in a vacuum." Without the culture around it, a work may often appear meaningless.

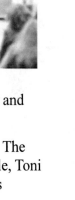

To give a very simple definition, *culture* is the attitudes, beliefs, practices, and habits of a society. Culture includes the media, entertainment, social customs, moral standards and value systems a group of people in the same region or nation share. It may be simpler to state that culture is everything in a given place and time besides politics and economics. **Relevance** means "the connection to the matter at hand."

Taken together, **cultural relevance** is the work's relationship to the culture in which it is produced. The extent to which something is culturally relevant sometimes determines its lasting appeal. For example, Toni Morrison's novel *Song of Solomon* directly addressed civil right issues after World War Two. It was published in the 1970s, a time when race relations were being re-evaluated after the Civil Rights Movement. Its main character, Macon "Milkman" Dead III, goes through a series of painful events trying to establish himself in the world without forsaking his racial or family identity.

GENRE FICTION AND CULTURAL RELEVANCE

Genre fiction (fiction of a specific type), such as science fiction and romance, also has cultural relevance. Some science fiction, especially, uses fantastic settings and situations as an allegory to real-life circumstances. *The Matrix* trilogy was created in the mid-1990s, a time when some were concerned that technology was advancing too fast for the human mind to handle. *Lost*, a mystery about survivors on a strange island, reflects the feelings of paranoia and helplessness many continue to feel after the events of September 11th, 2001.

Besides science fiction, historical dramas also often reflect the present by showing the past. While the film *Good Night and Good Luck* was set over fifty years ago, its meaning was clearly addressed to present-day concerns about censorship and political intimidation.

EVALUATING CULTURAL RELEVANCE

Cultural relevance can sometimes be harder to evaluate than historical context because often times the culture in which a book is written is the same in which the reader lives. But consider — using research if necessary — the time and place in which an author lived and worked. What issues and problems concerned people on a day-to-day basis? How did people feel about the world in that period?

You may also consider how a work from or set in another time period is relevant to our time and culture. For example, when criticizing a book about women written during the Civil War, you may choose to evaluate its modern value: does the book speak to women's issues today? To give another example, criticizing a memoir about growing up in the 1980s would probably include the details about the political anxiety and fashions of that time period, and if they have similarities to the current decade.

When evaluating cultural relevance in nonfiction, consider the author's motivations. Why did he feel the book needed to be written? Did it seem absolutely crucial at the time, given your research on the period? What about the book makes it necessary? If the book seems to have come "from a clear blue sky" — as if not in regards to a distinct need — its cultural relevance may be minimal.

Practice 10: Cultural Relevance

A. Choose a book or movie and evaluate its cultural relevance, using the methods described above. What about the work seems culturally relevant to you, both for its own time and for the present period? Do you think the work is valuable now? Why or why not? Discuss your results with a classmate or friend.

B. Search online or in your school/local library for books and movies considered famous for their cultural relevance, either now or from a previous time period. Books famous for their cultural relevance include *The Catcher In The Rye* by J.D. Salinger, *Catch-22* by Joseph Heller, *Invisible Man* by Ralph Ellison, and *Song of Solomon* by Toni Morrison. Films include *Fried Green Tomatoes* and *To Kill a Mockingbird*.

AUTOBIOGRAPHICAL PERSPECTIVE

History and culture are very large scales on which a writer works, but her own personal experiences come into play as well. Writing — as has been said previously — is often a deeply personal effort, and authors will bring their own lives and experiences into their work. Sometimes, that may involve something as simple as writing a memoir and recalling events from one's childhood or earlier life. At other times, the author may re-imagine, rework or even fabricate parts of her own life or past surroundings for literary effect.

Autobiographical perspective is the extent to which an author relied on personal experience to create a work. When criticizing a work using this criteria, consider *what* events led an author to write the work and also *how* his life may have affected his attitude towards his subject. For example, John Steinbeck's experiences in California during the Great Depression led him to write many of his most famous novels, including *the Grapes of Wrath* and *Of Mice and Men*. Steinbeck sympathized with the plight of poor migrant workers, and his experiences with them influenced much of his work.

Not all work comes from sympathy, though. Sometimes, a writer's time in a certain place may lead her to write **satire**, or work which pokes fun at a set of behaviors or attitudes. Jane Austen's time among the idle and wealthy British upper-middle-class led her to write *Emma* and *Pride and Prejudice*.

AUTOBIOGRAPHICAL PERSPECTIVE IN NONFICTION

Much of nonfiction is heavily influenced by autobiographical forces, as well. Someone writing an opinion piece will — obviously — be motivated and informed by personal experience. An author writing purely to inform, though largely objective in purpose, will still write from his own judgments about what is particularly important. This is a subtle form of autobiographical influence, but can be telling, particularly in works that criticize modern conditions or address a specific issue. For example, if someone who has spent his adult life in the Marine Corps writes in favor of reinstating the draft, that person's own experiences most likely affected his perspective. Similarly, someone who has lost all his money in the stock market will probably have a very definite opinion about financial investing.

Practice 11: Autobiographical Perspective

Match the titles with the people most likely to have written them.

1. Doctor of Psychology_____	A. *Bowery Days*
2. Construction foreman _____	B. "The local school lunch program is too expensive."
3. Orphan in 1920s New York_____	C. *Overcoming Hydrophobia*
4. Mother of three children_____	D. *The Road to Baghdad*
5. Veteran of Operation: Desert Storm_____	E. "The new city council building is unsafe."

Practice 12: More with Autobiographical Perspective

Recall a story from your English classes and consider what circumstances or events in the author's life might have played a part in the final creation of the work. Now find a biography of the author. Were your expectations close? If not, what about the work and the author's life surprised you?

IT ALL ADDS UP: YOUR REACTION TO THE MATERIAL

Reading a text is useless, however, if your ideas and thoughts go to waste. Remember that art is meant to be enjoyed and a creative work is meant to be puzzled over, held up and examined. The critical part of reading isn't really anything more than appreciating a work, recognizing its virtues while being able to identify its faults.

When you finish reading a book or watching a film, consider how you felt about it, and trust your reactions. Be open-minded, and willing to consider new ideas, thinking for yourself about the style of the work and how effectively it communicated its message. Some steps to help you reach decisions are on the opposite page:

Making Up Your Mind

1. Think For Yourself. Trust your own ability to interpret the information presented.

2. Keep an Open Mind. Don't dismiss new ideas or strange styles out-of-hand, but consider their worth and freshness to your experience.

3. Mull Over Your Reactions. Were there parts of a passage or book you felt worked better than others? What made you think so?

4. Discuss Your Ideas. Seek out the opinions of those you trust, teachers or mentors who may have more familiarity with a source than you; you will benefit from their knowledge.

5. Make Your Own Decisions. Base your decisions on what you learn from your literary criticism.

Practice 13: Conclusions

Read a short story, poem, or magazine article you otherwise might not be assigned or inclined to read. Consider the new information that was presented. Did you find your mind stimulated by the exotic information, or were you bored? If you were bored, was it because the information was too hard to understand, or because you didn't become interested in the material? Discuss your conclusions with a teacher, parent, or mentor.

SUMMARIZING

Being able to determine main ideas and supporting details in an information source is useful in writing effective summaries. Writing a summary is a way to increase reading comprehension. In order to write a summary of a source, you must first read the source carefully and determine the main ideas and supporting details. Writing a summary is also a valuable research tool. A **summary** condenses the ideas in an article and allows you to use the ideas as a reference without having to reread the entire source repeatedly. Summaries are also a useful means of reviewing information that you need for tests. In this way, summaries are good study tools.

Here are the steps to take in creating a summary of an information source.

> **NOTE:** Remember that it is important that what you write in a summary is in your own words. If you use exact words or phrases copied directly from the passage itself, be sure to put quotation marks around those words.

- Read the entire passage or source.
- Make a list of brief notes on the details and main idea of the passage. These notes will serve as a framework for creating the summary.
- Write down the main idea of the article. It is a good idea to put the main idea in complete sentence form.
- List the major details. These do not have to be in complete sentences; phrases are sufficient.
- Now you are ready to write your summary. The first sentence of your summary should include the title of the source and the author. Write the summary in paragraph form, using the notes you just created.

How long should your summary be? A general rule for summary length is to try and keep it to about one-fourth to one-third of the length of the original source. If your original text is two pages long, your summary should be about one-half to about three-fourths of a page.

Practice 14: Summarizing

Find a 1–2 page nonfiction article on the Internet or in a magazine or newspaper. Write notes about the main idea and some of the supporting details. Then using the guidelines on summarizing, create a summary based on your notes. Share your summary with the class or with your teachers for feedback. Then do one more summasry based on another article.

CHAPTER 1 SUMMARY

Diction refers to an author's choice of words, especially in regards to clearness and effectiveness in writing. Authors write with a purpose, either to comment on an issue or persuade others of a viewpoint or idea. An author's **audience** largely determines its use of voice, presentation of ideas, and tone.

An author's **style** is his own way of communicating through words and language. The words he chooses are called his **voice**. **Tone** is his attitude regarding the subject.

The **main idea** relates in a broad statement about what a given paragraph will be about. Main ideas are either **directly stated**, meaning they are put down in no uncertain terms within the paragraph or passage; or **implied**, in which their appearance is more subtle, often coming together only through careful arrangement of details.

Context clues are words used in combination with other words in their setting. Looking at the words around an unknown word can help you decipher the meaning of the unknown word.

Derivation is the process of building words using **roots** and **affixes: prefixes** and **suffixes.**

To **criticize** is to examine a creative work with an active mind, taking apart a work of literature or film and holding its different parts up to an appraising light.

- **historical context** means to apply knowledge of the time and place in which an author lived towards understanding a work.
- applying **cultural relevance** to a work means to consider what social pressures and influences affected a work's creation and purpose.
- **autobiographical perspective** involves looking at an author's own experiences and background to make a decision regarding the text.

Drawing conclusions involves making up your own mind about a work, approaching the work openly and without preconceived ideas about your enjoyment.

Summarizing condenses the key ideas and details from an article. It is used for research and review of large amounts of information.

CHAPTER 1 REVIEW

Read the following passage and answer questions 1–3. Then complete the remaining questions in this section.

Abaremasu*

Abaremasu: Japanese word for "storm"

Once upon a time, there was a son of a fisherman. One year, his family caught so many fish that the people of his village became weary of eating nothing else. The people of the village would buy no more fish. The boy's family was becoming poor. So, he decided to travel across the mountains to a village that had hardly any fish at all. He wrapped up one month's worth of dried cod and set the burden on his cow.

As he walked with the cow behind him, he began to sing aloud. A shout rudely broke into his song: Hai! Yes!" Impatient with the shouting, he looked around to see who was making the noise. At that moment, the ground began to shake. The boy looked up to see the largest, ugliest beast that had ever lived. The beast had short, white strands of hair, glistening like maggots on dead fish, and he had a hole for a mouth that reached to his ears. His ears were like a donkey's, and his one eye glinted with red and yellow sparks as he glared at the boy.

"*Abaremasu*!" howled the creature. "Give me fish!"

The boy being afraid of the beast threw a fish. Abaremasu swallowed it down in a gulp. Now after seeing the boy unwrap the fish, Abaremasu knew that the number of fish was great, and he demanded all of them in a great roaring voice. The boy tried to say no, but the beast shouted, "GIVE fish now or I eat YOU!"

So the boy threw all the work of a month, the whole catch of fish, to the beast. The fish disappeared down the terrible throat of the monster in a moment's time.

"Give me cow," snarled Abaremasu. But he did not wait for the boy to decide. The beast grabbed the cow and shoved it down his mouth, stretching the saggy, splotchy skin of his lips wide in a sickening slurp. Still hungry, the beast moved towards the boy howling, "I eat you now!"

Thinking fast, the boy cried, "Wait! How could you eat me with no tea to drink, no rice to eat? Your deeds of strength will go unsung if you should eat in a manner that has no honor. Tell me where the finest tea leaves and grains of rice grow, and I will bring them to you."

The beast pointed to the mountain and grunted the words, "Tea! Rice!"

"Stay here then, and use the wisdom you are known for, to decide on the best tea ceremony. I will soon return." With that, the son of the fisherman made his way quickly to the faraway fields of tea and rice. After harvesting as much as he could, the boy went back to his village. There he restored his family's fortune by selling the tea and rice. His village had hardly seen such foods before the boy overcame the beast.

Abaremasu, waiting by the mountain, believed the sweet words of the boy until he realized that he knew of no tea ceremonies at all. The beast never caught up to the swift child. The giant Abaremasu can still be heard in the mountains, howling his rage and disappointment to the clouds and to the rain, while his eye shoots off huge red and yellow lights through the skies.

1. What is the author's main purpose or motivation for writing this story? Give a reason with details from the story for your answer.

2. What is the author's purpose in having the boy trick the monster with "sweet words"? Use details from the story to support your response.

3. What is the author's attitude towards each of the two main characters in the story? Give specific details from the story to support your answer.

4. The attitude a writer takes towards his subject is known as his _____.
   A. style   B. tone   C. vocabulary   D. flavor

5. An author's personal way of conveying the point he wants to express is called his _____.
   A. style   B. technique   C. implication   D. range

6. Main ideas that are stated outright in the passage are known as _____ main ideas.
   A. inferred   B. implied   C. directly-stated   D. factual

7. Main ideas that must be discovered through careful reading of details are known as _____ main ideas.
   A. implied   B. direct   C. inferred   D. paraphrased

8. _____ is a writer's way of expressing his thoughts.
   A. Voice   B. Diction   C. Bias   D. Style

9. Read the following sentence: The prolific actor has starred in four movies this year alone. Taken in context, we can conclude that the underlined word means
   A. unemployed   B. hard-working   C. lazy   D. untalented

10. Criticism that evaluates the time and place in which an author lived is called _____ context.
   A. political   B. historical   C. social   D. cultural

11. Examining _____ involves considering what social factors, such as moral codes and belief systems, influenced the author's efforts.
   A. biographical context   C. modern criticism
   B. postcolonial theory   D. cultural relevance

12. All the personal events of an author's life lead him towards his _____ perspective when writing.
   A. biographical   C. biased
   B. autobiographical   D. misinformed

13. The beginning of a word is known as the _____..
   A.   prefix   B.   root   C.   suffix   D.   idiom

14. The actual meaning of a group of words is called the _____ meaning
   A.   figurative   B.   literal   C.   idiomatic   D.   main

Above each bolded word, write its meaning. Use context clues to help you.

15. The fire threatened to spread to the **adjacent** houses, potentially destroying the entire neighbor-hood.

16. After a **cursory** examination of only a minute or two, the doctor said he did not believe there was anything seriously wrong with the child.

17. Smoking too much is likely to have a **pernicious** effect on one's health; cigarettes are not called "cancer sticks" for nothing.

18. To drive home his point by repetition, John **reiterated** the facts again regarding the trial.

19. The bad odor from the leaking gas **permeated** the whole house.

20. The teacher **hypothesized** about the student's tardiness but couldn't prove it.

Chapter 2
Literary Elements and Devices

This chapter addresses the following performance standards:

Standards	ELA9RL1, ELA9RL2, ELA9RC2

Literature in its current form has existed for more than six centuries, but the techniques of conveying a story have not greatly changed. These techniques, which the writer uses to create an emotionally affecting story, are known as **literary elements**. These elements are found in all genres and have become a fundamental part of the narrative process.

When you read a novel or short story, your close mental involvement will reveal its basic components, by recognizing the parts that make a work complete and whole. This is the real power of critical reading and an important step in becoming a better reader. As we saw in the last chapter, rather than passively absorbing a story, close reading becomes a kind of detective work, because you're able to see the author's goals — and faults — in presenting a story.

LITERARY ELEMENTS

For a book or short story — or a stage play or poem — to function well, several elements must work together in perfect harmony, creating a final effect that is greater than themselves alone. These **literary elements** include:

Theme:	the story's message
Setting:	the story's place and time
Characterization:	the story's cast
Conflict:	the story's struggle
Imagery:	the story's description

In the next chapter, we'll take a look at fiction, nonfiction, poetry and stage genres one-by-one. Before we do that, though, let's "peel back" their surfaces and examine the basic working parts they have in common.

THEME

Writing is really the act of communicating through words, so a literary work always relates a central idea that its author wants to share with the audience. This "big idea" is the **theme** communicated in the work. Theme is not the *subject* of a work but rather *the insight about that subject* that the work relates to its audience. Themes are most often messages about life or human nature. For example, many stories are written about love. A very common theme in literature is that "love always triumphs over evil."

We sometimes understand themes without realizing. For example, have you ever watched a movie or television program and thought, "That was just preachy" or "That tried too hard"? When a work's theme is too obvious, we grow impatient because our mind feels "cheated" of reaching its own conclusions.

When a theme is obviously meant to reach an audience, we say it is an **explicit** theme. Fables and folk tales often include explicit, or directly stated, themes. The theme of "The Tortoise and the Hare" is clearly understood to be "slow and steady wins the race."

Themes may also be **abstract**, which in this sense means open to reader interpretation. Abstract themes usually appear in **genre** fiction such as science fiction or detective novels. But remember, any work of *literature* — which is to say, a story of great fame and stature — has a theme. For example, the implied theme of *Call of the Wild* is that loyalty and friendship conquer obstacles too big for one person to face alone. Sometimes great works have many themes, and scholars argue about the author's purpose in creating them. After 150 years, people are still discussing the themes of *Moby Dick*.

A theme is something the mind discovers for itself after considering the story as a whole. Do not confuse a book's theme with its subject. The **subject** is *who* and *what* the story is about — the characters, places and events.

The Tragedy of Romeo and Juliet	
Subject:	**Theme:**
Two young people fall in love, despite their families' wishes.	Love conquers everything, even the demand of the world around us.

On the left, you see the events of the story itself. But the theme (the "message") applies not just to the story but to life in general — at least, according to the author. That message is the **theme**.

UNIVERSAL THEMES

Some situations are shared by all peoples no matter when and where they live. Literature very often focuses on these **universal themes** of common human experience. For a theme to be universal, it must deal with human experiences that are found in any particular time period or cultural environment.

Some of the most common universal themes include good struggling against evil, the delicateness of life, and, of course, love in all its varieties. Family relationships, death and rebirth, man surviving against nature, and a young person's struggles to reach maturity (in works known as "coming of age" stories) are also common universal themes.

Universal Themes in Literature	
Theme	**Work**
Good always wins over evil	*The Chronicles of Narnia*
Power corrupts	*Animal Farm*
War forces men to change	*The Things They Carried*
Nature works by its own set of laws	*The Old Man & The Sea*
Individuals must think for themselves	*Ender's Game*

Practice 1: Identifying Universal Themes

Make a list of five novels or short stories you have read and five movies you have seen. Next to the title of each one, identify the universal theme. Write a sentence or two explaining why you decided on your answer. Compare lists with your classmates. If you listed some of the same titles but have different answers, discuss and defend your answers.

FINDING THEME

A theme is rarely stated outright: being so obvious robs the reader of discovering its meaning on his own. Rather, the reader has to infer the theme by looking at all the details from the work. Figuring out the theme in a work of literature is not always easy, but there are ways to make it less difficult:

- Look at the conflicts and how they are resolved. This resolution of the conflict, and how the conflicts change people or places, often points towards the theme.

- Look at the title of the work. Sometimes titles have special meaning or give clues about the theme. For example, the title of Sebastian Junger's book *The Perfect Storm* makes the reader think about what could trigger a storm of such size and power to be considered "perfect." Its theme — that great and terrible forces of nature and fate sometimes converge with devastating effect — echoes throughout the title and prepares the reader for the events related in the text.

Finding Themes

1. **Read** the passage carefully.

2. **Think of one statement** that summarizes the overall message.

3. **Make sure the details** in the passage support your answer. Sometimes a statement may be true but not relevant to the passage.

4. **Make sure your answer** summarizes the message of the *entire* passage, not just one part.

Practice 2: Theme

Read the following passages. Then choose the theme that best fits each one from the choices provided.

1.

     As the old man walked the beach at dawn, he noticed a young man ahead of him picking up starfish and flinging them into the sea. Finally, catching up with the youth, he asked why he was doing this. The young man explained that the stranded starfish would die if left until the morning sun.

     "But the beach goes on for miles, and there are millions of star-fish," commented the old man. "How can your effort make any difference?"

     The young man looked at the starfish in his hand and then threw it safely in the waves. "It makes a difference to this one," he said.

A.   The morning sun will kill stranded starfish.
B.   Starfish must be saved from extinction.
C.   Saving even one life can make a difference.
D.   Don't walk on a beach with starfish on it.

2.   It was market day. The narrow window of the jail looked down directly on the carts and wagons drawn up in a long line, where they had unloaded. He could see, too, and hear distinctly the clink of money as it changed hands, the busy crowd of whites and blacks shoving, pushing one another, and the haggling and swearing at the stalls. Somehow, the sound, more than anything else had done, wakened him up, — made the whole real to him. He was done with the world and the business of it. He let the tin fall, and looked out, pressing his face close to the rusty bars. How they crowded and pushed! And he, — he should never walk that pavement again!

– excerpted from *Life in the Iron Mills*, by Rebecca Davis

A.   When the busy marketplace wakes up, everyone around must awake as well.
B.   A person who retires should move away from overcrowded and noisy areas.
C.   Freedom is often taken for granted until it is lost.
D.   Some people prefer to act, while others prefer to watch.

SETTING

Setting is the background for the action of a story. Setting includes the *time*, *place* and *general surroundings* in which the story takes place. A setting can be realistic, as it would be in a historical novel, or it can be imaginary, as in science fiction or fantasy. For example, the New York City found in an episode of *Law & Order* would be for the most part true to life, while the world of *Star Wars* is purely make-believe.

The setting of a story affects the *mood*, creates *conflict*, and influences the *characters*. Below are three aspects of setting.

Time:	when the story takes place. It may be past, present, or future. For example, the novel *Ender's Game* takes place at least a hundred years in the future.
Place:	where the story happens, including such details as geographic place, scenery, or arrangement of a house or room. The place may be real or imaginary. In *The Outsiders*, the action takes place in Tulsa, Oklahoma during the 1950s.
General Surroundings:	the daily habits of characters, including their job, religious practices, or the economic or emotional spirit of the area in which they live. In Raymond Carver's "Where I'm Calling From," the characters are all patients in an alcohol rehabilitation clinic. The mood and routine there influence their actions and thoughts in every way.

Practice 3:

Read the passage below carefully. Then answer the questions which follow it:

> Paris was blockaded, starved, in its death agony. Sparrows were becoming scarcer and scarcer on the rooftops and the sewers were being depopulated. One ate whatever one could get. As he was strolling sadly along the outer boulevard one bright January morning, his hands in his trousers pockets and his stomach empty, M. Morissot, watchmaker by trade but local militiaman for the time being, stopped short before a fellow militiaman whom he recognized as a friend. It was M. Sauvage, a riverside acquaintance.

– excerpted from "Two Friends" by Guy de Maupassant

1. **Short answer.** Use your own paper to respond. The story takes place during a war between Germany and France in 1870. Write a list of words and phrases in the description of the setting, which indicate that the story takes place during a war.

2. **Short answer.** Use your own paper to respond. What details from the passage describe the characters and their lives?

MOOD & TONE

Any work of fiction has a feel to it, a sense of the place that comes from really engaging the description of its setting and characters. This feeling — the soul of a work, its atmosphere — is called **mood**. Authors create mood by carefully choosing the words they use to tell the story, using point of view, description and plot development to bring a sense of location and emotion to the work. For example, in the novel *My Antonia*, Willa Cather uses the vanished American prairie frontier to evoke a sense of nostalgia, regret, and sentimental memory.

Varieties of Mood				
dismal	peaceful	anxious	joyful	elated
melancholic	chaotic	mysterious	creepy	humorous

Mood is closely related to **tone**, which as we discussed in Chapter One is the writer's attitude toward his subject. Like mood, authors convey tone through language, word choice, and story pace. The novel *Tom Sawyer* has a tone of lighthearted nostalgia and humor. Sometimes, the tone can be reversed for humorous effect. In the novel *The Hitchhiker's Guide to the Galaxy*, the tone is light and carefree, even though the story is actually very dark. This type of reversal usually appears in **satires**.

CHARACTERIZATION

In literature, characters must have clear qualities that set them apart from other characters in the same work or characters in other works. Authors must portray these qualities in such a way that shows what to expect of the characters' behavior.

Characterization consists of the statements an author makes about a character through description or narration. It also includes what can be observed about a character, such as how the character speaks, other characters' opinions of him, his actions, and how he reacts to others.

Revealing Character Traits

Description	An author tells how characters look, dress, and their ages, just as you might describe a friend of yours to someone else. In Eudora Welty's story "A Worn Path," the narrator describes the main character, Phoenix Jackson, as an old, small Negro woman in plain but neat clothing.
Narration	the telling of the story through a speaker. The speaker could be one of the characters or could be an unknown observer. The speaker will tell how other characters feel or think about another character or will describe how they act towards that character. In *The Red Badge of Courage*, there is an unknown narrator who is limited to telling the story through the eyes of a young soldier.
Dialogue	conversation between two or more people. Mark Twain in *The Adventures of Huckleberry Finn* shows the character traits of Huck and Jim in the talks they share while rafting down the Mississippi River. • **Diction** is the *choice* of words a character uses. Authors usually use diction to reflect something about the character. For example, the uncomplicated language used by Jim demonstrates the character's honesty and good-hearted simplicity.
Actions	sometimes the actions of a character speak louder than words to show the character's true self. The main characters in O. Henry's "The Gift of the Magi" show their love for each other by placing the happiness of the other before themselves. There is a famous saying in literature that "action *is* character" - that characters reveal themselves most effectively by *doing* things.

Different characters also play different roles over the course of a story:

The **narrator** is the person telling the story. He or she will often be the main character. In *The Outsiders*, the narrator is Pony Boy Curtis, and he is also the main character. Sometimes another character or an outside voice narrates the story, as for example, Nick Carraway in *The Great Gatsby*.

The **protagonist** is the main character. He leads the plot, gets involved in the conflict and often changes by the end of the story. The protagonist is usually the hero, but not always. Many short stories by Edgar Allan Poe have protagonists who do evil things.

The **antagonist** struggles against the protagonist. An antagonist can also be a force blocking the protagonist, such as nature or society. In Jack London's "To Build a Fire," the antagonist is the freezing climate of the Alaskan wilderness.

Besides these central "actors," a narrative may also feature many other characters. A short story will have only a few, but authors use similar influences to reveal their characters as well.

INFLUENCES ON CHARACTERS

Relationships	The character's background and contact with other people. Through the narrator of a story, authors can describe a character's family life, job, and social position. An author can show through actions and words how a character thinks and feels about the story's relationships (family, friends, strangers). In Hemingway's *The Sun Also Rises*, Jake's tortured relationship with Lady Brett Ashley controls much of his attention.
Motivations	the reasons that characters have for acting a certain way. These reasons are often wants or desires. In human nature, we often find that the desire to *keep* something is often every bit as powerful as the desire to *obtain* something. For example, a character who is enslaved will want to gain freedom. A character who has freedom will want to keep it. In John Steinbeck's *The Pearl*, Kino and his family want to escape poverty.
Conflicts	In stories, an author creates interest by setting up conflicts or problems that the characters must resolve. How characters deal with problems says a lot about them. Do the characters run from difficulty, or do they work through problems? *Internal* conflicts are created inside the character's mind when trying to decide on the right way to act or how to understand life. *External* conflicts come from outside the character, like a test or a street fight.
Influences	To make a story as real as possible, an author will describe influences that help to shape the story's characters. An **influence** is an outside pressure or force that can change the thoughts and actions of a character. If a character knows that a certain way of dressing is the way to make friends, that is an outside pressure that may change how the character dresses. If a character knows something is illegal, the character may be influenced by the law not to act in a dangerous way. How a character reacts to influences says a lot about the character.

Practice 4: Characterization

Read the following passage and answer the questions that follow.

The transcontinental express swung along the windings of the Sand River Valley, and in the rear seat of the observation car a young man sat greatly at his ease, not in the least discomfited by the fierce sunlight which beat in upon his brown face and neck and strong back. There was a look of relaxation and of great passivity about his broad shoulders, which seemed almost too heavy until he stood up and squared them. He wore a pale flannel shirt and a blue silk necktie with loose ends. His trousers were wide and belted at the waist, and his short sack coat hung open. His heavy shoes had seen good service. His reddish-brown hair, like his clothes, had a foreign cut. He had deep-set, dark blue eyes under heavy reddish eyebrows. His face was kept clean only by close shaving, and even the sharpest razor left a glint of yellow in the smooth brown of his skin. His teeth and the palms of his hands were very white. His head, which looked hard and stubborn, lay indolently in the green cushion of the wicker chair, and as he looked out at the ripe summer country a teasing, not unkindly smile played over his lips. Once, as he basked thus comfortably, a quick light flashed in his eyes, curiously dilating the pupils, and his mouth became a hard, straight line, gradually relaxing into its former smile of rather kindly mockery. He told himself, apparently, that there was no point in getting excited; and he seemed a master hand at taking his ease when he could. Neither the sharp whistle of the locomotive nor the brakeman's call disturbed him. It was not until after the train had stopped that he rose, put on a Panama hat, took from the rack a small valise and a flute case, and stepped deliberately to the station platform. The baggage was already unloaded, and the stranger presented a check for a battered sole-leather steamer trunk.

– excerpted from "The Bohemian Girl," by Willa Cather

1. Which of the following sentences best describes the young man?

    A. He is poorly dressed and feeling uncomfortable.

    B. He is hard working and curious.

    C. He is dressed strangely and very excited.

    D. He is strong, relaxed, and a stranger in this place.

2. What does the following sentence say about the character?

    "His head, which looked hard and stubborn, lay indolently in the green cushion of the wicker chair, and as he looked out at the ripe summer country a teasing, not unkindly smile played over his lips."

    A. He is tired from his long trip and wishes it were over.

    B. He is a stubborn man and is feeling pleased.

    C. He enjoys teasing people.

    D. His head is very large and strange looking.

3. What three methods of characterization are used to describe the man?

    A. observation, dialogue, and narration   C. description, observation, and action

    B. dialogue, description, and action   D. thought, observation, and narration

4. On your own paper, find and write an example for each of the three methods of characterization used in this passage.

Practice 5: Characters and Characterization

Choose a fictional work from your literature textbook. After reading your selection, complete the following activities on your own paper.

1. Describe the character types from the work you selected. Who is the narrator? Who is the protagonist? Who or what is the antagonist?

2. Choose one main character from your fictional work, and describe how the author has shown the character. Which of the four methods of characterization did the author use to reveal the character? Then describe the character completely by listing as many character traits as you can.

POINT OF VIEW

Point of View is the perspective, or outlook, from which a writer tells a story. There may be a character narrating the story, or there may be an unknown, all-seeing speaker describing the action and thoughts of the main characters. It may help you to think of point of view as a "camera" from which the author shows you the story. The view shown by the camera is classified as one of three perspectives:

FEATURES OF POINT OF VIEW	
First Person	the narrator tells the story from his own point of view, saying "I did this" or "I did that." Perhaps the most famous example of recent times is J.D. Salinger's *The Catcher In The Rye*.
Second Person	the book itself addresses the reader, as if the reader is an active character in the book. For example, "You are walking down the street one morning when…" Second person narration is rarely used. Jay McInerney's *Bright Lights, Big City*, is one of only a few examples of second person narration.
Third Person	This point of view contains the majority of fiction written before the 20th century. In third person, a narrator moves unseen among the characters, relating their actions. There are two kinds of third person narration, with different advantages and difficulties:
• **omniscient**	narrators can see everything and everywhere, even relating the characters' thoughts. Charles Dickens' *Oliver Twist* is an example of omniscient third.
• **limited**	third person narration (sometimes called **approximate third**) centers on one character and observes only what he sees, hears, feels or does. It will also sometimes include his thoughts. Erich Maria Remarque's *All Quiet On The Western Front*, as it focuses on the soldier Baumer, is an example of this kind of work.

Practice 6: Point of View

Go through your literature text or local library, finding examples of each type of point of view. Read a few paragraphs of each, listening to the "feel" of the narration. Which one feels most comfortable to you? Why? On a separate piece of paper, record your thoughts. Then share them with a teacher or classmate.

CONFLICT

When speaking of literary devices, the term **conflict** has the same meaning as in everyday conversation — a struggle between two or more opposing forces. Conflicts are the obstacles or problems that the characters must resolve. How characters deal with such problems define them as people. Do they run from difficulty, or do they rise above? As mentioned on the chart, *internal conflicts* are created inside the character's mind when trying to decide on the right way to act or how to understand life. *External conflicts* come from outside the character. Protagonists usually struggle with both

kinds of conflict, and a good story will play off the tension between the two. In *The Old Man and the Sea*, the fisherman Santiago struggles to catch a giant marlin in the Gulf of Mexico while at the same time fighting feelings of doubt and hopelessness.

There are four basic types of conflict:

Four Types of Conflict	
Conflict Type	**Novel/Short Story**
Man vs. Man	*The Sea Wolf*
Man vs. Society	*1984*
Man vs. Nature	*Lord of the Flies*
Man vs. Self	*The Miracle Worker*

Practice 7: Conflict

On your own or with your class, complete the following activities. Review the answers with your teacher.

1. Discuss one or two recent popular films. Describe the main plot and any conflicts.

2. Choose a short story or novel you recently read in school. Identify the plot and subplots in those works. Or determine plots in one of the following novels or stories:

Novels	Short Stories
Across Five Aprils	"Masque of the Red Death"
Flowers for Algernon	"The Lottery"
The Red Badge of Courage	"The Monkey's Paw"
The Pearl	"The Rocking Horse Winner"

PLOT

Perhaps more than any other element, **plot** is essential to storytelling. It is the pattern of events in a story, or everything that happens to form a narrative. It is important to distinguish between plot and story, however. A story is a sequence of events in order. A plot is the events that happen, deliberately arranged in a way that shows cause and effect for the characters. Consider this famous quotation by E.M. Forster to tell the two apart:

> "The king died, and then the queen died" is a *story*.

> "The king died, and then the queen died of a broken heart" is a *plot*.

Traditionally, a plot has several parts. There is the **introduction**, the **rising action**, the **conflict**, the **climax**, the **falling action**, and the **resolution**.

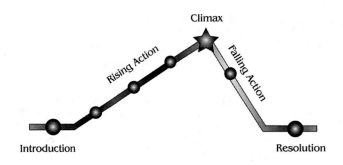

Introduction	sometimes called **exposition**, the introduction is the opening of a story. The author describes the setting, introduces the characters, and reveals conflict. Some authors choose to introduce a main character after revealing the conflict. For example, F. Scott Fitzgerald's short story "May Day" begins with an elaborate description of New York, then "zooms in" to several different groups of characters and their conflicts.
Conflict	occurs when the character encounters an obstacle to something he needs or wants. The struggle that takes place may be between a character and nature, between a character and himself (inner conflict), a character and other characters, or between the character and society — its laws, or its expectations and pressures.
Rising action	is the increasing tension and pressure the character feels to get the object of his need or desire. The rising action of *Romeo and Juliet* occurs when the two lovers attempt to be together despite their families' feud. When rising action reaches its highest degree of suspense, it attains the **climax**.
Climax	is the turning point in a story. It may occur when the conflict is at its worst, or when circumstances permanently change for the character. For example, at the climax of John Steinbeck's *The Grapes of Wrath*, the protagonist Tom Joad vows to spend his life avenging the suffering of poor people. His fate is sealed and his life is changed forever.
Falling action	is the easing of pressure on the main characters: the gradual return to a normal (possibly better) pattern in their lives. In *The Return of the King*, the falling action includes Aragorn becoming king and Frodo returning to the Shire. The falling action is almost always a shorter segment of the story than the rising action.
Resolution	also sometimes called the **denouement**, resolution is the very ending of a story. It is the point at which all conflict has been settled. In tragedy, the resolution is often a sad but final one. In Shakespeare's *MacBeth*, most of the main characters are killed by the final scene. However, in a comedy, the resolution is usually a happy solution to all problems.

Practice 8: Plot & Conflict

On your own or with your class, complete the following activities. Review the answers with your teacher.

1. Recall some of the characters and scenes from *The Wizard of Oz*. Describe the parts of the film, especially what you feel to be the exposition, climax, and denoument.

2. Discuss two recent popular films with a classmate or friend. Describe the main plot.

LITERARY DEVICES

As writers build their story with characters, conflict, and mood, they also use **devices** to help them effectively communicate. Since the earliest spoken epics such as *The Iliad*, writers have used devices to reach their audience. One of the most potent devices is **language**, the terms and words a writer uses to communicate. Language — all languages, both written down and spoken — carry limitless potential to stir human emotion. The right combination of words can amuse, sadden, terrify, reassure… the list includes the whole of human feeling. Writing itself can be described as an attempt to communicate directly with the human spirit, and language is one of the most powerful tools to that end.

The techniques with which writers work with language and story are known as **literary devices.** They number in the dozens, if not hundreds, and there are more invented every year. Perhaps the most fundamental of these techniques, **imagery**, has been around almost as long as the narrative itself.

IMAGERY

Imagery is the attempt to create a mental image for the reader by evoking any of the five senses. Authors use imagery to flesh out the world they create, to draw a reader in by giving them a sensuous, fully-developed sense of place. In *Ask The Dust*, the author John Fante describes a busy Los Angeles intersection:

> And so I was down on Fifth and Olive, where the big street cars chewed your ears with their noise, and the smell of gasoline made the palm trees seem sad, and the black pavement was still wet from the fog of the night before.

In only a few words, Fante creates images which stimulate the reader's sense of sight, sound, smell, and touch. Not surprisingly, the novel is famous for capturing the "feel" of living in California during the 1930s.

IRONY

Irony is the dramatic disparity between what is expected and what proves to be true during a narrative or sequence of events. Irony relates to theme in that many authors use irony to make a theme's emotional impact more powerful. Irony can be the difference between what is *stated* and what is *meant* (**verbal irony**), or between what is *expected* to happen and what *actually* happens (**irony of situation**).

For an example of *verbal irony*, imagine that you and some of your friends have been working on a project for school. It's been a long, hot, and tiring day. One friend suddenly announces to the group, "I've had about as much fun as I can stand!" That person is using verbal irony to express a wish to go home, saying that it's been too much fun — but meaning that it's really been too much work.

An example of *irony of situation* is displayed near the end of the movie *The Empire Strikes Back*. Darth Vader, the antagonist, reveals to Luke, the protagonist and his bitter enemy, that he is Luke's father. That the two have struggled for years is ironic because they are actually family.

Practice 9: Irony

Consider the last few movies you saw or the last books or stories you read. Can you recollect any examples of either kind of irony? Write several down and share them with a classmate. Then discuss them with your instructor or mentor.

SYMBOLISM

We use symbols such as signs, posters, and logos in everyday life, as shorthand for ideas or concepts. **Symbols**, over time and widespread use, have become universal — recognizable to everyone, regardless of heritage or language. For example, a skull and crossbones represents "poison," while a red hexagon means "stop."

Symbols appear in literature, as well, and while there are *universal symbols* that appear time and again, authors will create their own symbolism to reinforce and deepen their intended themes. Symbols may appear as characters, setting, plot events, or specific images or objects in the story. Each one points to a larger idea and/or theme the author wants to represent.

Book	Symbol	Meaning
The Great Gatsby	light across the bay	yearning, impossible goals
Song of Solomon	flight	freedom, escape
To Kill a Mockingbird	mockingbird	innocence, childhood, freedom
Adventures of Huckleberry Finn	the duke, the king	corruption, evil of the noble elite
A Raisin in the Sun	Mama's flower	hope for the future

When trying to determine the meaning of a symbol or image in a passage, consider the overall structure of the story. Often times, the writer will work in a set of symbols, called an *aesthetic* or *design*. As such, various symbols within a work are often related. For example, in *The Lord of the Flies,* both the Beastie and the pig's head — references to the Devil — represent the pervasive presence of evil on the island.

Practice 10: Symbolism

Read the passage below. Then answer the questions that follow.

He was quick and alert in the things in life, but only in the things, and not in the significant things. Fifty degrees below zero meant eighty degrees of frost. Such fact impressed him as being cold and uncomfortable, and that was all. It did not lead him to meditate upon his frailty as a creature of temperature, and upon man's frailty in general, able only to live within certain narrow limits of heat and cold; and from there on it did not lead him to the conjectural field of immortality and man's place in the universe. Fifty degrees below zero was to him just precisely fifty degrees below. That there should be anything more to it than that was a thought that never entered his head.

As he turned to go on, he spat speculatively. There was a sharp explosive crackle that startled him. He spat again. And again, in the air, before it could fall to the snow, the spittle crackled. He knew that at fifty below spittle crackled on the snow, but this spittle had crackled in the air. Undoubtedly it was colder than fifty below — how much colder he did not know. But the temperature did not matter. He was bound for the old claim on the left fork of Henderson Creek, where the boys were already. They had come over across the divide from the Indian Creek country, while he had come the roundabout way to take a look at the possibilities of getting out logs in the spring from the islands in the Yukon. He would be in to camp by six o'clock; a bit after dark, it was true, but the boys would be there, a fire would be going, and a hot supper would be ready. As for lunch, he pressed his hand against the protruding bundle under his jacket. It was also under his shirt, wrapped up in a handkerchief and lying against the naked skin. It was the only way to keep the biscuits from freezing. He smiled agreeably to himself as he thought of those biscuits, each cut open and sopped in bacon grease, and each enclosing a generous slice of fried bacon.

He plunged in among the big spruce trees. The trail was faint. A foot of snow had fallen since the last sled had passed over, and he was glad he was without a sled, traveling light. In fact, he carried nothing but the lunch wrapped in the handkerchief. He was surprised, however, at the cold. It certainly was cold, he concluded, as he rubbed his numb nose and cheekbones with his mittened hand. He was a warm-whiskered man, but the hair on his face did not protect the high cheekbones and the eager nose that thrust itself aggressively into the frosty air.

– excerpted from "To Build A Fire," by Jack London

1. What do the biscuits symbolize in the story? Why do you think so?

2. What does the old claim symbolize? Why do you think so?

3. From reading the passage, do you think the prospector will survive the cold? Why or why not?

FIGURATIVE LANGUAGE

Writers work in patterns of words to create their images. They may repeat ideas, images, sounds or words, compare two different things, or create a likeness between any two of the above.

An **extended metaphor** continues over several sentences or passages, sometimes over an entire work. George Orwell's *Animal Farm* is an elaborate re-imagining of the 1917 Bolshevik Revolution in Russia. The entire text is meant to represent the rise and ethical decline of the communists' control of Russian society. Works that use metaphor over their entire narrative belong in a special category, called **allegory**.

An **allusion** is a reference to a specific place, a historical event, a famous literary figure, real or fictitious, or a work of art. Allusions can be drawn from history, geography, science, math, religion, or literature. In order to identify an allusion in a piece of literature, the reader must have prior knowledge of the reference in question. In the film *The Matrix*, Morpheus alludes to Lewis Carroll's book *Alice in Wonderland* when he tells Neo he can either stay in the real world or see how far down "the rabbit hole" goes. Anyone not familiar with Lewis Carroll's "Alice in Wonderland" might not identify the allusion.

You probably use allusions all the time, as modern slang is filled with references to vivid images or famous people, quotations, events or locations. Some examples include:

- "a complete Pearl Harbor"
- "go postal"
- "uglier than a homemade sandwich

Practice 11: Allusions

Read the two excerpts below and see if you can identify the allusion in each.

1. "Two brothers devised what at sight

   Seemed a bicycle crossed with a kite.

   They predicted — rash pair!

   It would fly through the air!

   And what do you know? They were Wright!"
   – excerpted from "Two Brothers Devised what at Sight," by Laurence Perrine

2. "Jack, eating rotten cheese, did say,

   Like Samson I my thousands slay;

   I vow, quoth Roger, so you do.

   And with the self-same weapon, too."
   – excerpted from "Jack, Eating Rotten Cheese, Did Say," by Benjamin Franklin

3. **Extended Response.** Make a list of ten allusions you use or have heard others make. Did you understand the meaning of each allusion, or was the reference too obscure? Give reasons for your answers.

Foreshadowing is a literary device in which the author drops small clues about what is going to happen later in the story. Foreshadowing hints at the possible outcome without giving the ending details away before their appropriate time.

Authors use foreshadowing to tighten suspense for the audience and engage their minds into making predictions. Anton Chekhov, possibly the greatest short story writer of all time, explained foreshadowing as "the shotgun on the wall." If the reader or audience sees a shotgun on the wall of a scene, the shotgun has a purpose and should be used in the story. But its appearance *foreshadows* its use, keeping the audience anxious.

Practice 12: Foreshadowing

Think of three recent examples of foreshadowing you have read or experienced. Write them down, and also list if the event predicted came to pass. Share your results with a classmate or teacher.

CHAPTER 2 SUMMARY

Theme is the larger ideas a writer weaves into his work. A theme may be *explicit* or *abstract*. **Universal themes** apply to audiences of all ages and cultures.

Setting is the background of the story's action. It includes the **time, place,** and **general surroundings** in which the characters live and operate. A setting can be real or imaginary.

Mood is used to describe the atmosphere of a story — the feeling evoked by the writer's language and plot development. Mood is closely related to **tone**, which involves the writer's attitude towards the subject material.

Characterization consists of the writer's statements about a character using description or narration. Character is revealed through interaction with others, motivations, and conflict.

Point of View is the perspective, or outlook, from which a writer tells a story.

Conflict is the struggle, either with the self or with external forces, which a character endures over the course of a narrative.

Plot is the events that happen along the course of a story. It is not the same as story, which is a sequence of events in order.

Literary devices are techniques used by writers to stir emotion in their audience:

- **Imagery** is the use of language to evoke the reader's five senses.
- **Irony** is the dramatic disparity between what is expected and what proves to be true.
- **Symbolism** is the use of images, events, or characters in a narrative for dramatic and thematic effect.

Figurative language is the crafting of text in such a way that provokes a response in the audience.

- An **extended metaphor** is a comparison between two things that runs through the entire work.
- An **allusion** is a reference to a specific place, historical event, literary figure, or work of art.
- **Foreshadowing** involves giving the audience a glimpse of what is going to happen in a story, in order to heighten suspense.

CHAPTER 2 REVIEW

Questions 1 – 3 refer to the following passage:

      I had the story, bit by bit, from various people, and, as generally happens in such cases, each time it was a different story. If you know Starkfield, Massachusetts, you know the post office. If you know the post office you must have seen Ethan Frome drive up to it, drop the reins on his hollow-backed bay and drag himself across the brick pavement to the white colonnade: and you must have asked who he was.

      It was there that, several years ago, I saw him for the first time; and the sight pulled me up sharp. Even then he was the most striking figure in Starkfield, though he was but the ruin of a man. It was not so much his great height that marked him, for the "natives" were easily singled out by their lank longitude from the stockier foreign breed: it was the careless powerful look he had, in spite of a lameness checking each step like the jerk of a chain. There was something bleak and unapproachable in his face, and he was so stiffened and grizzled that I took him for an old man and was surprised to hear that he was not more than fifty-two. I had this from Harmon Gow, who had driven the stage from Bettsbridge to Starkfield in pre-trolley days and knew the chronicle of all the families on his line.

      "He's looked that way ever since he had his smash-up; and that's twenty-four years ago come next February," Harmon threw out between reminiscent pauses.

– excerpted from *Ethan Frome*, by Edith Wharton

1. How do you learn about Ethan Frome? Select all that apply.

    A. his actions   C. his appearance

    B. his thoughts   D. the comments of others

2. Which is a good description of Ethan Frome?

    A. a strong, powerful man   C. a tall, handicapped man

    B. an old, weak man   D. a strong, lean young man

3. **Extended Response.** Use your own paper to write your response. Write a detailed character description of Ethan Frome. Use passages from the selection to support your description. What does Ethan Frome's description tell us about the man?

Questions 4 – 6 refer to the following passage:

During the whole of a dull, dark, and soundless day in the autumn of the year, when the clouds hung oppressively low in the heavens, I had been passing alone, on horseback, through a singularly dreary tract of country; and at length found myself, as the shades of the evening drew on, within view of the melancholy House of Usher. I know not how it was — but, with the first glimpse of the building, a sense of insufferable gloom pervaded my spirit. I say insufferable; for the feeling was unrelieved by any of that half-pleasurable, because poetic, sentiment, with which the mind usually receives even the sternest natural images of the desolate or terrible. I looked upon the scene before me — upon the mere house, and the simple landscape features of the domain — upon the bleak walls — upon the vacant eye-like windows — upon a few rank sedges— and upon a few white trunks of decayed trees — with an utter depression of soul…

– excerpted from "The Fall of the House of Usher," by Edgar Allan Poe

4. Which of the following best describes the setting?
   A. a quiet, rainy day in the country
   B. a sunny afternoon at the Usher House
   C. a dark, gloomy day in autumn at the House of Usher in the country
   D. a simple landscape of trees, hedges, and quiet buildings

5. **Short answer.** Use your own paper for your response.

   What details from the passage show the mood? Do the ideas work together to give a vivid sense of the location? Do you think they imply what will happen in the story? Why or why not?

6. "I woke up every two hours waiting for the news."

The sentence above is an example of the _____ person point of view.

   A. first   B. second   C. third person   D. third person
                                            limited   omniscient

7. A story about a young man struggling to lose 100 lbs would most likely be described as having what kind of conflict?
   A. man vs. nature   C. man vs. self
   B. man vs. society
                                         D. man vs. man

8. The difference between what is stated and what is meant is known as _____ irony.
   A. verbal   B. situational   C. metaphorical   D. symbolic

9. The turning point of a story occurs during the _____.
   A. rising action   B. exposition   C. falling action   D. climax

10. Language used to evoke the five senses is known as _____.
    A. symbolism   B. tone   C. voice   D. imagery

11. The following sentence uses what kind of figurative language?
    "He's pretty much the Quentin Tarantino of his generation."
    A. irony   B. allusion   C. symbolism   D. archetype

12. Giving the audience a glimpse of something still to come is called_____.
    A. teasing   C. foreshadowing.
    B. flash-forwards   D. rising action

13. Which of the following is *not* a segment of plot?
    A. rising action   B. exposition   C. allusion   D. climax

14. Situations shared by people of all times and cultures are known as _____ themes.
    A. universal   B. common   C. international   D. hypothetical

15. The choice of words a character uses is known as his_____.
    A. inflection   B. dialogue   C. pronuncia-   D. diction
                                                      tion

Chapter 3
Fiction, Nonfiction, Poetry & Drama

This chapter addresses the following performance standards:

Standards	ELA9RL1, ELA9RL3, ELA9RL4, ELA9RC1, ELA9RC4

In Chapter Two, we discussed the inner workings of prose fiction and nonfiction, how many different elements combine to create a work of writing that is more than the sum of its parts. Authors carefully craft setting, characterization, mood and plot to create a unified work that conveys observations, beliefs, and emotions to the reader.

The techniques of theme, setting and mood also apply to the genres of poetry and theatre, as well, though their methods of execution vary in many important ways. Because the act of reading a poem or watching a stage play is different than reading a prose text, it is only natural that the delivery of such ideas vary according to the **genre**, or type of writing. That's not to say their *substance* changes, because the use of ideas and the desire to communicate cut across all literary and artistic efforts. Rather, their delivery and appearance varies according to the demands each genre places upon both the writer and the audience.

In this chapter, we'll run the course of literary genres, exploring fiction and nonfiction, poetry and drama. We'll also look at unique elements within each and determine how they differ from one another. We'll begin by looking at *prose*: the intersecting worlds of fiction and nonfiction.

FICTION AND NONFICTION

The majority of **prose writing** — which is to say, writing that is not script writing or poetry — usually, but not always, falls into the categories of fiction and nonfiction.

FICTION

Fiction is a literary work produced by the imagination, not necessarily based on fact. Fiction is easily distinguished from nonfiction because it almost always takes the shape of a **narrative**: it tells a story with a *beginning*, *middle*, and *end*. While fiction is "made up" in that the events described didn't actually happen, for thousands of years authors have based fiction on real-life events. They change names, locations, and other details, but the basic truths of inspiration remain. A famous example is the novel *All The King's Men* by Robert

Penn Warren. It was based on the life of controversial Louisiana governor Huey P. Long, but not actually true. Other types of fiction, such as *fantasy* and *science fiction*, exist in a world almost completely created by the author's imagination.

It may help you to think of fiction as having a scale, like a car's fuel gauge. At one end is extremely realistic fiction, made-up stories with such attention to detail that they seem like watching the evening news. Such works include the movies *Saving Private Ryan* and *United 93*. At the other end are purely imaginative works like the Harry Potter series or *The Chronicles of Narnia*. One is almost lifelike and the other fantastic. That's not to say one is better — both serve to educate and entertain. But the two extremes are both considered fiction, despite huge differences in both style and purpose.

Fiction most commonly appears in two lengths: the **novel** and the **short story**. A novel is a longer work, usually consisting of more than 85,000 words. A short story is much shorter, almost always less than 15,000 words. While it may be tempting to think of a short story as a brief novel, in fact, the two are very different in their approach to theme, *pacing* (the speed at which the story moves) and *plot structure* (the course of events in the story). Some famous short stories include "The Darling" by Anton Chekhov and "The Lottery" by Shirley Jackson.

The following are the major types of fiction genres:

Novel	Any long, fictional story usually written in prose. Two examples are James F. Cooper's *The Last of the Mohicans* and Alice Walker's *The Color Purple*.
Short Story	Works that tell a complete story in 500 to 15,000 words. Most often, the story has a clear beginning, middle, and end. It reveals the characters' personalities through actions and thoughts. Examples include Eudora Welty's "A Worn Path," John Steinbeck's "The Chrysanthemums," and Flannery O'Connor's "A Good Man Is Hard To Find."
Fantasy	Takes place in another world with magical or otherwise amazing creatures. Examples: *The Lord of the Rings* trilogy by J.R.R. Tolkien; the Harry Potter series.
Romance	Stories of passionate love and heroic deeds, sometimes set in faraway places or historic times. Example: *The English Patient* by Michael Ondaatje.
Science Fiction	A story in which science facts, theories or beliefs are used to interpret the future, others planets and dimensions, or time travel. Examples: *2001: A Space Odyssey*; *Ender's Game* by Orson Scott Card.
Mystery	A story in which the characters face a problem which seems to be beyond explanation; mood and tone convey high degrees of suspense. Examples: the television series *Lost*; *The Long Goodbye* by Raymond Chandler.

Some other types of fiction include:

Allegory	A work in which the characters, setting, or objects represent ideas or beliefs that are more than their place in the story itself. In an allegory, everything symbolically stands for something. Examples include Jonathan Swift's *A Tale of a Tub* and William Golding's *Lord of the Flies*.
Fable	A brief story that teaches a moral lesson, for example the tales in *Aesop's Fables*.
Folk Tale	A story passed on by word of mouth through centuries, sometimes meant to convey a moral lesson. Examples include Grimm's *Fairy Tales*.
Tall Tale	A story of exaggerated, unrealistic acts and deeds, passed down from the American frontier. Examples include the legends of Paul Bunyan, Pecos Bill, and Mike Fink.
Legend	Stories connected with some period in the history of a culture, written to glorify a hero or object. Examples include epic poems such as the Sumerian legend of *Gilgamesh* from India and Homer's *The Iliad*. Epics will be discussed later in this chapter.
Myth	A story with supernatural characters and events, sometimes including religious beliefs or rituals. Myths try to explain the natural order of the world or why things happen. A wealth of examples can be found in the collection *Bullfinch's Mythology*.

Practice 1: Fiction

Go through your literature book or your school or classroom library, finding examples of each kind of fiction. Leaf through them, examining their format and structure. Is there one format you prefer over the others? Why and why not?

NONFICTION

Nonfiction, as its name suggests, deals not with the true-to-life or imaginary but with the concrete facts of the actual world, with events and information that can be scientifically proven. Nonfiction is sometimes also called **journalism.** Its **purpose** or intent is to persuade, to teach, or to inform. Examples include historical accounts, scientific explanations, instructional manuals, and information in newspapers, magazines, or books. Biographies and autobiographies also fit this category. Their purpose is to entertain and to inform.

Informational Article	Writing that gives facts and details, such as in a newspaper or journal. Examples include *Time* magazine articles on the war in Iraq and newspaper features on athletic events. Such articles are *objective*: they do not let the author's personal feelings determine the tone of the writing. • informational articles can also take the form of **pamphlets**, **brochures**, or **manuals** printed by your school, the government, or private companies and representatives such as your doctor or employer. • **technical documents** are another form of informational article. These include the instructions for operating machines or directions on how to use medication.
Biography	The story of a person's life written by someone else. Examples include William Roper's *Life of Sir Thomas Moore* and Lee Server's *Robert Mitchum: Baby, I Don't Care.*
Autobiography	The story of a person's life written by that person. Two very different examples are *Anne Frank: Diary of a Young Girl,* and *Brother Ray: Ray Charles' Own Story.* • a **memoir** is a recollection of a particular event or period in a person's life, rather than an overview of the life as a whole. Jimmy Carter's *An Hour Before Daylight* recounts the former president's boyhood in southwest Georgia.
Diary	A book arranged for entering information by date. Diaries are sometimes published as memoirs. Some examples of *fictitious* diaries — written about imaginary experiences, by authors — have also been published.
Essay	A short work that addresses a topic from an individual's point of view, often using the author's own personal recollections.

Practice 2: Nonfiction

As with Practice 1, go through your literature book or your class or school library, finding examples of each of the types of nonfiction listed above. Take note of their formats, and decide which one you find most absorbing.

POETRY

The words **poetry** and **poem** apply to a vast variety of literary forms, both spoken and written. They also include a wide variety of subjects. There is so much difference in so many different kinds of work considered poetry that it is not easy to nail down a complete definition.

Part of the problem is that **verse** — which is to say, formal writing that is not the **prose** of novels and short stories — is among the oldest forms of human communication. Poetry also often involves **rhythm** and **rhyme**, although neither is necessary for a work to be called poetry. Also, poetry conveys powerful images, feelings, and figurative language in fewer words than prose. Often it uses only phrases, single words, or figures of speech to provoke ideas. Prose, which is much longer, follows standard rules of paragraph and sentence structure.

Some common types of poetry include:

Epic Poems	Long, complicated story-poems. They tell of extraordinary deeds by supernatural heroes and villains. Epics include the literary devices of *invocation* and *epithet*. **Invocation** is asking a god or muse for help. **Epithet** involves naming a character's qualities. Examples include Homer's *The Iliad* and *The Odyssey*, *Beowulf*, and *The Epic of Gilgamesh*.
Lyric Poetry	Conveys an exact mood or feeling to the reader. The poet speaks directly to the reader and asks for the reader's sympathy. Examples of a lyric poem include *The Book of Psalms*. • An important type of lyric poem is the **sonnet**, which is a fourteen line poem with strict formatting. William Shakespeare made the sonnet popular in the 17th century.
Ballads	Part of the oral tradition, ballads tell a story in song. Their subjects can be heroic, satirical, romantic, or political. Ballads focus on the actions and dialogue of a story, not on the characters. They usually end in tragedy. "The Ballad of Jesse James" is an example of an American folk ballad.

POETIC DEVICES

Poetry has a variety of figurative language techniques. These help its effectiveness:

Personification is the device of giving human qualities to something not human. For example, "the stars stare down on us" implies that the inanimate stars watch us as other people might. Other examples include:

- "The stop sign jumped out at me."
- "Summer waited just around the corner."
- "The moon winked at the young lovers."

A **simile** is a comparison of one thing to another, using the words *like* or *as*. Because they make direct connections between two things, similes are said to be *explicit* comparisons:

- "The cold wind howled like a starving wolf."
- "Talking to him is like taking sleeping pills."
- "Her skin was as soft as a rose."

Metaphor is the comparison of two objects without using the words *like* or *as*; it is an *implicit* comparison. For example, in Shakespeare's "As You Like It," a character observes:

> "All the world's a stage.
> And all the men and women merely players.
> They have their exits and their entrances."

Shakespeare connects life itself with a theatrical production, with birth and death akin to the comings and goings of actors in a drama. The speech goes on to list the stages of a man's life as different parts to be played.

Hyperbole (pronounced *hy-PER-buh-lee*) is another way of saying "a figure of speech," a saying that involves gross exaggeration or overstatement to make a point:

- He's as big as a car.
- She's got more money than Bill Gates.
- That was pretty much the worst movie ever made.

Hyperbole is different from idiom, in that with idioms, the meaning of the words is not literal; hyperbole makes a literal — if exaggerated — comparison between two or more things.

POETIC LANGUAGE

In addition to choice of words, poetry often uses specialized sounds of language to convey imagery.

Alliteration is the repetition of consonant sounds at the beginning of words or in stressed syllables. Examples of alliteration in poetry include:

- "Droning a drowsy syncopated tune," – Langston Hughes (repetition of the "d" sound)
- "Ah! Slowly sink/ Behind the western ridge, thou glorious Sun!/ Shine in the slant beams of the sinking orb," – Samuel Taylor Coleridge (repetition of the "s" sound).

Alliteration is perhaps most famously found in childhood tongue twisters, such as "Peter Piper picked a peck of pickled peppers" and "Sally sold seashells down by the seashore." Although it is more commonly used in poetry, alliteration can be found in certain works of prose as well.

Onomatopoeia involves using words whose sound suggest their meaning, such as "whoosh," "splash," "buzz," "hiss" or "kaboom." Onomatopoeia is considered a "spice" by most writers — as with cooking, a little of it goes a long way. Sometimes, onomatopoeic words are used so often they become cliché, such as the phrase "gravel crunching underfoot." However, new onomatopoeias become invented all the time, replenishing the stock of phrases.

Practice 3: Poetic Devices & Language

Read the following sentences. Then identify the figurative language used in each.

1. "I slept like a baby: I woke up every two hours screaming."

   A. simile   B. metaphor   C. onomatopoeia   D. allusion

2. The car screeched to a halt in the driveway.

   A. simile   B. alliteration   C. onomatopoeia   D. symbolism

3. "I had rather be a canker in his hedge than a rose in his grace." – from *Much Ado About Nothing*.

   A. simile   B. metaphor   C. onomatopoeia   D. irony

4. The car told me it was running out of gas.
    A. alliteration   B. symbolism   C. simile   D. personification

5. Whistle while you work.
    A. simile   B. onomatopoeia   C. allusion   D. alliteration

RHYTHM AND RHYME SCHEME

Many forms of poetry require a definite structure to the words used. Such structures, called **fixed forms**, appear in poetry such as sonnets, odes, and ballads. The opposite of this structure is called **free forms** or **free verse**, which has no regular meter or rhythm. Until the 20th century, however, free verse was not widely respected.

It may help you to think of rhythm and rhyme scheme as the skeleton or structure of a poem. From these two components, poets "build" their poems, developing a sense of where certain words must go for the poem to conform to its shape.

RHYTHM

We understand **rhythm** as the arrangement of sounds or movement, in a definite pattern, over a period of time. Rhythm appears in music, in athletics, dance, and even in some fiction. Our minds and bodies react instantly to a perceived pattern of sound. If you've ever found yourself nodding your head or tapping your foot along to music, you've participated in the effects that patterns of sound can have on our consciousness.

Rhythm in poetry is the movement or sense of movement conveyed by a pattern of stressed or unstressed syllables. The pattern has a regular *repetition*, or rate of repeated use.

Rhythm is similar to **meter** (a word pattern of stressed and unstressed syllables) except that rhythm includes the duration of the pattern. To express this another way, rhythm is meter drawn out through the whole of the poem. While meter is the pattern itself, rhythm is its beat. The two work together within the poem's design.

Poets use rhythm to create a movement of words the reader will appreciate. In this excerpt from Edgar Allan Poe's "The Raven," rhythm figures prominently in the poem's sound. Note the stressed and unstressed syllables. Stressed sounds are marked with a (`) and unstressed syllables with a (~)

For the rare and radiant maiden whom the angels name Lenore –

Read the line aloud, stressing the syllables indicated. Do you "hear" its rhythm and meter?

Practice 4: Rhythm

Consider the lines from the following poem by Alfred Lord Tennyson. Mark the lines for rhythm and meter, noting each stressed and unstressed syllable. When you are finished, read the lines aloud. Do your markings fit the rhythm, or do they seem somehow out of whack? Mark them again if they do not fit. Compare your markings with your teacher or classmate.

The Eagle

by Alfred Lord Tennyson

He clasps the crag with crooked hands;
Close to the sun in lonely lands,
Ringed with the azure world, he stands.

The wrinkled sea beneath him crawls;
He watches from his mountain walls,
And like a thunderbolt he falls.

RHYME SCHEME

We define **rhyme** as repeating similar sounds in words that appear close together in a poem. Rhymes can appear several places in poetry:

Internal rhyme is found inside a single line of poetry:

> **Example:** "Poor Jesse had a *wife* to mourn his *life*"

Slant rhymes, also known as *half* rhymes, are words that almost — but don't quite — rhyme. The final consonant sounds of the words rhyme, but the final vowel sounds do not.

> **Example:** I heard a fly buzz when I died —
> The stillness in the *room*
> Was like the stillness in the air
> Between the heaves of *storm*.

> – From "I Heard A Fly Buzz When I Died," by Emily Dickenson

End rhymes are the most common rhyme type; they occur at the end of lines:

> **Example:** "You did not walk with *me*
>
> Of late to the hilltop *tree*."

> – From "The Walk," by Thomas Hardy

Rhyme scheme is the arrangement of rhymes formed by end rhyme. To denote these on paper, we mark them with letters.

> Tyger! Tyger! burning bright (a)
> In the forests of the night, (a)
> What immortal hand or eye (b)
> Could frame thy fearful symmetry? (b)
>
> In what distant deeps or skies (c)
> Burnt the fire of thine eyes? (c)
> On what wings dare he aspire? (d)
> What the hand dare seize the fire? (d)
>
> And what shoulder, & what art. (e)
> Could twist the sinews of thy heart? (e)
> And when thy heart began to beat, (f)
> What dread hand? & what dread feet? (f)
>
> – From "The Tyger," by William Blake

A new letter of the alphabet is given to each new rhyme, so that **couplets** — two-line rhyme pairs — are easily identified. This continues until the poem is finished.

An important difference exists between rhyme schemes that apply to only one **stanza** (or group of lines), and those that continue through an entire poem. Poems with such elaborate rhyme schemes are called *chain rhymes*. Also, in the first stanza, "eye" and "symmetry," though technically a slant rhyme, are marked down as a normal end rhyme.

When reading a poem, pay attention to the rhyme scheme. You will notice how cleverly some poets choose their words both for rhyme and meaning. Sometimes, you will find two words rhyme or have a meaning together you wouldn't expect. Finding such unexpected word usage is one of the joys of reading poetry.

Practice 5: Rhyme Scheme

Read the poem listed below. Then, mark the rhyme scheme on a separate sheet of paper. When you have finished, go back and read the poem, looking for unexpected rhyming word choices. Did the poem surprise you? Why or why not?

The World Is Too Much With Us
by William Wordsworth

> The world is too much with us; late and soon,
> Getting and spending, we lay waste our powers;
> Little we see in Nature that is ours;
> We have given our hearts away, a sordid boon!
> This Sea that bares her bosom to the moon,
> The winds that will be howling at all hours,
> And are up-gathered now like sleeping flowers,
> For this, for everything, we are out of tune;
> It moves us not.— Great God! I'd rather be
> A Pagan suckled in a creed outworn;
> So might I, standing on this pleasant lea,
> Have glimpses that would make me less forlorn;
> Have sight of Proteus rising from the sea;
> Or hear old Triton blow his wreathed horn.

DRAMA

Long before stories and poetry were written down, the ancient Greeks wrote and performed **plays** to communicate ideas and entertain their audiences. Before there were even stages in the modern sense, there were plays and scenes acted for Greek citizens on hillsides and in city plazas.

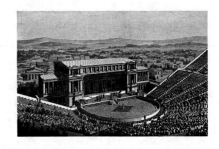

The word *drama* comes from the Greek word for "to do" and "action." Drama as a work of performance craft involves *action* and **dialogue** between the characters. The work is usually performed on a stage or soundstage, and there is almost always conflict, resolution, and character growth. Since the time of the ancient Greeks, through Shakespeare and up to the present period, there have been two main types of drama, the **tragedy** and the **comedy**.

TRAGEDY

Tragedies are plays or films about a central character that end with a sad or unfortunate outcome. Most tragedies descend from the tradition of the Greek philosopher Aristotle, who taught that tragedy should involve conflict between man and either the gods, nature, or society. Tragedy continued through the time of Shakespeare but vanished from the stage for centuries, before becoming resurrected in the 1940s by the playwright Arthur Miller. His classic *Death of a Salesman* involved the tragedy not of a king or great warrior but a beaten-down everyman named Willie Loman. Modern examples of the tragedy include the feature films *American Beauty*, *Gladiator,* and *King Kong*.

WILLIAM SHAKESPEARE AND TRAGEDY

Four centuries after his death, it remains difficult to overstate the impact of William Shakespeare on literature published in the English language. His work has been adapted countless times into all genres, and new versions of his tragedies are constantly appearing on television, on stage, and in film. Moreover, his influence on playwrights, authors, and filmmakers remains unequalled.

SHAKESPEARE

Shakespearean tragedies typically depict a once-revered protagonist who falls from grace, usually through a combination of his own central weakness (called his **tragic flaw**) and the events which surround him. The protagonist almost always dies in the end, along with a good portion of the cast. Shakespeare's four major tragedies are *Hamlet*, *Othello*, *King Lear*, and *MacBeth*.

When evaluating a play for Shakespearean tragic qualities, consider the following:

- What is the protagonist's central conflict(s)? What is his tragic flaw?
- What mistakes does the protagonist make that contribute to his downfall?
- What is the motive of the antagonist? How does he go about committing evil acts?
- Do the protagonist and antagonist ever show regret or remorse for their actions?

Practice 6: Tragedy and The Bard

Consider a Shakespearean tragedy you may have studied the past year or in your lifetime, for example *Hamlet, Romeo & Juliet,* or *Julius Caesar.* Apply the criteria above to the main characters and share your answers with classmates or your mentor. Keep in mind that the character of Brutus is considered the protagonist of *Julius Caesar*, not Caesar himself as the title would suggest.

COMEDY

Dying is easy; comedy is hard.

– Sir Donald Wolfit, famed British thespian

Compared to tragedy, **comedies** are more light-hearted works that attempt to amuse the audience or otherwise lift the spirits. Comedies often mock the conventions of society, particularly the customs of the ruling elite. There is a long tradition that comedies end with the wedding of one or more main characters, as a wedding by its nature signals the promise of a new life.

As Sir Donald Wolfit suggests, comedy is difficult to write and more difficult to perform because provoking laughter requires not just good writing but also precise timing and modes of speech by the actors. Comedy is also "in the eye of the beholder" — what an audience finds funny largely depends on its individual members' tastes and sense of humor. These tastes change over many years, so comedy also runs the risk of seeming dated.

Nevertheless, some comedies have been found intelligent and insightful enough to stand the test of time. Classical examples of comedy include George Bernard Shaw's *Arms and The Man* and Oscar Wilde's *The Importance of Being Earnest*. Modern examples of comedies that follow the classical formulae are *10 Things I Hate About You* (an adaptation of Shakespeare's *Taming of the Shrew*) and the television series *Arrested Development*.

DRAMATIC AND COMEDIC ELEMENTS & DEVICES

Theatrical dramas and comedies are like prose and poetry in that they contain a theme, mood, tone, characterization and plot. However, by their nature they are driven largely by characterization and dialogue, as the physical limits of the stage and theatre building prevent drastic shifts in plot and setting.

Dialogue is the conversation between two characters in a written or acted-out work. Characters speak and are spoken to in turn. Because of the limits of stage production, most dramas are driven by dialogue; it is dialogue that moves the story forward.

Dialogue varies by playwright and its interpretation by the actor. Playwrights develop their own particular sense of speech rhythm, tone, and cadence, often becoming famous as much for their individual style as for the strength of their narratives. The playwright David Mamet, author of the plays *Glengarry Glenn Ross* and *Oleanna*, is sometimes regarded most highly for his intricate and rhythmic dialogue patterns. The 19th century playwright Oscar Wilde is famous for his cutting wit and the observations his characters shared.

A **monologue** is a speech given by one character speaking directly to the audience. Monologues are most famous in our time because of stand-up comedians and talk-show hosts. With a monologue, the action of a play stops, and a character is able to meditate aloud, sharing his thoughts with the audience. Monologues are also sometimes called **soliloquies**, especially in plays by Shakespeare. Perhaps the most famous soliloquy in the English language is Hamlet's "To be or not to be" meditation on life and death:

To be, or not to be—that is the question:

Whether 'tis nobler in the mind to suffer

The slings and arrows of outrageous fortune

Or to take arms against a sea of troubles

And by opposing end them. To die, to sleep—

No more—and by a sleep to say we end

The heartache, and the thousand natural shocks

That flesh is heir to. 'Tis a consummation

Devoutly to be wished. To die, to sleep—

To sleep—perchance to dream: ay, there's the rub*,

For in that sleep of death what dreams may come

When we have shuffled off this mortal coil,

Must give us pause. There's the respect

That makes calamity of so long life.

For who would bear the whips and scorns of time,

Th' oppressor's wrong, the proud man's contumely**

The pangs of despised love, the law's delay,

The insolence of office, and the spurns

That patient merit of th' unworthy takes,

When he himself might his quietus [death] make

With a bare bodkin***? Who would fardels **** bear,

To grunt and sweat under a weary life,

But that the dread of something after death,

The undiscovered country, from whose bourn

No traveller returns, puzzles the will,

And makes us rather bear those ills we have

Than fly to others that we know not of?

Thus conscience does make cowards of us all,

And thus the native hue of resolution

Is sicklied o'er with the pale cast of thought,

And enterprise of great pitch and moment

With this regard their currents turn awry

And lose the name of action. — Soft you now,

The fair Ophelia! — Nymph, in thy orisons [eyes]

Be all my sins remembered.

*catch
**arrogance
***dagger
****burdens

**Edwin Booth
as Hamlet**

**Sir Lawrence Olivier
as Hamlet**

An **aside** is a short comment or observation made by a character in a play directly to the audience. It is sometimes mocking but almost always meant to inform or amuse the audience. It is assumed that the other characters do not hear asides, as if the characters speaking them had expressed the comment or observation to himself.

Example: The television series *Malcolm In the Middle* used asides by its main character, Malcolm (Frankie Muniz) to explain family members' actions and motivations.

Practice 7: Comedic Elements and Devices

Find examples of dialogue, monologues, asides and soliloquies in a book of plays or by researching online. Read them over carefully, absorbing their meanings. Then, read them out loud. Can you hear the rhythm of the language? Share your results with a classmate, teacher, or family member.

CHAPTER 3 SUMMARY

Fiction is written work at least partially inspired by the imagination. It may be based on actual events.

- A **narrative** is a story with a beginning, middle, and end.
- Fiction types include the *short story* and the *novel*. They may be romance, science-fiction, fantasy, mysteries, tall tales, folk tales, myths, or legends.

Nonfiction is writing based on actual events, facts, and people. Sometimes called *journalism*, nonfiction articles such as magazine and newspaper articles sometimes include the author's personal feelings and/or opinions. Types of nonfiction work include manuals, informational pamphlets, essays, diaries, and memoirs.

Poetry is written work that is not **prose** but has **rhythm and rhyme**.

- **Epics** are long story-poems that tell of extraordinary deeds by supernatural characters and villains.
- **Ballads** tell a story in song. Their subjects can be heroic, satirical, romantic, or political.
- A **lyric poem** conveys an exact mood or feeling to the reader.

Poetic Devices are used to enhance the effectiveness of poetry.

- **Personification** is the technique of giving human qualities to something not human.
- A **simile** is a comparison of two things using the words *like* or *as*; a **metaphor** is a comparison without using *like* or *as*.
- **Hyperbole** is another way of saying "a figure of speech," in which the words in the phrase do not match their literal meanings.

Poetic Language is the specialized kinds of language used to convey imagery within a poem.

- **Alliteration** is the repetition of consonant sounds at the beginning of words or stressed syllables.
- **Onomatopoeia** involves using words whose sounds suggest their meaning.

Rhythm is the arrangement of sounds in a definite pattern within a written work. **Rhyme** is the repetition of words with similar-sounding endings.

Drama is a story told through action and dialogue between actors.

- **Tragedies** involve a character's struggle against larger forces; they do not end happily.
- **Comedies** are meant to lift the audience's spirits and end happily.

Dialogue is conversation between two characters that moves the plot forward in a theatrical drama or comedy.

- A **monologue** is a speech given by one character speaking directly to the audience. It is also called a **soliloquy**.
- An **aside** is a short, usually humorous remark made by a character to the audience.

CHAPTER 3 REVIEW

Read each question and write the answer on a separate sheet of paper.

1. A written work that has a clear beginning, middle, and end is called_____.
   A. fiction   B. nonfiction   C. a narrative   D. drama

2. A work of fiction longer than 85,000 words is considered a_____.
   A. novel   B. short story   C. myth   D. tragedy

3. The course of events in a work of fiction is known as the_____.
   A. summary   B. pacing   C. short story   D. plot structure

For questions 4 – 10, match the kind of writing with its description or feature:

Title	Source
4. science fiction	A. record of a single period in someone's life
5. tragedy	B. speech given by a character describing his thoughts
6. autobiography	C. story where characters and settings represent ideas or beliefs
7. memoir	D. a brief, fictional work written in prose
8. short story	E. the story of someone's life, told in a person's own words
9. allegory	F. use of other planets and space travel to predict the future
10. monologue	G. a flawed character's struggle against larger forces

11. Long, complicated story poems are known as_____.
    A. tragedies   B. comedies   C. epics   D. lyric poems

12. To compare two dissimilar things using the words *like* or *as* is known as a_____.
    A. metaphor   B. allusion   C. onomato-poeia   D. simile

13. Another word for an exaggerated figure of speech is_____.
    A. hyperbole   B. metaphor   C. simile   D. rhythm

14. Which of the following is *not* a trait of a lyric poem?
    A. It speaks directly to the reader.   C. It tells a story.
    B. It conveys a mood.   D. It relates the poet's feelings.

15. Rhyme scheme involves all of the following except
    A. words close together that sound alike.   C. placement within lines or stanzas.
    B. a definite pattern.   D. use of suggestive detail.

16. Which of the following is *not* one of Shakespeare's four major tragedies?
    A. *Hamlet*   B. *Othello*   C. *Twelfth Night*   D. *King Lear*

17. Comedy is difficult for all of the following reasons *except*
    A. not all actors can do comedy well.
    B. audiences' tastes may vary.
    C. tastes change over the years.
    D. delivering the dialogue requires precise timing.

18. *Wham*, *bang*, and *hiss* are all examples of
    A. metaphor.   C. onomatopoeia.
    B. rhyme scheme.   D. pop bands from the 1980s.

19. Another name for monologue is_____.
    A. sermon   B. soliloquy   C. drone   D. memoir

20. You're watching a play when suddenly an actor turns to the audience and says, "Pay attention, people. You won't believe what happens next." The actor's comment is called a(n)
    A. aside.   B. monologue.   C. soliloquy.   D. vignette.

Chapter 4
Information Gathering & Research Skills

This chapter addresses the following performance standards:

Standards	ELA9W2, ELA9W3

Sometimes, you'll hear something and only later realize it may have been important. However, many times you'll be able to prepare to listen effectively. An example is the way you read in class when you know the teacher is reviewing material that will be tested. Think about the way you pay attention to major points and details and the questions you ask to clarify what you are reading. This is an example of a **reading strategy**.

READING STRATEGIES

At some point in your life, you may have watched running or track events, perhaps during the Olympics or at your school. Runners learn an important skill that they apply to their individual events—they learn to pace themselves and follow a set course, even as their mind reacts to the world around them.

When reading, you think about the material your mind is consuming, while your eyes "follow the course" of print across a page. Your thoughts probably take the form of an **interior dialogue**, or conversation with yourself, about the events of the narrative or the evidence presented in an essay. This is your mind's way of communicating ideas and may be an idle conversation running through your more conscious thoughts. It might also be an active "attack" on the material. Such an attack would take the form of a deliberate effort to confront the text and pull out every scrap of information and meaning.

THINK-ALOUDS

A **think-aloud** is a reading strategy that allows you to "pump up" free-floating inner thoughts into an active, aggressive interior monologue. It allows you to:

- Verbalize (in your mind) your thoughts and feelings
- Think about and understand the topic
- Connect the information you have learned to your own experiences
- Form thoughts, opinions and questions about the material

With think-alouds, you create ideas and thoughts as you scan each passage or sentence, creating ideas and inspiration for discussion as you go. These ideas can be jotted down quickly or held in your memory for later use.

THE SPEED OF PRINT: KNOWING HOW FAST TO READ

As runners vary their speed, so too will you sometimes need to change the pace at which you read. There are three main reading speeds: **skimming**, **scanning**, and **in-depth reading**.

Skimming is a way to look over material and get a general idea what it is about without reading the details. When skimming, you read over **titles, headings**, **subtitles** and **subheadings**, and **topic sentences** as you "sprint" over a page. You also note any **words or terms that are bolded**, since they are obviously important. Noticing any **illustrations**, **charts**, or **graphs** is also helpful. Skimming is useful when determining if a magazine article has any useful information for a report. If you have some difficult material to read, skimming it first will give you an idea of what the material is about.

Scanning is a technique used to find a particular piece or item of information on a page. When you see the particular item, you stop and read more slowly. An example would be looking for a date or a name within a chapter, in order to answer a test or homework question.

In-depth reading is used to absorb difficult or obscure material. It helps you **focus on details**, **processes**, and **concepts**. As you read, you think about and notice the main ideas and subordinate ideas in the material. However, not all materials will need in-depth reading.

Practice 1: Listening and Taking Notes

A. Go through an article in your text, in a book, magazine or in the newspaper, practicing the three reading methods listed above. For scanning, pick a term at random from the article. Then, close the book or magazine and reopen it to the article, scanning for the word over again. Practice this several times.

B. Skim the same article for main ideas. Then read the article from beginning to end. Did you find skimming improved your speed and understanding? Share your results with your teacher or classmates.

RESEARCH AND RESEARCH MATERIALS

Research is the study and investigation of some topic or field of knowledge. The ability to do research and to choose and use **resource materials** is an essential life skill in today's Information Age society. Whether doing research in the library or reading a schedule or map, you will face situations where you will need the best resources available. Obtaining and using the information from these sources can help you answer questions or complete a task in school, at home, or on the job.

PRIMARY AND SECONDARY SOURCES

A **primary source** is any source of information created *at the time* something happens, *by* the people involved in the event. It is "firsthand" information. Primary sources include official reports, speeches or letters by participants, and interviews given by participants years after the fact. When compiling information, most historians prefer to use primary sources.

For example, primary sources for a report on the Battle of Fallujah in 2004 would include interviews and reports by soldiers and war correspondents in Iraq who were present at the conflict. They would probably appear in both popular magazines and political science journals.

Secondary sources are historical works built up by primary sources. They include scholarly work, news reports, and interviews with experts in a field. Secondary sources for the Battle of Fallujah would include news service articles compiled by staff writers, books published today, and interviews with military strategy experts.

Practice 2: Primary and Secondary Sources

Read the following sources and determine whether each one is a primary or secondary source:

1. a book published today on the American Revolution

2. an interview with the commander of the latest Space Shuttle mission

3. the autobiography of the first man to land on Mars

4. a biography of Ray Charles, written by a nationally-respected music critic

5. a speech about the Great Depression, given by a professor of American History

CHOOSING A TOPIC FOR RESEARCH

Inevitably, you will need to demonstrate that you can research a topic given to you, or you may have to **choose a topic** on your own. If you are choosing your own topic, the choices are almost endless. You will probably be given some guidelines as far as the general area of research you are to do. A good way to start your decision process is to think of a topic you're truly interested in that fits within the given guidelines.

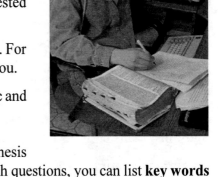

When deciding on your own topic, **prewriting** exercises may be helpful. For example, try freewriting or brainstorming about subjects that interest you.

Next, formulate your research question or questions. Based on your topic and your brainstorming exercises, narrowing your field of research by composing research questions will help determine exactly what to investigate. Your research question(s) can later lead to good ideas for a thesis statement, if you are writing a research paper. Using a topic and research questions, you can list **key words** to guide your research efforts.

Topic:	the ancient art of scrimshaw	hot peppers
What I know:	carvings in ivory; no longer done because ivory is protected	spices up food; can aid digestion; popular in certain cultures
What I want to know:	is anyone still doing it? what are the most creative & valuable examples?	how many kinds of hot peppers are there? how else are they used?
Research question:	how did scrimshaw get started, and why did it end?	are hot peppers good for health? what are all their uses?

FINDING AND EVALUATING RESEARCH SOURCES

Information comes from many places, including **libraries**, **educational software**, **television and radio**, and the **Internet**. In some cases, people also do field research, meaning that they make first-hand observations or conduct **interviews** about a topic, creating primary sources for you to use.

LIBRARY RESEARCH

Performing **research in libraries** is convenient because most modern libraries feature electronic and print materials enclosed in a single space. Some libraries also offer large back catalogs of **periodicals**, **magazines**, and **technical journals**. However, libraries sometimes fail to have the specific document you're looking for and can consume time travelling back and forth. Check to see if a libraries' catalog is available online before making the trip.

Some resource materials typical of a library include:

DICTIONARIES

As you are almost certainly already aware, a **dictionary** is a reference book listing words and their meanings in alphabetical order. For each word, a dictionary generally includes spelling, pronunciation, definitions, parts of speech, usage, etymology or word origin, and sometimes synonyms and antonyms. The information given in a dictionary is described in detail below.

Word Division	Each word is divided into a syllable or syllables. Each syllable is pronounced with a single sounding of the voice. For example, the word **swallow** is divided into two syllables, **swal** and **low**. In a dictionary, this is written as **swal·low**.
Principal parts	Each verb in a dictionary entry is immediately followed by the principal parts of that verb. For instance, the verb **see** is found in the various verb tenses as **saw, seen,** and **see′ ing**
Pronunciation	Each entry in a dictionary is followed by its pronunciation. For example, the word **radius** is shown to be pronounced **ray-dee-uhss** (rā′ dē us). A pronunciation guide appears in the front of the dictionary for unfamiliar symbols.
Plural form	Some words in a dictionary entry are also shown in their plural form. For example, the word **child** in the dictionary is immediately followed by the plural form, **children.**
Part of speech	Each dictionary entry also notes the word's part of speech. Before the first definition or entry, the part of speech appears in italics as an abbreviation. For example:

transitive verb = **vt.**   adjective = **adj.**

intransitive verb = **vi.**   preposition = **prep.**

noun = **n.**   conjunction = **conj.**

adverb = **adv.**   interjection = **interj.**

pronoun = **pron.**   article = **article**

Example: the word **foliage** is a noun, so the abbreviation **n.** follows it.

Definition	Each dictionary entry also contains a definition, which gives the meaning of the entry word.
	Example: mascot - any person, animal, or thing supposed to bring good luck) There are sometimes several definitions listed for an entry.
Etymology	The etymology (word origin) of each word is also part of some dictionaries' entries. Consult the etymology guide in the front of the dictionary to discover the meanings of abbreviations. **(Example: OE means Old English, Fr means French, L means Latin, Gr means Greek)**

The following is an example of a dictionary entry:

> **gris·ly** (griz′ lē) **adj.**[ME *grislich*] terrifying; horrible - SYN. See *ghastly*

From this definition, we know that the word *grisly* is divided into two syllables as gris•ly. We also know that *grisly* is an adjective. This word came from Middle English and has *ghastly* as a synonym.

Here is another dictionary entry:

> **cher•ry** (cher′ ē) *n., pl.* **-ries.** [OFr. *cerise*] 1. a small fleshy fruit containing a smooth, hard pit and ranging from yellow to very dark red   2. any of various trees (genus *Prunus)* of the rose family which bear this fruit

We know that the word *cherry* is correctly divided as cher•ry. We also know that **cherry** is a noun and that its plural form is *cherries*. The word comes from Old French and has no synonyms or antonyms.

Practice 3: Dictionary Skills

Read the following dictionary entries. Fill in the appropriate blanks with the correct answer.

1.

> **know** (nō) *vt.* **knew, known, know′ing** [ME *knowen*] 1. to have a clear perception or understanding of; to be sure or well-informed about (to *know* the truth) to be aware or cognizant of; have perceived or learned (to *know* that one is in control) SYN. See UNDERSTAND

A. Word Division_____   D. Pronunciation_____

B. Part of Speech_____   E. Verb Parts_____

C. Etymology_____   F. Synonym_____

2.

> **flur•ry** (flur′ i) *n., pl,* **-ries** [unk]1. a sudden, brief rush of wind; gust   2. a gust of rain or snow   3. a sudden confusion or commotion

A. Word Division_____   D. Pronunciation_____

B. Part of Speech_____   E. Noun Forms_____

C. Etymology_____   F. Synonym_____

THESAURUS

A **thesaurus** is a book containing lists of synonyms and antonyms in alphabetical order. Remember that not all words have the exact same meaning. Some words may be similar in meaning but have different connotations.

```
┌─────────────────────────────────────────────┐
│              Thesaurus Entry                  │
├─────────────────────────────────────────────┤
│                 88. HEIGHT                    │
│  NOUNS:                                       │
│  1. height, tip, stature, elevation           │
│  2. top, highest point, ceiling, zenith       │
│  3. hill, knoll, volcano, mountain            │
│                                               │
│  VERBS:                                       │
│  4. heighten, elevate, raise, rear, erect     │
│  5. intensify, strengthen, increase, advance  │
│  6. command, rise above, crown, surmount      │
│                                               │
│  ADJECTIVES:                                  │
│  7. high, towering, exalted, supreme          │
│                                               │
│       Antonyms:  depth, descent               │
└─────────────────────────────────────────────┘
```

Practice 4: Using a Thesaurus

Answer the following questions based on the sample thesaurus page shown above. For questions 1–3, choose the word that would best provide a synonym for the bolded word in each sentence below.

1. With a **height** of 20,320 feet, Mt. McKinley is an impressive sight.

    A. stature   B. top   C. elevation   D. zenith

2. The **high** skyscraper stood in the center of the city.
    A. exalted   B. supreme   C. towering   D. elevated

3. The frequent thunder **heightened** our fears.
    A. intensified   B. erected   C. crowned   D. commanded

4. True or False: **increase** is the same part of speech as **heighten**.

5. True or False: A mountain is lower than a hill.

6. What part of speech is **height**?

7. What are the antonyms for **height**?

8. List the synonyms for **intensify**.

READER'S GUIDE TO PERIODICAL LITERATURE

The Reader's Guide To Periodical Literature is an index to articles from periodicals and magazines. Annual volumes are published, but there are monthly update volumes available through the year before the single annual volume is published. The Reader's Guide is also available online in many libraries. If you use the print version, the first few pages of the volume contain information on the abbreviations used in the entries.

Articles are arranged alphabetically by subject and by author. Cross references to other subject headings are commonly used to guide you to other entries that may contain articles. You will need to check which of the magazines indexed are actually available in your library.

Here is a sample entry with an explanation of the information contained in it.

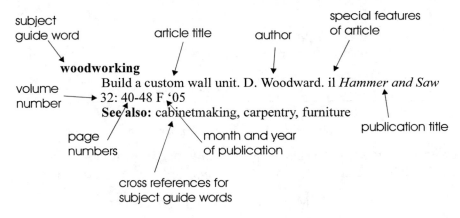

Practice 5: Using the Reader's Guide to Periodical Literature

Using the sample on the next page, answer the following questions.

1. On which pages would you find the pasta article by R. Stokes?

2. Who is the author of "Washable Pastes for Kids"?

3. What other topic in the Reader's Guide should you look under for articles about passports?

4. What is the volume and date of the article about pâté?

5. Which article discusses traveling?

Sample Page of Reader's Guide to Periodical Literature

Abbreviations Used: il: illustrated article   *Am Games: American Games;*
Gov Qterly: Government Quarter;   Jrnl Relign Socty: Journal of Religion and Society;
Tightwad Trvler: The Tightwad Traveler

---

passport – pâté

passport
  Avoid rush: order passports early.
  T Kelley. il. *Gov Qterly* 48:22-24
  F '05
  See also: immigration
password
  New twist to an old game. O.
  Vinson. il. *Am Games* 14:6-7 Ja
  '05
pasta
  Choose the new pastas. L. Fideli.
  il. *Cooking Today* 28:14-17 F '05
  Pasta is healthy. R. Stokes, MD.
  il. *Wellness* 6:9-11 Ja '05
  Pick a sauce and pick a shape! W.
  Thomas. il *Tuscan Kitchen* 8: 25-
  29 F '05
  See also: macaroni, spaghetti

29

paste
  Paste for wallpaper projects. B.
  West. il. *Decorator* 41:18-22 F
  '05
  Washable pastes for kids. il.
  Homemade Fun 34:60-64 Ja
  '05
  See also: cement, glue
pastor
  The pastor as a good shepherd.
  il. *Jrnl Relign Socty* 64:28-33 F
  '05
  See also: minister, priest
Patagonia
  Awesome adventure in the
  Andes. il. *Tightwad Trvler*
  14:6-7 Ja '05
pâté
  A palette of pate: varieties for
  every palate. H. Wolfe. il.
  Cooking Today 28: 18-23 F '05

STYLE MANUALS

Because the correct use of grammar as well as **citation** (the official technique of quoting or citing an existing work) is frequently a tricky proposition, the use of a good **style manual** is often encouraged by editors, teachers, and writing teachers.

Style manuals, such as *The Chicago Manual of Style* and *Associated Press Stylebook,* are concise, easy to use guides to proper use of titles, good grammar, and ways to write with authority. They are available at most book stores and feature advice on everything from the correct way to include a movie title (all italics) to grammar involving states and countries. *The Modern Language Association Handbook* and *The MLA Handbook for Writers of Research Papers* are also especially helpful. General MLA guidelines can be found at Purdue University's online English lab: http://owl.english.purdue.edu/handouts/research/r_mla.html

EDUCATIONAL SOFTWARE

Educational software includes CD-ROMs and DVDs that are specifically created to inform or educate the user. Examples include an encyclopedia software suite and *National Geographic* specials available in DVD or downloadable format. These are available in most electronics stores and at public and university libraries.

TELEVISION AND RADIO

While not as predominant in the age of the Internet and software, educational programs on **television** and **public radio** are still a vital source of information. Transcripts of their broadcasts can usually be found online.

When using television and radio sources as research, it is vitally important to consider the **objectivity** (neutrality) of the program you intend to use. With the rise of cable television and a reduction in government standards, **biased** (having a preference for one particular side of an issue over another) programming has become more widespread than ever and often appears to be even-handed even when it is not. So, be careful.

Practice 6: Television and Radio

Find a television or radio program you believe will be helpful in a research report. Search for a transcript online, and determine if others found the piece objective or biased. As always, share your results with a classmate, teacher, or mentor.

INTERNET RESEARCH

The **Internet** has in just ten years managed to dominate the research process. Still and all, using the Internet can challenge your research skills. When using a search engine or content site:

- Decide which **key words** to use to find the material you want.
- **Validate** the material by checking the site for its credibility or the material for accuracy.
- Decide how best to use the material and if it is an appropriate source for your topic.

RESEARCH KEY WORDS

Key words are tools to find the most useful sites in the shortest amount of time. These key words are arranged with other words to broaden a search that is too narrow or narrowing one that is too broad.

Using the earlier example of the art of scrimshaw on page 90, we can decide that key words include *scrimshaw*, *carving*, and *ivory*. While *scrimshaw* is specific enough that a search would probably yield good results, using just the word *carving* would be too broad. In that case you might combine it, for example with *ivory*, to narrow your search and access more relevant material.

- Make a list of words that describe what you are looking for in a site, such as words that you would use in describing the topic to a friend.
- Make a list of synonyms for these words. This will give you ways to narrow your topic.
- Try using both the singular and plural forms of the search words for your topic.

VALIDATION: CHECKING SOURCES

Many Web sites are created by students and ordinary citizens, who may believe what they have posted is true but are mistaken in that belief. Researchers protect their work by screening the material they find for quality and accuracy. Steps to solid validation include:

- **Corroboration:** find two or more sources that agree with the information you wish to use.

- **Evaluation:** read material carefully, watching for bias or particularly strong opinion.

- **Certification:** Look at the **URL** (Uniform Resource Locator, or Web address) for the source of the material, which is usually an organization or individual. If the organization is an educational, government, or professional center, the material is most likely valid.

- **Dating:** Check the date on the material. Obviously if your topic is on a current event, the more recent the date, the better the information. Also keep in mind that recent data and theories are valuable for any topic.

Some sites on the Internet have been validated already. These are listed in online catalogues known as **database sites**. The organization which creates the database checks the material to ensure both accuracy and relevancy. Many databases are offered through educational organizations and are free to use. One example is *thinkquest.org,* a site that indexes award-winning, student-created Web sites. The site covers many topics and many levels of study.

Practice 7: Web sites

Choose a topic to research on the Internet. Search for your topic and then look at several Web sites. Find one site that is an ureliable source, one that is questionable, and one that is definitely reliable. Explain why you believe each site is reliable, unreliable, or questionable. Indicate what information you used to make your judgements.

CONCLUSION: THE RIGHT RESOURCE MATERIAL

Different sources present information in different ways. Research becomes more interesting when you read an assortment of sources. It is also important to choose the correct resource material to find information. Before beginning research, you need to have a clear idea of what information you are looking for. Then you need to evaluate the resource materials and decide which source will provide the best information.

Regardless of your topic, your sources should always be:

- **Reliable:** written by respected authors and published in dependable books, magazines, newspapers, and so on.

- **Timely:** current information

- **Suitable:** appropriate to your topic

Practice 8:   Choosing the Right Resource Material

Choose the most appropriate resource material to find the information.

1. Alex is writing an essay and needs to find another word for *boring*.
    A.   dictionary   B.   Internet   C.   thesaurus   D.   encyclopedia

2. Michelle is working on a science project about bats.
    A.   dictionary   B.   newspaper   C.   glossary   D.   encyclopedia

3. Anthony is reviewing words for a vocabulary test.
    A.   dictionary   B.   Internet   C.   thesaurus   D.   encyclopedia

4. Latisha needs to bring in an example of an event that happened that day.
    A.   Internet   B.   encyclopedia   C.   journal   D.   thesaurus

5. Lewis is writing about a baseball player's current season.
    A.   newspaper   B.   magazine   C.   journal   D.   dictionary

CHAPTER 4 SUMMARY

A **think-aloud** is a strategy used to "pump up" free-floating interior dialogues into an active reading process. It allows you to absorb information more quickly and also more effectively.

Skimming is a way to quickly absorb material, paying attention to illustrations, key words and phrases and important subheadings. **Scanning** is a means of searching for a particular term or word within a text. **In-depth reading** is used to absorb more difficult material that requires your complete attention.

A **primary source** is any information created at the time something happened by its participants. **Secondary sources** are historical or informational sources built up "after the fact."

When choosing a topic to research, **brainstorming** what you already know is frequently helpful.

Libraries include vast amounts of information centered in one place.

- **Dictionaries** are reference works that include words and their meanings, listed in alphabetical order.
- **Thesauruses** are alphabetical listings of words with their antonyms and synonyms.
- **The Reader's Guide To Periodical Literature** is an index to articles from magazines and periodicals. Articles are arranged alphabetically and by author.

Educational software includes CD-ROMs and DVDs specially designed for educational or informational value.

Television and radio features can be helpful in gathering research, but be careful that the information presented is not **biased**.

Internet should be focused on-topic and conducted with a clear idea of what information to consider relevant to the research topic.

- **Key words** will help narrow the search criteria.
- **Material** should be validated for **credibility** and **authenticity**.
- Material should also be judged for its usefulness and value in preparing the research presentation.

Research should always be **reliable**, **timely**, and **suitable** for your audience.

CHAPTER 4 REVIEW

Read each question and write the answer on a separate sheet of paper.

1. _____ is a technique used to quickly find the important points of a text.

   A. Scanning   B. Skimming   C. Skipping   D. In-depth reading

2. Diane is writing a paper and needs another word to use for the word "trip." Which reference should she use?

   A. appendix   C. thesaurus
   B. bibliography   D. encyclopedia

3. Where would Serena look to find an article about African-American folktales?

   A. encyclopedia   C. advertisement
   B. periodical   D. Reader's Guide

4. Brittany needs to know the definition of the word "lugubrious." Where should she look?

   A. dictionary   C. electronic library catalog
   B. thesaurus   D. encyclopedia

5. Quickly moving your eyes over a printed page to locate a particular term or phrase is known as _____.

   A. skimming   C. in-depth reading
   B. scanning   D. research

For questions 6 - 10, determine whether each listed source is primary or secondary:

6. a textbook on Georgia state history

7. an interview with a famous heart surgeon on the world's first heart transplant

8. a speech given by George Washington about the American Revolution

9. an interview with Jerry Seinfeld about comedy

10. the autobiography of a movie star from the 1940s about life in Hollywood

11. Which of the following would *not* be found in a library?

    A. dictionary   C. Reader's Guide
    B. thesaurus   D. FM radio announcer

12. An alphabetical listing of words and their meanings is called a(n)

    A. dictionary.   C. Reader's Guide.
    B. thesaurus.   D. encyclopedia.

13. In the *Reader's Guide to Periodical Literature*, articles are arranged by _____ and subject matter.

    A. author

    B. date

    C. order of importance

    D. country of origin

14. To _____ a source is to determine its credibility and usefulness.

    A. research

    B. skim

    C. validate

    D. discredit

15. **Extended Response.** Find research sources for a topic of your choice, using any of the types of sources discussed in this chapter. Then, evaluate them for validity, usefulness, and whether or not the sources are primary or secondary.

Chapter 5
Planning & Drafting The Written Composition

This chapter addresses the following performance standards:

Standards	ELA9W1, ELA9W2, ELA9W3

Literature and writing — much like life — are filled with struggle. Almost all writers want to make a point, and most use arguments to try and convince the reader to agree with their point of view, opinions, or philosophies.

In this chapter, we'll examine how to prepare **arguments**, both in the construction of a sound line of reasoning and in presenting your findings to an audience. We'll look at how to build stronger vocabulary to be persuasive; how to structure a strong, durable position; and how to summarize information for better reference. The more you improve your skills in these areas, the better you become at critical thinking, reasoning, weighing evidence and making decisions. We'll also look at the ways media and presentation techniques can help you communicate a message more effectively. Finally, we'll measure ways to gauge and enhance **audience awareness.**

WHY WE WRITE

Some people do a certain amount of **personal writing**, such as a diary. Some people also keep travel journals when they go on vacations. Another type of personal writing is sometimes called **social writing**. Letters and thank you notes to friends or family, in either print or via email, are considered social writing.

Business writing is an important though frequently under-appreciated skill. In today's information-driven economy, virtually every business or career requires some degree of writing skill. As an employee, you might need to record procedures for a new employee or to explain processes for employees in another location. Business writing can convey basic information, or it can be used to document technical information.

Any piece of good writing has certain elements in common. A **clear focus and voice**, **solid evidence**, and **an awareness of the audience** are all crucial to writing well.

DEVELOPING A CLEAR, PRECISE STYLE

Your **style** is an important way to interest the reader, accurately convey your ideas, and provide convincing reasons for your position on a topic. Improving style greatly depends on word choice and involves selecting **specific words**; **avoiding clichés and sweeping generalizations;** developing **coherence**; and correctly using **formal** and **informal language**. Also, almost all effective writing uses the **active voice**.

SELECT SPECIFIC WORDS

One aspect of good word choice is selecting **specific and concrete words** rather than general or abstract words. Overused words like *thing, nice, great, bad, good,* and *a lot* "water down" your writing with vagueness and lack of clarity. Specific words provide the reader with a clear image of what you are describing:

> **Example 1:** He hit the home run, and the crowd cheered.

This sentence tells the basic facts but consider the following questions: Who hit the ball? How did he hit it? Where did it go? How did it get there? In what way did the crowd cheer? To answer these questions, one might write the following:

> **Example 2:** Myers' swing sent the ball hurtling out towards the full moon. The crowd exploded to its feet, roaring their approval.

In Example 2, the writer gives detailed answers to the above questions and provides a vivid picture of what happened. The writer describes the sights and sounds of the game. Using concrete words makes all the difference.

	Ways To Evoke The Various Senses
Sight	size, color, shape, surface appearance, action, comparison to other sights
Sound	volume, pitch, sound quality or character, comparison to other sounds
Touch	texture, temperature, weight, density, comparison to other textures
Taste	texture, comparison to other tastes

Practice 1:   Using Specific Words

Choose the best answer to rewrite each of the following sentences using specific words.

1.   The dog barked all night long.

   A.   The dog was barking all night, so I had to get up and put in some ear plugs.

   B.   The mutt next door yipped from the time I went to bed until the sun came up.

   C.   The poor dog could not sleep, and he wandered around making lots of noise.

2. He wanted a new video game, but he didn't have any money.
   A. He liked playing video games, and he was tired of all the old ones he already had.
   B. What he really wanted was a new game and a new system on which to play it.
   C. He longed to play the new adventure game, but his wallet was empty.

3. It was very cold and windy on the shore.
   A. As the chilling wind came in from the sea, we shrank into our heavy blankets.
   B. We all felt cold standing on the shore because we had not worn the right clothes.
   C. It seemed to get colder as we stood there, on the shore, in the cold and the wind.

4. I was so happy to get a new scooter for my birthday.
   A. It was so nice of my cousins to get me the scooter I wanted so much for my birthday.
   B. When I pulled the yellow wrapping off the bright metallic scooter, I shrieked with surprise.
   C. I absolutely loved the scooter I got for my birthday, and it made me very happy.

Practice 2: Using Specific Words

Rewrite the following sentences, using specific words to create more vivid descriptions. Replace as many original words as you can with specific and descriptive words.

1. The dog barked all night long.

2. The strong wind caused a tree to fall on our house.

3. It was so hot, we had to jump into the pool.

4. He almost cried when he saw his son graduate.

5. That book was boring.

AVOID CLICHÉS AND SWEEPING GENERALIZATIONS

Avoid using **clichés** in your writing. These familiar expressions include popular phrases such as "busy as a bee" and "to make a long story short." Simple, straightforward language is far more effective.

Clichés	Simple Language
busy as a bee	very active
to make a long story short	to get to the point
cute as a button	endearing
stop beating around the bush	stop wasting time
save it for a rainy day	save it for when you need it

Also, avoid sweeping generalizations, such as "No one ever calls me." Instead, replace vague claims with accurate, to-the-point descriptions.

Sweeping Generalization	Accurate Description
No one ever calls me.	I almost never get phone calls.
It always rains on my birthday.	It seems like every year it rains on my birthday.
Everybody knows the Falcons are the best team.	Many people believe the Falcons will win the championship.

DEVELOP COHERENCE

Coherence means "sticking together." You want the ideas of your essay to be connected and to lead from one to the other in a logical way.

- **Plan an Order: Organizing your ideas** in a certain order is the first step to developing a coherent extended response. If something is out of order or doesn't belong, it can throw off your readers and interfere with their understanding of what you wrote.

- **Use Transitions: Transitional words** link ideas from one sentence to another. They also link ideas between paragraphs to make the whole work "stick together." Without these transitional words and phrases, the writing becomes less interesting and may even become less clear to an audience. Examples of transitional words include *meanwhile, eventually, currently, especially, above all, as a result, therefore, since, also, as well as,* and *similarly.*

- **Repeat Key Words and Phrases:** By including **key words** or **phrases** from your controlling idea in the topic sentences of your paragraphs, you make it easier for the reader to follow your train of thought. These repeated words are like landmarks along the road of your presentation.

Practice 3: Developing Coherence

Read the following passage. Then answer the questions that follow it.

(**1**) Many people are familiar with the Civil War monument and museum of Fort Sumter. (**2**) How many know that Fort Sumter is named after a true patriot and hero who served his country long before the Civil War? (**3**) Fort Sumter has a very interesting museum that is open year-round. (**4**) General Thomas Sumter (1734 – 1832) started his famous military career in the French and Indian War. (**5**) He fought heroically against the British to win freedom in the American Revolution. (**6**) He became a U.S. Representative and Senator from South Carolina, and he served a year as minister to Brazil. (**7**) He founded the town of Stateburg. (**8**) Sumter never gave in to British occupation, fought for many years to ensure America's independence, and continued to serve his country after the Revolution. (**9**) In fact, he was called "the gamecock of the Revolution" because of his tenacious fighting style.

Thomas Sumter

1. What is the most logical place to put sentence number 9?

   A. immediately after sentence 4   C. immediately after sentence 6

   B. immediately after sentence 5   D. correct as is

2. Which sentence interrupts the logical progression of ideas?

   A. sentence 2   C. sentence 6

   B. sentence 3   D. sentence 7

3. Which sentence provides the most support for the central idea that Thomas Sumter was a true patriot and hero?

   A. sentence 4   C. sentence 7

   B. sentence 5   D. sentence 8

FORMAL AND INFORMAL LANGUAGE

You should use **formal language** for any writing assignments in school or for any standardized tests. Formal language is appropriate for business letters or letters to people who hold a particular office, such as a superintendent, mayor, or newspaper editor. **Informal** language is used when addressing friends, family members or people with whom you feel comfortable and relaxed.

Formal Language	Informal Language
Characteristics	
broader vocabulary	simple words
more complex sentence structure	simple sentences
strict attention to proper grammar	loose following of grammar rules
no slang	can use slang, depending on audience
Appropriate Uses	
written assignments for school	conversations with friends or relatives
business letters	personal letters, e-mails

ACTIVE AND PASSIVE VOICE

A good trick for powerful writing that clearly communicates its message is to use only **active voice**, which combines good sentence structure with a sense of timeliness. In active voice, the subject is the agent (or doer) of the verb. For example,

He threw the ball for the touchdown.

Active voice, as its name implies, achieves a level of *action* that **passive voice** does not. In passive voice, the verb's direct object is the subject of the sentence:

The ball was thrown by him for the touchdown.

Passive voice makes the action described seem after-the-fact and lacks immediacy. You might be aware that all electronic journalism, such as on television and radio, is written in the active voice. Newscasters want their listeners to feel a part of the story, which active voice encourages. When you write, you want the reader to feel involved as well.

Practice 4: Active and Passive Voice

Rewrite the following passive sentences into active voice:

1. The shooting was explained by the vice president.

2. The suspect was held in custody by the police.

3. The couch was jumped upon by the movie star.

4. The exam was failed by over two-thirds of the graduating class.

5. The wall was jumped by her in the hurry to get away from the house.

BUILDING A STRONG ARGUMENT

Many writers use both **facts** (information which can be proven true) and **opinions** (an individual's personal beliefs) in their writing to persuade readers. Politicians, for example, use facts to support their stance on a given topic as a means of swaying voters. Facts strengthen an argument, making it credible and persuasive. An argument consisting of nothing but opinions does not have the same credibility as one which also contains verifiable facts. It will most likely *not* persuade the reader to agree with its writer's point of view.

Your ability to persuade depends not just on *how* you say something but also on *what* you have to say. Learning to build a **strong argument** is a vital skill. Most of the writing you will do for tests such as the EOCT — and others you will certainly encounter later in high school and in college — will ask you to produce an argument. The process of building an argument can be compared to constructing a pyramid:

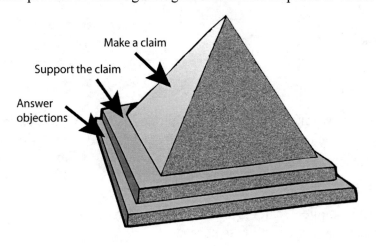

Make a claim

Support the claim

Answer objections

MAKING A CLAIM

The first step in building a good argument is to *make a claim*. A **claim** is the position taken on a particular issue and argues for one side of a debate or controversy.

Read the following three statements and decide which *claims* provide a good starting point for arguments.

1. According to a 1999 Harris poll for the National Consumers League, a majority of Americans believe that water is our second most-threatened natural resource, after clean air. – Sarah Milstein

2. Through personal choices, economic reform, and improved schools, we, the citizens of this great democracy, must stop the irreversible destruction of our most precious resources: air, water, and children.

3. We ought to be increasing programs that help the hungry children in our country rather than giving more money to an already well-financed program like the military.

Statement 1 presents information in a factual, non-persuasive way. The information presented could be used to persuade but doesn't encourage one belief over another. Statements 2 and 3 urge the reader to take a certain action or have a certain belief. In other words, they make a claim. You may also notice that the persuasive statements sometimes use the subject "we" in an attempt to involve the reader in the position or idea.

Statement 2 requires a special note. It makes a claim that requires support, but the claim is not focused. Air, water, and children are indeed precious resources. However, protecting the environment and improving schools are two topics that would be better addressed by two separate arguments. When writing, remember to always try to pick one side of a single issue and take a stand. Make sure your "pyramid" has a focused point.

SUPPORTING THE CLAIM

Once you've made your claim, you need to support it with **evidence** or provable facts. Again, a strong argument is supported by good logic, solid evidence, and appropriate reasons or examples. Such evidence could be had by:

*   finding expert opinions, either published or through interviews you conduct.
*   making your own observations and documenting them
*   gathering print and electronic sources

A weak argument suffers from poor logic, weak evidence, and **fallacies** (faulty reasons or examples). How you support your claim can make or break your argument, so take the time to research and use good resources and solid evidence. A well-supported claim, like a pyramid, will stand the test of time.

Read the following two passages about weight loss, and decide whether the arguments are strong or weak.

Rapidly Burn Off Pounds And Inches With SUPER DIET PILL!

You can lose 10, 20, 50, even 100 pounds! This is it! This is the diet pill researchers around the world have hailed for its powerful, quick-working ingredients that help people shed stubborn fat — fast! Super Diet Pill satisfies the need for fast action without strenuous dieting.

So fast-working, you can see a dramatic difference in just two days, without complicated calorie counting or suffering from biting hunger pains. Even people with long-term weight problems find they can burn off up to a pound of fat and fluid every five hours.

50% Fat Loss In 14 To 21 Days

The longer you use the super diet pill, the more weight you lose. You don't have to stop until you reach the weight that you want. Without making major sacrifices or drastic changes, you can shed as much as 50% of your fat in just 2 or 3 weeks.

Increased Metabolism Means Weight Loss

One-half of the women and one-fourth of the men in the United States are trying to lose weight and become fit. The sad truth is that most of us will regain our original weight in a year or less. What's the real secret for losing weight and keeping it off? The answer is developing and maintaining a healthy metabolism. Metabolism refers to how the body burns energy. A person with a high metabolism burns more calories than a person with a low metabolism. Consequently, the person who burns more calories has an easier time losing weight. Here are some tips for improving your metabolism and melting away that extra fat:

1) Drink plenty of water. Filling up on water decreases the appetite. Three quarts of water each day are ideal. 2) Don't skip meals, especially breakfast. Eat small meals every two to three hours. In this way, carbohydrates and protein will not be converted into fat. 3) Eat fat-burning foods. Raw vegetables, whole grains, fruits, and legumes are your best choices. Consume fruits between meals for extra energy. This healthy snack won't be converted to fat. 4) Exercise regularly. Aerobic exercises like swimming, running, and walking are best. Also try lifting weights — a good muscle builder and fat burner. Exercise before you eat. It will decrease your appetite and increase your metabolism.

Each passage strongly suggests a way to lose weight and provides reasons to support its method of weight reduction. But which one is based on valid reasons, and which one is based on falsehoods?

An examination of the evidence shows that the diet pill advertisement offers very limited factual information about the diet pill. Little proof is presented to support its dramatic claims. The ad never mentions the names of the diet pill researchers, the people who lost weight, or where and when the testing was done.

The description of metabolism, however, bases its argument on biological principles and well-established medical fact. It provides logical explanations of how to increase your body's metabolism. The author is not selling anything and does not offer an easy solution. A decision to follow the suggestions for changes in diet would be based on much better information than a choice to try the diet pill.

Four Ways to Build a Strong Argument

1. **Use clear logic and valid facts.** Avoid falsehoods and use readily proven facts.

2. **Illustrate your point of view with a personal story.** Readers will likely understand or empathize with events from your life that illustrate your point of view. Be careful, however, that you remain objective and do not turn the argument into an opinion.

3. **Contrast your claim** or position with another, opposing point of view. One way to show the strength of your choice is to show the weakness of another choice.

4. **Use credible sources** to support your argument. Quoting one or more credible resources can help to validate your entire argument.

ANTICIPATING OBJECTIONS

A strong argument **anticipates objections**, making a "preemptive strike" against them through careful wording. When writing, you should research contrasting opinions. Knowing about an opposing viewpoint and incorporating it convinces an audience that your argument is both sincere and knowledgeable.

Read the following passage regarding capital punishment and decide which objections the author is trying to answer.

No More Executions

I want to applaud the governor of Illinois for his recent decision to stop all executions in his state until further review of the capital punishment system. Contrary to popular belief, capital punishment is not a deterrent to crime. In fact, statistics show that states without capital punishment had a lower rate of violent crime in 2005: 3.6 murders per 100,000 persons. States with capital punishment had a higher rate of violent crime in 2005: 5.5 murders per 100,000 persons. Some people claim that the appeals process takes too long, and that's why the death penalty is not a deterrent. However, the Death Penalty Information Center reports that 21 condemned inmates have been released from death row since 2003. This includes seven from the state of Illinois. We cannot risk the execution of innocent people by speeding up the appeals process. The lengthy appeals process also makes capital punishment very expensive. Anyone who has been in a court case knows how much lawyers cost. Those who do not want tax money wasted on criminals should oppose capital punishment because it is actually more expensive to execute someone than to imprison him or her for life. Overall, the system is terribly flawed. The other 38 states with capital punishment laws should join Illinois in placing a moratorium on all executions.

The author of this passage opposes capital punishment and wants to convince others to oppose it as well. In doing so, the writer addresses and refutes three popular reasons for supporting the death penalty:

- capital punishment deters crime
- capital punishment would be a deterrent if the appeals process were shorter
- execution is less expensive than life imprisonment

The author answers these objections to her argument with statistics, authoritative information, and common sense.

Practice 5: Analyzing an Argument

Read the following argument for CFLs (compact fluorescent lamps). What is the claim? Is the argument strong or weak? Cite examples from the passage to support your viewpoint.

Light Up Your Life!

The best improvement to our house this year was the addition of compact fluorescent lamps (CFLs), a type of energy efficient light bulb. This, no doubt, sounds like an incredibly boring change. However, if you consider the environmental and economic impact of these little gadgets, it can be quite "enlightening." For example, nearly 99% of the energy used by a regular incandescent bulb is turned into heat. I don't know about you, but I don't think light bulbs are a very efficient way to heat a house — I want light bulbs to give off light. That's what fluorescent lamps use 90% of their energy to do. Another great thing about compact fluorescent lamps is that you hardly ever need to change them. Unlike traditional light bulbs that last a month or two, CFLs last from five to seven years. Yes, that's years, not months! Of course, these long-lasting bulbs are more expensive to buy than the old bulbs. However, when you add up the money that you save in using less electricity, a CFL pays for itself three times over the course of five years. So as you can see, a simple change in your life can have a big impact.

Anticipating objections is a key part of knowing and being aware of your audience.

AUDIENCE AWARENESS

As we discussed in Chapter One, considering a passage's audience involves more than just anticipating objections. Rather, **knowing your audience** gives you important information. Here again is the chart from Chapter One:

interest:	what topics or information is of interest to the audience.
prior knowledge:	what the audience already knows.
vocabulary:	words that the readers understand.
what the audience needs to know:	information or explanations that you want the audience to know.

Read the following two paragraphs that appeared as Practice 2 of Chapter One.

Example: Since you're in the market for a new car, I wanted to tell you about mine. My new car is the best one I've owned. It's a 2005 Puma. It's got a 5.0 L overhead cam engine with multi-port fuel injection. It can do 0–60 m.p.h. in 5 seconds. With that much engine, passing cars on the highway is a breeze, but handling corners on back roads is a little trickier than with my old pickup. I love the rush I get when I'm cruising around with my new wheels. You should consider buying one, too.

Example: Since you're in the market for a new car, I wanted to tell you about mine. My new car is the best one I've owned. It's a 2005 Puma. This sporty two-door is canary yellow with electric blue racing stripes and silver mag wheels. It has cordovan leather seats and a concert hall quality sound system. The sunroof is the perfect finishing touch. You should see the looks I get when I'm cruising around with my new wheels. You should consider buying one, too.

In both paragraphs, the author is telling someone about a new car, but each paragraph includes very different details about the car. You may have come to the same conclusions when you wrote your answers. If not, review the explanations both here and in Chapter One, "second-guessing" the author's intentions when he wrote the paragraphs.

AUDIENCE INTEREST

How does the writer try to catch the audience's interest in each paragraph? Clearly, the first paragraph is intended for a reader who is interested in a car's power and performance. The writer describes the car's engine, as well as its speed and handling. The second paragraph, on the other hand, mentions nothing about performance. The writer assumes that the audience is concerned with appearance and style, so the description focuses on colors and high-priced options.

AUDIENCE KNOWLEDGE

What does the writer assume the audience already knows? Since the reader of the first paragraph is interested in performance, the writer assumes that the reader knows what a Puma is and that going 0–60 m.p.h. in 5 seconds is fast. The reader of the second paragraph may need the author to describe the Puma as a "sporty two-door," but the reader understands the stunning colors and fine accessories of the new car.

AUDIENCE VOCABULARY

What kinds of words will the audience be familiar with and understand easily? The writer expects the reader of the first paragraph to know technical terms like "5.0 L" and "multi-port fuel injection." While these terms may speak loudly and clearly to the reader of the first paragraph, they may mean nothing to the reader of the second paragraph who appreciates "cordovan leather" and a "concert hall quality sound system." Likewise, the reader of the first paragraph may have no use for these terms since they have nothing to do with power or performance.

WHAT THE AUDIENCE SHOULD KNOW

What does the writer want the audience to know? In both paragraphs, the writer wants to share excitement about a new car purchase in order to encourage readers to purchase the same kind of car. The writer shares information that will be of interest to two kinds of audiences and that will encourage readers to purchase a Puma.

Many writing assignments will require you to address a particular audience, such as parents, teachers, other students, or the editor of a local newspaper. Knowing your audience and taking their interest, level of information, and vocabulary into account will make your writing more concise, appealing, and powerful.

Practice 6: Audience

For each of the following topics, describe the interest, knowledge, and vocabulary of the given audience, as well as what you think the audience should know.

1. Topic: parental advisory stickers on music CDs

    Audience: students

    Audience Interest

    Audience Knowledge

    Audience Vocabulary

    Audience Should Know

3. Topic: high salaries of professional athletes

    Audience: stadium worker

    Audience Interest

    Audience Knowledge

    Audience Vocabulary

    Audience Should Know

2. Topic: using lottery to fund public education

    Audience: governor of state

    Audience Interest

    Audience Knowledge

    Audience Vocabulary

    Audience Should Know

THE WRITING PROCESS

When you write, your mind organizes ideas into paragraphs, creating a body of sentences that communicate ideas. With a pen and paper in hand, you set out to record your thoughts and opinions. Unfortunately, the human mind does not work in a straightforward fashion, and our first attempts at writing are seldom our best. Fortunately, there are steps to take to increase the effectiveness of our writing.

As mentioned in the previous chapter, **prewriting** is the act of brainstorming ideas, either quickly jotting them down or making an organized chart of thoughts. A prewriting chart on the pros and cons of video games might look like this:

The benefit of prewriting is that, since the writing has yet to take shape, any idea is theoretically as good as any other. Many ideas are better than only a few, so quality takes a backseat to quantity.

The **first draft**, as its name implies, is the stage in which ideas are loosely organized on paper. Many writers believe the first draft is the easiest part of writing, since the "creative juices" flow freely and critical review is not yet important. With a first draft, the ideas taken from prewriting are put into written form. A first draft can be as messy and convoluted as possible, so long as its ideas "line up" in a way that makes sense.

With **revision**, a composition is "worked over" — given a thorough examination and rebuilt, rewritten and re-imagined in order to shore up its weaknesses and augment its strengths. If that seems tedious to you, don't worry. A more expansive look at revising the written composition follows in the next chapter, where we'll discuss ways to improve compositions with speed, accuracy, and vision.

Editing is the final marking up of a paper for grammar and punctuation, looking out for mechanical and stylistic errors that could weaken the piece's strength. Remember, a clean, error-free style will subconsciously impress the reader more than a piece filled with typos and vague or awkward sentences. The editing process allows you to weed out the small, inevitable mistakes that come with the creative process. In many ways, editing is putting your passage in its fanciest set of clothes, grooming it for its big debut.

Practice 7: The Writing Process

1. Brainstorming all your ideas onto paper is called

   A. prewriting.　　B. editing.　　C. publishing.　　D. revising.

2. Fill in the blank: _____ includes the process of casting out pretty thoughts or turns of phrase that don't really help a passage.

   A. editing　　B. publishing　　C. prewriting　　D. revising

3. To_____ a work includes building up its strengths.
    A. revise   B. brainstorm   C. edit   D. draft

4. Eliminating any spelling and grammatical errors comes in this stage:
    A. publishing   B. editing   C. first draft   D. revising

5. In this stage, you set all your ideas onto paper:
    A. publishing   B. editing   C. first draft   D. revising

THESIS STATEMENTS

Perhaps the most important part of a composition is its **thesis statement**, which articulates its argument or position in a single, concise sentence. The word "thesis" descends from a Greek word meaning "to put" and "to see." So consider a thesis as a means of putting your ideas out where other people can see them. The thesis statement includes the basic idea you want to impart to your audience or the belief that you want to persuade them to agree with.

When you write, remember that the best thesis statements focus on issues for which you have strong personal feelings. A topic doesn't necessarily have to concern a subject about which you are deeply passionate, but you should stay away from areas of which you have no interest. Find your opinion on a subject, think it through, and write from there.

Practice 8: Thesis Statements

Choose five essays out of your English textbook and/or magazines, and identify the thesis statements in each. Write them down and share your findings with a teacher or classmate.

TOPIC SENTENCES

A thesis statement is the main idea of a composition. Within a composition, however, **topic sentences** summarize the main idea of a particular paragraph. Topic sentences usually work to reinforce or support the thesis by including and summarizing additional information that is important to the composition.

In writing a paragraph, however, there are sometimes ways to tinker with or replace a topic sentence so that the meaning of the evidence becomes clearer and stronger. Consider the paragraph below, in which the topic sentence is italicized.

> *As President Kennedy implied, knowledge and peace seem to be ideals best looked for somewhere over the rainbow or beyond.* Knowledge found here on earth often takes the form of learning new devious technologies to destroy and corrupt social fabrics and societies. Advantages in physics in the 1940s were turned to mass destruction by the atomic bomb. Peace on this earth is so fleeting and rare, that even in utopias no peace could last. What turns knowledge to the evil side and twists yearnings for peace into power struggles? We may never know, and so we should learn to live with it. Looking for knowledge and peace must then be found in places so alien that human nature may be transcended.

The italicized sentence works as a topic sentence because it introduces the main idea of the paragraph. The key idea is that true knowledge and peace cannot be found on this earth but in a place beyond our world. The remaining sentences provide support for this topic sentence.

When reading topic sentences on the Ninth Grade EOCT, search for a statement that conveys the most information with the strongest possible message. A good topic sentence will take a position and assert it with confidence. It will also make sense within the context of the composition — that is, it won't contradict the evidence found elsewhere.

Practice 9: Topic Sentences

Read this introductory paragraph about the use of natural resources:

> The natural historian, Stephen Jay Gould, uses the phrase 'less is more" when describing the workings of human DNA. There are fewer genes needed for humans than originally thought. The explanation is that each gene is responsible for several types of physical traits. Gould notes that <u>humans tend to be greedier than nature, and use more than we should</u>.

1. Which sentence would be a better topic sentence than the one underlined?

    A.   Human DNA operates with fewer genes but more physical traits.

    B.   Humans tend to not think in terms of less is more, and often squander earth's resources.

    C.   Nature shouldn't use as few resources as she does.

    D.   Humans shouldn't use natural resources.

> <u>I've been thinking lately that living well is a good thing</u>. It will bring peace of mind. When bills must be paid, people will have fewer bills. It will bring respect for individuals at their own worth, instead of the false respect for what they own. It will bring back a life based on strong values like integrity, hard work, and community spirit, instead of a life based on the value of possessions.

2. Which sentence would be a better thesis statement than the one underlined?

    A.   The process of living with less will bring people more rewards than is immediately apparent.

    B.   The process of living well should be mandated by the government.

    C.   If we live well, we'll live without so much distraction.

    D.   Living well is something everyone should do.

ORGANIZATION

Organizational patterns shape how an author arranges and links details or ideas, either within a paragraph or over a series of paragraphs. Questions dealing with patterns require you to find the types of connections the author uses in a passage and to identify how the organization of a composition helps communicate its meaning.

ORGANIZING PARAGRAPHS

When organizing paragraphs, look for a clear progression of ideas, either according to the time they happened, the best sequence of actions to take, or a direct cause/effect relationship:

(**1**) If a fire should occur during the night in your home, follow these steps for survival. (**2**) First, roll out of bed. (**3**) Next, crawl to the door, and feel the door. If it is hot, do not open the door. (**4**) Or, if smoke or hot gases rush into the room when you open the door, close it and find another method of escape. (**5**) If the door is not hot, then brace yourself against it very slowly. (**6**)Toxic gases or fire may be on the other side. (**7**) Third, if no smoke enters the room, open the door, covering your nose and mouth with a moist cloth. (**8**) Then crawl quickly to safety. (**9**) Most importantly, get out by the quickest, safest route. (**10**) Finally, use an escape ladder, knotted rope, or a fire escape to leave your home. (**11**) Or you may be able to climb out a window on the roof and drop to the ground. (**12**) Then find a phone, and call the fire department.

– Shriners' Burn Institute, Cincinnati, Ohio

The above paragraph lists which actions to take, in their most logical order, to escape a burning house. If the sentences were rearranged, the proper flow of information would be disrupted, possibly leading to mistakes in a real-life situation. Though this is a dramatic example, when arranging paragraphs look for the choice that "makes the most sense" — that is, conveys the most logical flow of thought — when answering a sentence order question.

CHRONOLOGICAL ORDER

One of the more common patterns is the **chronological order,** which starts with a first event, followed by a second event, then a third event, and so forth. The passage and questions about it will usually contain **key words** that help you locate answers. Some key words are listed below:

first	before	next	second	after	until	now	afterwards
third	then	finally	when	last	between	later	most important

You can also use chronological order to organize other types of writing, such as **expository writing** that explains a process.

SPATIAL ORDER

When you describe a scene or a location, you can sometimes use **spatial order** to arrange your ideas among paragraphs. Imagine yourself holding a camcorder and moving it in every direction. You can order your observations from top to bottom, left to right, clockwise, near to far, front to back, inside to outside, east to west, north to south, etc., and all of these directions reversed (e.g., bottom to top). The following description is organized in spatial order:

When I saw the horse, I knew I was looking at a creature of great athletic beauty and ability. The horse's head was finely shaped, as if sculpted by an artist. On either side of its head, the eyes were alert and far-seeing. The ears were pointed and moved attentively to the slightest sound. The horse's neck was crested in a proud arch, and its muscular shoulders tapered down to powerful legs. The spine of the horse was perfectly aligned, and the back legs were unblemished and moved freely. The hindquarters of the horse were well rounded, and the horse's tail flowed like silk in the wind. In short, this horse was a magnificent animal.

In the passage, the details of the horse are organized in a front to back order. The writer discusses the horse's head, along with the eyes and ears. Next, the writer provides details about the neck, shoulders, and front legs. Third, the writer describes the spine and the back legs. Finally, the author tells us about the horse's hindquarters and tail.

Spatial order can also be an effective way to organize persuasive writing.

It's time for the city to clean up Jones Park. As visitors enter the park, they are greeted by a broken sign that is smeared with graffiti. Next, they pass the pond where they must hold their noses because of the smell of decaying trash. If visitors make it past all of this, they reach the playground in the middle of the park. Here they find swings with ripped seats hanging limp beside slides with broken steps. The park, in its current state, is a hazardous waste area that must be cleaned up.

ORDER OF IMPORTANCE

Another way to organize a paragraph is in **order of importance.** All of the details should be relevant to the topic, but some details should be emphasized more than others. You can emphasize a certain idea by placing it either at the beginning or the end of a paragraph. The following letter provides a good example.

Dear Aunt Jenny,

I would really like to spend the summer with you because I have never spent much time in Oregon. Also, I am interested in earning some extra money for my college savings, and many jobs are available in your area. Most importantly, I really enjoy our short visits when we get together over the holidays, and I want to spend more time with you so we can be closer.

Please write back soon, and let me know what you think.

Love,

Sandra

In this letter, Sandra begins with a simple wish that may be of some interest to her aunt. Aunt Jenny would be more likely to respect Sandra's second reason. However, Sandra's desire for a closer relationship will make the greatest impression upon her aunt's decision.

The letter could be arranged so that the most important idea comes first.

> Dear Aunt Jenny,
>
> I would like to spend the summer with you because I really enjoy our short visits when we get together over the holidays, and I want to spend more time with you so we can be closer. I am also interested in earning some extra money for my college savings, and many jobs are available in your area. Besides, I have never spent much time in Oregon.
>
> Please write back soon, and let me know what you think.
>
> Love,
>
> Sandra

Sometimes you will want to start off with the most important idea. Other times you will want to "save the best for last." The writer usually bases this decision on the audience, the topic, and personal preference.

CONTRASTING IDEAS

Occasionally, writing assignments require that you choose one side of an issue or topic and convince the reader of the validity of your position. One way to do this is to **contrast** your position with its opposite, pointing out differences and showing why your position is better. For example, look at the paragraph below, in which the writer is trying to convince his or her family to get a cat instead of a dog.

> Since our family spends a lot of time traveling, a cat is definitely a better choice than a dog for a family pet. Dogs need to be let outside several times a day, while a cat knows how to use a litter box. Dogs also need to be fed regularly, whereas a cat can snack on one bowl of food for a few days. Dogs are very social animals and get lonely if they don't have people or other dogs to play with. Cats, on the other hand, are affectionate sometimes, but they can also get along just fine by themselves. A dog would not be treated well enough in our busy household. A cat would be much happier.

In this example, the writer contrasts the qualities of a dog with those of a cat. The writer points out the reasons why a cat would fit better in a family that likes to travel. Someone with a different family situation could write a paragraph like the one below.

> For our young family, a dog would be a much better choice as a family pet than a cat. Dogs are social animals who love to be around people, especially kids. Cats, on the other hand, avoid crowds and often run from children. Dogs require regular feeding, which is a great opportunity to teach children responsibility. Cats require much less regular care. A dog offers great security for a home and family by barking when strangers approach. A cat can do little more than hiss at someone it doesn't like. A cat just doesn't offer our family the benefits a dog would offer.

This second paragraph also shows how awareness of audience is important in writing. The writers know that each of their families have different needs and interests. Therefore, the writers choose reasons and examples that are appropriate for each family's unique situation.

Practice 10:   Organizing Within Paragraphs

The following is a list of sentences taken from a paragraph. In the blank provided, write the order in which the sentences should appear when made into a clear, logical paragraph. The first is given as an example to help you.

___1___   His bedroom was a disaster zone.

_____   He hoped he could find them under one of the many laundry piles before his final exam, but all he found was a small garter snake.

_____   He had to run if he was going to be on time for class.

_____   His mother would be here soon to help pack, but he had no time to straighten up.

_____   There were clean, folded clothes mixed with dirty, crumpled clothes all over the floor, and even some old t-shirts slung across a lamp shade.

_____   Somewhere in this smelly pile of junk were the textbooks he was searching for.

_____   Damp, mildewed towels were draped over the door and foot of the bed.

_____   The trash can, teetering on top of three old pizza boxes, overflowed with snack wrappers and empty soda bottles.

Practice 11:   Organizing Multiple Paragraphs

Read the following composition and answer the question that follows:

1.   If I were to try to change the ages for driving and working, I would start a campaign. First, I would talk to my friends and tell them my ideas. Then, I would ask them to tell their friends and have their friends tell their friends. Finally, I would get everyone to write letters to their congressman to lower the driving and working ages because kids shouldn't have to wait.

2.   I want to change the driving age so that I can go places. I live far away from any kind of civilization. Any time I want to go to the mall with my friends, I have to ask my older brother or my parents. My parents are always busy working on something. My brother doesn't want to be seen anywhere with his little sister. He says it would kill his social life. If I could drive myself, I wouldn't have to bother any of them when I wanted to go somewhere. I could go where I want and do what I want. I could even get a job to buy a car and pay for the gas.

3.   I wish I were older so that I could drive and have money for things I want. But since I can't change time, I'll have to figure out how to get the government to change the driving age and the working age.

4.   If the working age were changed, then I could work to earn money for the things I want. I could buy my own clothes and wouldn't have to wear the things my mom buys for me. I could even buy some things for my family. My dad needs a new briefcase. My mom could use a new cell phone. My brother could use a new attitude, but I can't buy that. He'll have to settle for a new CD burner.

How should the paragraphs of the composition above be arranged, in order to put them in order of importance?

      A.   3, 1, 2, 3   B.   4, 3, 2, 1   C.   2, 4, 1, 3   D.   3, 2, 4, 1

SUPPORTING SENTENCES

Your composition leads with a thesis statement, and your paragraphs lead with topic sentences. However, their bodies and strengths lie in their supporting sentences. **Supporting sentences** add detail, embellish existing ideas, offer opinions or quotations, and make references to existing work that back up your thesis or topic sentences. As you might imagine, the proper placement and editing of supporting sentences can reinforce or weaken your composition as a whole.

1. **Supporting details are more than restatements of the topic sentence.** They provide reasons and examples that show why the main idea is true.

> **Example:** <u>Researchers have proven that smoking is bad for your health.</u> Many researchers have determined smoking is unhealthy. In addition, researchers have publicized smoking's harmful components.

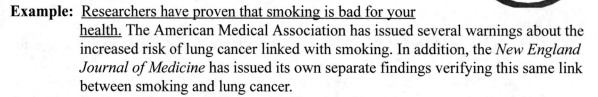

The underlined topic sentence is not supported with details. Instead, the next two sentences simply restate the topic sentence in different words.

> **Example:** <u>Researchers have proven that smoking is bad for your health.</u> The American Medical Association has issued several warnings about the increased risk of lung cancer linked with smoking. In addition, the *New England Journal of Medicine* has issued its own separate findings verifying this same link between smoking and lung cancer.

The same underlined topic sentence is supported by details. The writer cites the American Medical Association and the *New England Journal of Medicine* as providing examples of research that have shown the relationship between lung cancer and smoking.

2. **Supporting details are related to the topic.** If the details digress from the topic, these unrelated ideas can weaken the coherence of the paragraph and confuse the reader.

> **Example:** <u>It is easier than ever to learn a new language.</u> Sometimes it's hard to find someone who speaks another language. It's also fun to learn martial arts. Sometimes I just can't learn how to memorize things.

Each of the sentences may have one or two words in common, but they all refer to different topics. Each sentence should relate to the idea, "It is easy to learn a new language."

Example: <u>It is easier than ever to learn a new language.</u> Right now, you can learn a language by taking an elective course in high school. Then, if you go to college, you may have the opportunity to live in a foreign country as an exchange student. All along, you can join chat rooms on the Internet or conversation meetings in your area that will help you practice speaking your new language.

The supporting sentences in the paragraph explain and relate to the underlined topic sentence. The sentences provide specific examples of ways to learn a foreign language.

3. Supporting details are specific, not general, statements. The topic sentence is a general statement but should be explained in detail.

Example: <u>Opinion polls question small samples of the population in order to indicate larger trends.</u> An important part of polling is making sure that different kinds of people are represented. Even though this country is made up of many different kinds of people, opinion polls are pretty accurate.

All of the sentences above discuss opinion polls, but each one is general enough to be a topic for its own paragraph. They are related to the same idea, but they don't focus on one aspect of that idea.

Example: <u>Opinion polls question small samples of the population in order to indicate larger trends.</u> Pollsters must be careful to select people of different age, gender, occupation, location, and ethnic background. In this way, a sample of as few as 200 people can give a good indication of public opinion throughout the country. Despite the small sample, the margin of error is usually between four and six percent.

The author chose one general statement as the topic sentence (underlined) and supported it with specific details that emphasize the accuracy of polls based only on small samples of the population. Each supporting sentence elaborates on this single idea.

Practice 12: Supporting Sentences

Read each paragraph below. Strike out any sentences that don't fit the topic, are unwieldy or unnecessary, or do not "fit in" with the rest of the supporting details. You may add details if you wish. If the supporting sentences relate to the topic sentence, write "correct" next to the paragraph.

1. Swimming is really the healthiest exercise anyone can do. Jumping rope is also healthy, and it's a lot of fun. Sometimes just talking on the phone with friends can be fun, but you don't get much exercise. Going to the movies can be amusing, and if you walk there, it might be healthy. Just don't get butter on your popcorn because that's not healthy.

2. Something should be done about the cafeteria food because it tastes bad. Every time I gobble a mouthful, the taste is foul. Everyone agrees that the food tastes bad, and they bring in sack lunches instead. The food just does not taste good.

3. Scientists have a new theory to explain the mass extinction of aquatic life 186 million years ago. Using chemical analysis, researchers have determined that a large amount of methane gas was released from ocean floor sediment about that time. The methane combined with oxygen in the ocean and formed carbon dioxide. Without oxygen available, marine life could not breathe. Researchers believe this was the cause of death for many ancient underwater creatures.

4. I enjoy the smell of the air after a good rain. The air smells very good when the rain ends. After the water comes down from the clouds, the air smells very clean. Everyone enjoys the smell outside after a long soaking downpour. Nothing refreshes the air like a spring rain.

5. Many people wonder whether there is life on other planets in the universe. All around the world, people claim to see UFOs. The idea of creatures from other planets visiting Earth has been the topic of many books and movies. Science fiction clubs are very popular and often have large annual meetings.

USING TRANSITIONS BETWEEN PARAGRAPHS

Transitional words link ideas from one sentence to another, but they also link ideas between paragraphs to make the whole composition "stick together." Without these transitional words and phrases, the writing becomes less interesting or even less understandable.

REPEATING KEY WORDS AND PHRASES

While repetition is usually boring, repeating important key words and phrases will improve reader understanding. By including key words or ideas from your thesis in the topic sentences of your paragraphs, you make it easier to follow your train of thought. These repeated words are like landmarks along the road of your composition, reminding the reader where you have been and where you're going. For example, look at the following plan for a composition, in which the topic sentences repeat key words from the thesis:

Thesis: Citizens of the United States could greatly improve the country by obeying the law, protecting the environment, and being kind to other people.

Topic Sentence: The first and most basic step to improving the country is to obey the law.

Topic Sentence: In addition to obeying the law, citizens can make this country even more beautiful by protecting the environment.

Topic Sentence: A third way to make the United States a better place to live is for citizens to reach beyond their own self-interest and be kind to one another.

CONCLUDING SENTENCES

The **concluding sentence** of a paragraph brings closure to the paragraph by providing a summary of the topic and the supporting details. It may also suggest what action the reader should take, especially in persuasive writing. If another paragraph follows, the concluding sentence serves as a link between the two paragraphs.

A paragraph that lacks a concluding sentence may leave the reader wondering if the author left something out. Read the example below to understand the importance of concluding sentences.

Example: The federal government should increase spending for defense. Now that the war on terrorism has started, there is a need to keep this country well-armed. Currently, the United States spends more for defense than all other countries in the world combined! Congress continues to approve larger amounts of money for defense.

This paragraph lacks an ending. The addition of a concluding sentence would make a big difference:

Write to your representatives to say the terrorist attacks have justified every penny spent on defense and more.

This one sentence ties the paragraph together by summarizing the main idea and supporting details while urging the reader to take action. The reader may agree or disagree with the writer's ideas, but the reader understands that the writer has brought the paragraph to a close.

Practice 13:   Concluding Sentences

Read the following paragraphs, and write a concluding sentence that best completes the topic. If the paragraph has a concluding sentence, write *correct*.

1.   The global economy is moving toward the East. By 2020, China is projected to have an economy that is roughly eleven times as large as the economy of the United States! In addition, Japan, India, and Indonesia will have production levels that rival the United States. Only four nations in Europe will even make the top twenty list of the world's largest economies.

2.   The dancing craze is back in full force in the United States. After years of obscurity, swing music and dancing have made a rapid comeback. Also, the Latin rhythms of salsa, merengue, and cumbia can be heard in many cities. Two-stepping in clubs playing country music is also popular. In addition, the clubs playing techno, hip hop, and R&B music continue to draw larger crowds.

3.   Lifting weights is both mentally and physically demanding. It takes a great amount of concentration to lift large weights safely. Every lifter knows that form is crucial. The lifter must understand and visualize what he or she is doing during every second of a lift. People who do not exercise their mind in this manner end up with strains, sprains, and back and neck injuries.

CHAPTER 5 SUMMARY

Preparing **arguments** involves **using a good vocabulary, clearly supporting a definite claim**, and **knowing your audience**.

A good **writing style** includes:

- using specific words and phrases
- avoiding sweeping generalizations and cliches
- developing coherence
- using active rather than passive voice

Formal language is used when addressing an audience in professional or business surroundings. **Informal** language is used among friends and people with whom you have a friendly, cordial relationship.

Building a strong argument involves **making a claim, supporting the claim** with solid evidence, and **anticipating objections.**

Audience awareness concerns knowing the audience's interest, level of prior knowledge, vocabulary, and their need-to-know.

The **writing process** has four stages**:**

- *Prewriting* involves brainstorming for ideas and writing down whatever comes to mind.
- A *first draft* is the initial composition made to organize your ideas into prose form.
- *Revision* is the process of eliminating a work's weaknesses and building its strengths.
- *Editing* involves proofreading the final draft.

A **thesis statement** gives the author's position or theory on a given subject, putting it out for public display and discussion. A topic sentence is the main idea of a paragraph.

Organizational patterns determine how an author arranges details and ideas, either within a paragraph or over a series of paragraphs.

- *Chronological order* lists events in the direct order in which they happened.
- *Spatial order* describes objects as they appear when placed around each other.
- The *order of importance* organizes information according to which is either most important or least important.
- *Contrasting ideas* set up information in a kind of point-counterpoint, letting their value play off each other.

Supporting sentences add detail, embellish and add strength to a thesis statement and to topic sentences. They are related to the thesis and topic and offer specific information.

Concluding sentences provide a summary of the passage and challenge readers to come to their own conclusion about the evidence presented within.

CHAPTER 5 REVIEW

1. Rewrite the following paragraph, using vivid images and concrete words to enhance the description.

   There is a park not far from the center of town. At its edges, a variety of trees provide shade. In the center is an open field and a baseball diamond. Many people use this area for different sports and recreation. They can also just relax there and take in nature. In nice weather, many people gather in the park. All summer long, there are festivals and other fun activities that keep the area lively. The park is a favorite place for young and old alike.

For questions 2 – 6, decide if the word used is a cliche or an example of simple language.

2. old as the hills

3. black as night

4. full of energy and vigor

5. blue as the sky

6. expect the unexpected

7. Which of the following will **not** help develop coherence?
   A. planning an order
   B. using transitions
   C. avoiding generalizations
   D. repeating key words and phrases

8. Which of the following is **not** a feature of informal language?
   A. broader vocabulary
   B. simple sentences
   C. loose following of grammatical rules
   D. use of slang

9. Rewrite the following sentence in active voice:
   All the controls were damaged by him prior to landing.

10. A strong argument includes all **but** which of the following?
    A. clear logic
    B. valid facts
    C. blind, idiot shouting
    D. credible sources

11. When gauging audience awareness, consider all of the following factors *except*:
    A. the audience's interest.
    B. the audience's idea of a good joke.
    C. the audience's prior knowledge.
    D. what the audience needs to know.

12. The _____ stage involves putting all your brainstorming ideas onto paper.
    A. first draft
    B. revision
    C. editing
    D. audience analysis

13. The final markup of a draft is called the _____ stage.
    A. arguing   B. editing   C. revising   D. prewriting

14. The sentence that articulates your written composition's position, opinion, or argument is called the
    A. analysis.   C. introduction.
    B. active voice.   D. thesis statement.

15. The pattern in which things are arranged in the order in which they happened is called
    A. chronological order.   C. cause and effect order.
    B. spatial order.   D. order of importance.

16. _____ sentences add detail, embellish existing ideas, and offer opinions and quotations.
    A. Thesis   B. Argument   C. Exposition   D. Supporting

17. Which of the following is *not* true of supporting details?
    A. They're related to the topic.
    B. The offer specific statements.
    C. They're restatements of the topic sentence.
    D. They're explained in detail.

18. One way to improve reader understanding of a difficult concept is to
    A. repeat key words and phrases.
    B. explain the details in smaller, easier to understand words.
    C. taunt and insult the reader's poor comprehension skills.
    D. change the composition's argument mid-paragraph.

Read this introductory paragraph about film in the 1930s:

> People were going to the movies by the 1930s, largely because of their quality. Because tickets cost only pennies and offered hours of diversion, they existed for millions as a cheap way to kill time. Movies had also yet to escape the public perception as a "working class" medium — entertainment fit not for the cultured elite but for the blue-collar laborer. Hollywood responded with films that appealed to peoples' dreams of release from economic want. Other films attacked the social and government systems blamed by many for the Depression. Films such as *Public Enemy* and *White Heat* held up as heroes those who defied the status quo, while comedies like the work of the Marx brothers satirized the very rich.

19. Which sentence would be a better topic sentence than the one underlined?
    A. People went to the movies in the 1930s because it was trendy.
    B. Movies in the 1930s were better than ever.
    C. By the height of the Great Depression, Americans were flocking to movies more than ever.
    D. The Great Depression made Hollywood make better movies.

20. For the following topic, describe the interest, knowledge, and vocabulary of the given audience, as well as what you think the audience should know.

Topic: Parental Advisory Stickers on Music CDs

Audience: concerned parents

Audience Interest

Audience Knowledge

Audience Vocabulary

Audience Should Know

Chapter 6
Revising the Written Composition

This chapter addresses the following performance standards:

Standards	ELA9W3, ELA9W4

With revision, a work is taken apart and put back together again. The writer discards thoughts or wording that become unnecessary or incidental to the main idea, honing the passage down to its most effective, elegant form.

The word *revise* literally means "to see again." When revising, take a fresh look at your work and see if better ideas don't present themselves. These ideas could involve the substance of your work— the ideas your passage contains — or it may include a better way to express a thought or write a sentence. In almost every instance of revision, both will be involved. Don't be afraid to make changes if it will help the larger piece, and don't be afraid to "murder your darlings"— to cast out phrases that sound pretty or clever (and make you feel proud) but don't truly help the passage. Beginning writers sometimes see revision as having to write the same piece over again. It's closer to the truth to say revision is a means to write the same piece, but better.

HOW TO REVISE

Before revising your draft, you may want to "step back" to think about something else. Then, return to your composition, and read it as if you were the audience. Reading aloud will help you to hear the mistakes you might have made in grammar and mechanics, as well as give you a sense of how the piece will sound when you present it in the "mind's ear" of your reader.

While you read your composition during the revising stage, ask yourself the questions listed on the next page. You may wish to use the chart as a checklist to help you navigate the revision process:

Revision Checklist

_____	1.	Is the introduction a good preview of the rest of the composition?
_____	2.	Does my statement of the thesis give my composition a clear purpose?
_____	3.	Do the body paragraphs support the thesis with logically arranged supporting details?
_____	4.	Will my audience clearly understand how my ideas fit together?
_____	5.	Is there any irrelevant or repeated information that I can cut out?
_____	6.	Is there information that I need to add to make my ideas clearer?
_____	7.	Do my sentences fall into a repetitive and uninteresting pattern?
_____	8.	Have I used transitional words appropriately?
_____	9.	How can I improve my word choice?
_____	10.	Are there unexpected shifts in person or tense?
_____	11.	Are there unnecessary words that I can delete?
_____	12.	Does my conclusion tie the composition together and leave the reader with the sense that the composition is whole and complete?

ADDING OR REORGANIZING INFORMATION

When you write your draft, *you* know what you mean. As you revise your composition, imagine that you are the intended audience reading the composition for the first time. Make sure your readers have enough information and that the information is presented in a logical, organized manner. Ask yourself if switching the order of paragraphs to reorganize information will clarify your composition. Also, determine if adding information, more detail, or another example would make your writing clearer. Consider the following example:

> **Example:** The proposal will be considered by the school board at its next meeting.

The writer may have provided enough information for someone who is familiar with the situation described. However, another reader might ask, *"Which school board?" "What proposal?"* or *"When's the next meeting?"* The writer must add information to make the description clearer, as in the sentence below.

> **Example:** The DeKalb county school board will discuss the controversial recycling proposal at its regular Thursday night meeting.

Under the revisions, the five Ws of journalism (*who, what, where, when, why*) are identified. Vague generalities, such as "the school board," are replaced with specifics — DeKalb, recycling — and background information is filled in. Finally, a definite time is given. Notice also that the revised sentence has been changed to active voice, from the passive voice of the original.

Practice 1: Adding Information

Revise the following sentences by adding information.

1. I went with them to our favorite hangout, and we saw her.

   _____

   _____

2. The lines were down because of the storm.

   _____

   _____

3. Few people have big families these days.

   _____

   _____

4. Trees clean the air.

   _____

   _____

5. I bought a new lens to take better pictures.

   _____

   _____

DELETING UNRELATED SENTENCES

In some cases, you will want to eliminate information, ideas, or examples if they do not relate directly to the topic of your composition. Consider the paragraph below:

> I got a lot of great deals at the Clothing Mart. All the shoes were 50% off, so I bought two new pairs. I bought four new shirts because they were on sale — buy one, get one free. I'm so glad my friend, Chris, was there to help me pick out clothes. The pants were reduced by only 10%, but I really liked a green pair, so I bought it. I've never seen such a great sale.

Each sentence in the paragraph relates to the writer's purchasing new clothes at a big sale. The writer's appreciation of Chris' help, however, is not related closely enough to the other sentences, so it weakens paragraph coherence.

Practice 2: Deleting Unrelated Sentences

Read each of the following paragraphs, and draw a line through the unrelated sentence.

1. Out of all the classes you take in high school, not <u>one</u> of them deals with real-life situations. For example, you can get your diploma and not once have you been taught how to apply for college admission or for a full-time job. It seems like no one knows what's going on! Also, nobody has taught you how to communicate effectively or what skills are necessary in the interview process. Even if you get a job or go to college, no one has taught you how to get a checking account, apply for a lease, or even file your federal and state tax returns. It's a wonder any of us can make it to adulthood given our lack of education!

2. My first day in high school was pretty challenging. For the first time, I changed to a different class every fifty minutes. The school was huge, and I got lost during every move. I showed up to every class late. To top it all off, the combination to my locker didn't work, so I had to carry all of my books the entire day. I was not looking forward to going home, either, because I had to mow the lawn. My only consolation was that the other students in my classes were really friendly, and the teachers were understanding of what happens that first day.

3. When Leah turned the corner and entered the perfume shop at the mall, she got more than she bargained for. The most horrid smell in the world assaulted her nose. Customers and sales associates in this store were coughing and gagging! Leah pinched her nose immediately and ran for her life. After running for about fifty feet with her nose pinched, she let go of her nose and breathed some fresh air. There's nothing like fresh air to increase your mental functioning. After that incident, Leah thought it would be best to go home. Then, the next morning, she read about someone placing a stink bomb in the store as a prank.

4. I look forward to a solution to the problem of the super-sensitive security motion sensor. Once that type of motion sensor is activated, the slightest movement can set it off. A flying moth or even my cat scratching the litter box after a large dinner can send loud sounds pulsating through my house. I know the sensor needs to detect the sounds and motions of a thief, but how many thieves are actually as small as a moth or as silent as a cat? A home security system is very expensive.

5. Spelunking had always been a passion for Aaron. Every weekend he would explore the small caves and sinkholes in the Blue Ridge Mountains of Northern Georgia where he lived. He had no interest, however, in delving into the local "famous" cave, named Mystery. Fortunately, Aaron's teachers at school did not mind that the cave was famous and set up a field trip for the park. There were several families who owned large vehicles, like Suburbans and Explorers, and these parents volunteered to drive. Aaron discovered that Mystery cave was well-named because of its twelve  miles of corridors which were linear and maze-like in their complexity. Aaron enjoyed the cave's features of underground pools, stalactites, stalagmites and its temperature, which was 48° F in January. Aaron was impressed and returned to the park to roam the interior of the cave as often as he could.

ELIMINATING UNNECESSARY WORDS

Along with unrelated sentences, you also want to eliminate unnecessary words. Good writing does not necessarily involve lengthy sentences full of big words. Good writing expresses ideas clearly through effective words — the fewer the better. As an example, read the following sentence.

Unnecessary Words: As I was reflecting the other day, I thought about the very great number of people who, as of yet, have had very little experience of their own with using the Internet by going on-line.

This sentence includes various words that do not help the reader understand the writer's idea. Such extra words cloud the meaning.

Simple Language: Two days ago, I thought about the many people who have never used the Internet.

This shorter sentence provides the same information, but it does so more directly and clearly.

As you write your draft, don't worry too much about extra words. Let the ideas flow. However, when you are revising, eliminate unnecessary words and replace them with a simpler way of expressing the same ideas. Use the chart below to help you.

Unnecessary Words	Simple Language
due to the fact that	because
with respect to	about
hurried quickly	hurried
at that point in time	then
conduct an investigation	investigate
circular in shape	circular
there are many students who join	many students join
has a preference for	prefers
it is my belief that	I believe that
In Nathaniel Hawthorne's novel *The Scarlet Letter*, he writes about	In *The Scarlet Letter*, Nathaniel Hawthorne writes about
she is the kind of person who doesn't tolerate rudeness	she doesn't tolerate rudeness

Practice 3: Eliminating Unnecessary Words

Rewrite the following sentences and eliminate the unnecessary words.

1. I received various and many compliments while attending the cast party due to the fact that the peers of my own age have a preference for acting that is less formal in style.

_____

_____

2. At this point in time, the county commissioners are taking into consideration the reasons for or against pursuing formal and official charges against the sheriff.

    _____

    _____

3. These are the issues that will determine who will be elected president.

    _____

    _____

4. In my mind, I was thinking that the class's poor results on the tests that were administered in physics class were due in large part to the short amount of preparation time.

    _____

    _____

5. There are many people who do not realize that the first original name of St. Paul was Pig's Eye due to the fact that a French-Canadian whiskey trader, Pierre "Pig's Eye" Parrant, was the leader of settlers to that particular spot.

    _____

    _____

DEVELOPING SENTENCE VARIETY

Sentence variety involves writing sentences of various structures and lengths. Three ways to develop sentence variety are by **combining simple sentences into longer ones**, **starting a sentence with something other than the subject**, and **using a question or exclamation.**

COMBINING SIMPLE SENTENCES

Simple, direct sentences are often the best way to convey ideas. But if they become repetitive, they make your prose uninteresting. Compare the two examples below.

Example 1: We went to the basketball game. We were late. There was a huge crowd of cheering fans. The team won. Everybody celebrated in the parking lot. Then, some jubilant fans had parties at their houses. It was a great night.

Example 2: We got to the basketball game late, and the gym was already thronged with fans. Our team won, and, before we knew it, we were whisked out again to the parties in the parking lot. Some other fans invited us to party. What a night!

In Example 2, the writer has combined several of these simple sentences into a few longer ones. Both passages tell the same story, but the second one is more interesting because of sentence variety.

STARTING A SENTENCE WITH SOMETHING BESIDES THE SUBJECT

The simplest form of sentence construction places the subject first, followed by the verb, and finally a direct object or phrase. While grammatically sound , such writing can become dull and mechanical.

Example 1: We went to the movies last Friday. We saw X-Men3. It was okay, though my friends preferred X2: X-Men United. I thought the special effects were good.

The sentences in the above example are fine but bore the reader with over-simplicity and a somewhat monotonous tome. Sentence variety involves using phrases, different sentence construction, and subject variety to make the topic more interesting:

Example 2: Last Friday, my friends and I went to see X-Men 3. I thought is was okay, but they seemed to feel the second X-Men movie was better. The special effects were good, though.

Be careful, however, that when exploring sentence variety you do not lapse into passive voice.

USING A QUESTION OR EXCLAMATION

Using a **question** or **exclamation** occasionally can provide a welcomed change of pace.

Example 3: I didn't like it when my best friend told me he was going out with my ex-girlfriend. It was the worst feeling I've ever experienced.

Example 4: How would you like it if your best friend told you he was going out with your ex-girlfriend? It's the worst feeling I've ever experienced!

Examples 3 and 4 show how to use a question or exclamation to add variety to your writing. Example 4 also shows how a shift in person can be used effectively. Use them sparingly, however. Using exclamation marks too much can sometimes seem like laughing at your jokes.

Practice 4: Sentence Variety

Rewrite the following paragraphs by varying the sentences.

1. My friends and I went to the Philips Arena to see professional wrestling. There was a huge crowd. Everybody was screaming and yelling. All the fans were cheering for their favorite wrestlers. My favorite wrestler won all her matches. She flipped one of her opponents off the mat. She flew into the crowd. I was scared that she was going to land on me. She fell right next to me. I saw her up close. I saw that she was very big.

2. My best friend is a guy. We've known each other forever. Other girls ask me about him. They ask me why we are good friends. I tell them he is funny. He thinks of weird stuff. He tells me this stuff to hear me laugh. Sometimes I just tell him that he is too strange. He will listen to my opinion. He says that he is glad that he knows someone who will both laugh and tell him different.

3. You never know what effect you can have on other people. Sometimes it can be a big effect. Our school held a talent show. My friends and I did a lipsync to a song by System of a Down. The crowd cheered. Everyone thought it was great. After the show, everyone wanted to tell us how

great we were. I shook everybody's hand. I had a little fever that day. I found out later that I had strep throat. A lot of students were out sick the next week.

4. There's a new student in our school. His name is Omar. Most of his friends are in the chess club. He wasn't very popular. He wanted to run for student council. There was another student who was coming up for re-election. Her name is Theresa. Omar's friends were excited about his campaign. They put up a lot of posters all around the school. Omar gave a good speech. He had some good ideas. This was the first time he did something like this. He won by a small margin.

Practice 5: Revising

Based on the skills you learned in this chapter, revise the following paragraphs.

1. I do not believe in superstitions. But I like to learn about them. The one I'm reading about now says that people act weirder than usual during a full moon. The last full moon was the Worm Moon on March 9th. Different studies have recorded the number of people taken into mental wards, jails, and morgues when the moon lights the sky "as bright as day." The results, though, do not enlighten you. Some studies showed an increase in violent behavior. Some don't. There are theories that the added time of light helps people to do mischief or act out in weird ways. There are other which place blame for believed weirdness on the particular gravitational pull due to the fact  of the moon's position. I know only that I always enjoyed seeing the full moon and that is all I need to know.

2. At first, do not be scared when people in public tried to talk with you. We Americans are much more outgoing than I saw in Britain. They are the kind of people who are more subdued. They put a smile on their face that is polite. People were very emotional here in the United States. When Americans are happy and cheerful, they will show it. When they are unhappy and sad, they are not embarrassed to cry in front of the other many people.

3. Becoming popular in life has one big part of people getting into groups. To become popular may cause a person to join a group because they want to prove themselves to someone. This happens usually to new students at a new school. Becoming popular and well-known in the working area is about the same as school. This happens when someone gets a job they would like to keep. They try to impress the boss. People also join groups to become popular to be cool, so other people around them will like them.

CHAPTER 6 SUMMARY

- Make sure you provide the audience with enough organized information, in the correct order, to understand your ideas.

- Delete sentences or phrases that are not directly related to the paragraph or composition.

- Good writing expresses ideas clearly through effective words—the fewer the better.

- Vary your sentences by combining simple sentences into longer ones, starting sentences with something other than the subject, or using a question or exclamation occasionally.

CHAPTER 6 REVIEW

A.   **Using the skills you practiced in this chapter, revise the composition below. It was written as a response to the following writing prompt.**

Your teacher has asked you to write about the career you wish to pursue and why you have chosen that career.

State your choice of career, and give specific reasons why you have chosen it. Give enough details so your teacher will understand your ideas.

I would like to show you why I am now choosing to pursue a medical career. While I have been growing up I have had many doctors to inspire me. When I was diagnosed with cancer as a young seven-year-old, I was very scared. However, the doctors and nurses at the Mayo Clinic took the time to explain how they would help me. In the end I would like to be a doctor to help others in an important way, provide an income for my family, and make important contributions to the medical field.

Most importantly, I want to be in a profession where I can help people in the way I was helped. Being a doctor would give me the ability to touch the lives of people because being there for some one when their health is at risk and being able to give them the advice they need is a great feeling. I look forward to looking at my patients as people. not cases. I want to make them laugh, as well as give them the medicine they need. I want to make their lives better by giving them real support and lending them my expertise. The best kind of knowledge to have is the kind that you can share with the world.

Secondly, providing an income for the family I will have one day concerns me. I don't want to have to work sixty hours a week in a job I hate so that I can bring in enough money, to keep my family taken care of. I want to have time to spend with my family instead of being with a company that becomes my family because I spend so much time there. I want to be able to earn enough in a regular work-week to not need to work over-time hours. Being a doctor will give me the opportunity to work the hours I want while still being able to provide for my family.

Thirdly, I want to pursue a career in medicine so that one day I can make important discoveries to help patients. I believe there are other cures to cancers waiting out there in the world. I find it hard to believe that the only way today to cure people from cancer is to inject them with poisonous chemicals. I was really scared when I was a kid and all my hair fell out. Those chemicals do things to your body that nature didn't intend. And they damage you. I want to find cures for diseases from the natural world. Our bodies are natural, so we shouldn't be surprised to find cures for diseases coming from nature. I would like to be at the front of efforts to find natural remedies to many of the diseases afflicting the people.

To tell you the truth, I want to be a doctor because I can help people in an important way, provide a good income for my future family without having to work too hard, and contribute important natural discoveries for cures for diseases. Being able to work my own hours will help balance my future family responsibilities and work. Helping people is why I feel I have been put on this earth, and I want to help someone in the way someone else helped me. In addition, producing natural cures for diseases will help me to leave this earth feeling I have made a lasting difference while I was here.

Now discuss your revision with your teacher or your classmates.

Chapter 7
Grammar & Conventions

This chapter addresses the following performance standards::

Standards	ELA9C1, ELA9C2

Grammar and convention rules are probably no one's favorite part of writing and reading, and even the most distinguished scholars are sometimes hard-pressed to insist on their proper use. Nonetheless, grammar remains important and continues to be taught in schools.

Grammar is in many ways similar to the laws and customs of a society, the rules everyone agrees by to keep the language in good running order. Among English-speaking cultures, language varies somewhat, determined by local customs and habits formed over centuries. We call these local variations **conventions**. Indeed, the English language is a living thing, constantly incorporating new words and phrases as a means of adapting to an ever-changing world.

SENTENCE TYPES

Sentences are classified by structure in one of four ways: **simple, compound, complex,** and **compound-complex sentences**. In the examples below, independent clauses are underlined, and dependent clauses are kept in regular type:

A **simple sentence** is a sentence made of one independent clause. It may have more than one subject or more than one predicate. It may have phrases also.

> **Example:** Billy took the boys fishing after school.

> **Example:** Today was hot and dry.

A **compound sentence** is a sentence made of two or more simple sentences joined by a semicolon or a comma and the conjunctions *and, but, or, nor, for, so,* or *yet.* It can contain two or more independent clauses.

> **Example:** Gladis took the car to the mechanic, but she forgot to bring her checkbook.

> **Example:** We ate a large breakfast; then we skipped lunch.

A **complex sentence** is a sentence containing one independent clause and one or more dependent clauses. Relative pronouns or subordinating conjunctions are used to connect the sentences together.

> **Example:** Because the lobby was filled with smoke, the elderly man could not enter the building.

> **Example:** The car that she likes the best is a Lexus.

A **compound-complex sentence** is a sentence containing two or more compound sentences and one or more complex sentences.

> **Example:** When her mother planned Crystal's birthday party, she first made an invitation list, and then she planned the food menu and the cake design.

> **Example:** Before we buy shoes, my mom looks for bargains, but sometimes we splurge.

Practice 1: Sentences

Read the following sentences. On a separate sheet of paper, write *S* if the sentence is simple, *Cd* if the sentence is compound, *Cx* if the sentence is complex, and *CC* if the sentence is compound-complex.

1. Mary pruned the bushes while Ben mowed the lawn. _____

2. Dolores and Ricki went canoeing with their friends after church on Sunday. _____

3. Eve sewed her feather-filled coat to prepare for the onslaught of winter. _____

4. Three divers are trying out for a spot on the team, and there is only one dive remaining. _____

5. At 6:30 p.m., Phil Moore left his house; we have no record of him after that. _____

6. After his car hit the bridge and flipped over, Rodney needed to get to the doctor quickly, and his wife turned on her cellular phone and dialed 911. _____

7. Since Paul ran faster than all of his classmates, he won the prize. _____

8. I was late for school because I missed the school bus. _____

9. Never talk to strangers, and call 911 if you have an emergency. _____

10. They enjoy playing kickball during gym class. _____

FRAGMENTS, RUN-ONS, AND COMMA SPLICES

SENTENCE FRAGMENTS

A **sentence fragment** is a collection of words that do not express a complete thought.

     Example: All this year's best peaches..

     Example: The long way back to the house.

To correct a sentence fragment, simply add the parts of the sentence that are missing. If the sentence is missing a subject, add a subject. If the sentence is missing a verb or predicate, add a verb or predicate.

     Example: All this year's best peaches are headed to the grocery stores.

     Example: Calvin took the long way back to the house.

RUN-ON SENTENCES

A **run-on** sentence occurs when a comma is used in place of a period, semicolon, or comma and coordinating conjunction **(and, but, or, for, nor, yet, so)** to join two complete sentences. Sometimes all punctuation is omitted between the complete sentences.

     Example: Joseph went to school the dog stayed at home..

There are three ways to fix run-ons:

- break the two **independent clauses** into separate sentences:
  Example: Joseph went to school. The dog stayed at home.

- add a **semicolon** that separates the two complete sentences:
  Example: Joseph went to school; the dog stayed at home.

- add a **comma + coordinating conjunction** to separate the two complete sentences:
  Example: Joseph went to school, but the dog stayed at home.

Practice 2: Fragments and Run-Ons

Tell whether each of the questions below is a sentence, run-on, or sentence fragment. If the example is a run-on or a sentence fragment, rewrite it to make it into a proper sentence.

1. The cat fell out of the tree onto the roof.

2. Just in time for that midnight snack.

3. Running all the way up the stairs.

4. We're going through the house, you should stay outside.

5. Fishing in the lake brought back childhood memories.

6. Tracy took the shortcut home she didn't want to walk far in the heat.

7. At that time, all people will rise up and demand justice.

8. He was batting left-handed, the ball went deep into right field.

9. The soccer game begins at noon the players are here an hour early.

10. Living in this climate under these conditions.

COMMA SPLICES

Comma splices are punctuation errors in which two independent clauses are joined only by a comma, with no conjunction.

> **Example:** You're going to a concert, you can't wear that.

As with run-on sentences, there are several ways to correct comma splices.

- replace the comma with a **semicolon**:

  > **Example:** You're going to a concert; you can't wear that.

- write the separate clauses as **distinct sentences**:

  > **Example:** You're going to a concert. You can't wear that.

- insert a **coordinating conjunction** between the two clauses:

  > **Example:** You're going to a concert, but you can't wear that.

- make one **clause dependent** upon the other.

  > **Example:** If you're going to a concert, you'd better not wear that.

Note that simply removing the comma from a comma splice does not fix the error. Rather, it creates a run-on sentence.

Practice 3: Comma Splices

Correct the comma splices below by using one of the methods described above. If the sentence is correct, write *C*.

1. She's tall for her age, she's probably not going to get a prom date.

2. I'm going out later, but I'll be back in relatively early.

3. No one wants to be lonely, everyone wants someone to dance with.

4. You know what I think, she's probably the prettiest girl here.

5. How can anyone say that, he's such a cool dude.

CHECKING FOR PARALLEL SENTENCE STRUCTURE

Parallel sentence structure means that the parts of the sentence which are equally important are expressed with equal emphasis. In other words, verbs match with verbs, adjectives with adjectives, prepositional phrases with prepositional phrases, and so on. *We didn't lose the game; we just ran out of time.* – Vince Lombardi

> **Example:** Not everything that can be counted counts, and not everything that counts can be counted. – Albert Einstein

> **Example:** First they ignore you, then they laugh at you, then they fight you, then you win. – Mahatma Gandhi

These sentences have rhythm and power because they are written in parallel structure. Writing that is not parallel can be difficult to read. Read the following examples and listen to the flow and logic of the words.

Gandhi

- **Non Parallel:**   Janine likes to dance, sing, *and even plays* the flute.
- **Parallel**:   Janine likes to dance, sing, *and play* the flute.
- **Non Parallel:**   When I think the rain will never stop, the sun comes out, *I hear* the birds begin to sing, and the flowers raise their little heads.
- **Parallel:**   When I think the rain will never stop, the sun comes out, the birds begin to sing, and the flowers raise their little heads.

VERBS

Verbs are "doing words" - they relate action, and writing is impossible without them. The following are some matters of good verb usage. To start, there are three solid rules for **subject-verb agreement**.

SUBJECT-VERB AGREEMENT

Rule 1.   **Grammar rules state that the *subject* of the sentence must agree with its corresponding *verb*. The *subject* is the word performing the action (*verb*). In the examples below, each subject is underlined, and each verb is bolded.**

> **Example:** My older brothers **play** baseball in the park.

> **Example:** The frog **croaks** in the pond every night.

Rule 2.   **The subject of a sentence does not necessarily have to appear before the verb. In questions and sentences with here and there, the verb usually comes before the subject:**

> **Example:** When **is** Dorothy coming to plant her flowers?

Remember that some words having an *s* at the end are also singular subjects: for example, *news, physics, mathematics.*

Rule 3. Sentences containing compound singular subjects have verbs that are written as compound singular.

Example: In addition to Keri, Rick is entered in the contest.

Keri and Rick are both subjects of this sentence. Because the sentence interrupter, **in addition to** is used, the verb **is entered** becomes singular.

Practice 4: Subject-Verb Agreement

Read the following sentences. Write a *C* next to the sentence if the subject and the underlined present tense verb agree. Correct the verb in the present tense if it does not agree with the subject.

1. Mickey Mouse <u>makes</u> funny comments during his cartoons.

2. Mrs. Nally and her friends <u>plays</u> cards during the night.

3. The new riding lawn mower <u>run</u> smoothly.

4. Now <u>is</u> the time to change the future.

5. Theresa <u>want</u> to be the class president.

6. There <u>is</u> five pencils on the floor.

7. Instead of steak, <u>eat</u> the shrimp.

8. The genie <u>grant</u> three wishes to the one who releases him.

9. I <u>smile</u> whenever I see a clown.

10. Louise and Rita <u>is</u> going to Disneyland.

SHIFTS IN VERB TENSE

It is important to choose **one verb tense** and use it throughout your composition. Although you should change tense to show time relationship, you should not change without appropriate reason. Read the following passage, and notice how the underlined verbs shift from present tense to past tense.

Example: The Mojave Desert <u>stretches</u> from the Sierra Nevada mountains to the Colorado Plateau. On its southwest border <u>lies</u> Death Valley, the lowest point in North America. The arid basin <u>received</u> less than five inches of rain annually. Sparse vegetation <u>grew</u> throughout the region. Even so, a variety of life <u>flourished</u>, especially after sunset.

The shift in tense can confuse a reader about the writer's relationship to the events. To make this paragraph clearer, the last three verbs should be revised to the present tense (*receives, grows, flourishes*).

PARALLEL VERB TENSE

To keep verbs parallel, make sure there are no unnecessary shifts in tense and that tenses match their intended meaning.

Non-Parallel	Tiffany <u>finishes</u> her homework and <u>will do</u> the dishes.
Parallel	Tiffany <u>finished</u> her homework and <u>did</u> the dishes. Tiffany <u>will finish</u> her homework and <u>will do</u> the dishes.

Practice 5: Parallel Verb Tense

In the following passage, correct the verbs so that they contain parallel tenses. Use a separate sheet of paper for your revisions.

(**1**) Tamika is quite adventurous and liked to take action-packed vacations. (**2**) Last year, she rode a bike through Tuscany and see the beautiful countryside. (**3**) She had never tasted so many delicious dishes and was glad the cycling works off all the calories in them! (**4**) Before that, she visits the pyramids in Egypt and stayed for a week in Cairo. (**5**) During that trip, she rides a camel in the desert and learned to belly dance! (**6**) On another excursion, she will raft down the Snake River and then exchanged her raft for a kayak in the middle of the trip. (**7**) She says that traveling makes her feel alive and helped her understand other cultures. (**8**) Considering all the activities she includes in her trips, she'll get plenty of exercise, too! (**9**) On her upcoming vacation, Tamika hiked in Tibet and will backpack in the Himalayas. (**10**) While there, she learns more about the small country's traditions and will meet some of its people. (**11**) One day, Tamika likes to write a book about her adventures and would like the sale of that book to fund further travels.

MISPLACED AND DANGLING MODIFIERS

A **modifier** is a phrase or clause that helps to clarify the meaning of another word.

> **Example:** Tripping over the trash can, our cat was looking for food.

In this sentence, the phrase *tripping over the trash can* modifies the word **cat**. It describes a condition or tells of a circumstance relevant to the subject.

In modern English usage, however, modifiers are frequently misused, leading to their either becoming **misplaced** or left **dangling**.

MISPLACED MODIFIERS

A misplaced modifier is a word or phrase that modifies a clause ambiguously; the modifier could possibly apply to either the subject or object of the clause.

> **Example:** Two students competed against the school record diving in the swimming pool.

It is unclear whether the phrase *diving in the swimming pool* describes the **students** or **the school record**. To correct this problem, we place the modifying phrase closer to the word it describes:

> **Example:** Diving in the swimming pool, two students competed against the school record.

A **modifying clause** is a dependent or independent clause that clarifies the meaning of another word.

> **Example:** Raymond waited for his test results pacing nervously on the steps.

Here it is unclear whether the clause *pacing nervously on the steps* describes **Raymond** or his **test results**.

> **Example:** Pacing nervously on the steps, Raymond waited for his test results.

Practice 6: Misplaced Modifiers

The following sentences contain misplaced modifiers. Rewrite each on a separate sheet of paper, placing the modifiers and modifying clauses in their proper place within the sentence. Write *C* if the modifier is correctly placed.

1. Grandpa Frank who was called Carlene brought a set of clothes for the baby girl.

2. Neal worked hard on his farm raising beef cattle to support his family.

3. The teacher announced that next week's class, which would encourage more participation, would be about international foods.

4. The travel agency is now providing added incentives for customers vacationing in October.

5. One of our scouts sighted a tank through night vision glasses that he could not identify.

DANGLING MODIFIERS

A **dangling modifier** is a phrase or clause that comes at the beginning of a sentence but does not modify the subject in the sentence.

> **Example:** Listening to hip hop music, her arms began to move with the rhythm.

The phrase *Listening to hip hop music* modifies the subject **arms**. Since arms cannot listen to music, the phrase *Listening to hip hop music* cannot be the modifier of **arms**.

> **Example:** Listening to hip hop music, Latasha began to move to the rhythm.

Listening to hip hop music correctly describes **Latasha** instead of **arms**.

Practice 7: Dangling Modifiers

On a separate sheet of paper, rewrite the following sentences so that they no longer contain dangling modifiers. Write *C* if the modifier is used correctly in a sentence.

1. While fishing in the river, a large piece of driftwood floated by.

2. Left penniless by the taxes, his hunger grew larger.

3. To decide a military action, the long-term outcome must be planned by the generals.

4. While flying high above the Rocky Mountains in the clouds, a flash of lightning hit the front of our plane.

5. Working in this beach side resort for many months, the sunstroke was caught by many lifeguards.

CAPITALIZATION

Capitalization involves the practice of using a mixture of capital ("A") and lower case letters ("a"). In the early development of English, writers used only capital letters. In modern English, there are rules for capitalizing certain words in order to emphasize their importance. One example is the first word of every sentence; another example of capitalized words are proper nouns, like "Savannah, Georgia."

Some common rules for capitalization include:

Rule 1. **Capitalize the first word of a sentence.**

    Example: We went to the candy store.

Rule 2. **The first word of a sentence following a colon can begin with a small letter or a capital letter. Be consistent throughout your writing.**

    Example: Listen to the following announcement: aliens will now rule **all** people living on planet Earth.

    Example: The aliens are benevolent: **They** come from the Polaris system.

Rule 3. **Capitalize the first word of a direct quotation that is a complete sentence, even if it is within another sentence. When a quotation is interrupted by words such as *he said*, do not use a capital letter to begin the second part of the quotation.**

    Example: Mr. White said, "**Be** here next Saturday at 9:00 a.m."

Rule 4. **Capitalize the pronoun *I* and the interjection *O*. Capitalize the word *oh* only when it appears at the beginning of a sentence.**

    Example: Help us, **O** great one!

Rule 5. **Capitalize the names of specific persons, places, things, or ideas. Capitalize the adjectives that are formed from proper nouns:**

- **races and nationalities** - The food of **Asian** people is popular with **Canadians**.
- **geographical features** - When did you drive through the **Smoky Mountains**?
- **historical periods** - The **Great Awakening** was a time of religious fervor.
- **titles of courses** - My **math** class is now **Introduction to Algebra**.
- **names of buildings, monuments, bridges** - I work in the **Forsyth Center**.
- **names of celestial bodies** - **Saturn** is part of the **Milky Way**.
- **names of streets and roads** - He lives near **Vermillion Street** and **Route 27**.
- **names of religions and terms for the sacred** - Most **Muslims** read the **Koran**.

Practice 8: Capitalization

Carefully read the letter below, proofreading for errors in capitalization. Circle all of the words with capitalization errors, including words that should have been capitalized and were not and words with capitalization that should not.

july 24, 2004

dear mr. Golden,

My Family and i finally went on our vacation to the grand canyon in arizona. we got there on a Wednesday Morning. My brother, will, and I both wanted to go on the Helicopter tour first, but mom and dad said "Later!"

When we first walked to the Edge of the South Rim, our jaws dropped, and we exclaimed "oh, wow!" at one time. Mom took a step back. "Oh," She said, "I don't think I can hike this!"

Some german Tourists, hearing our english voices, stopped by us at that moment to ask about the horseback tours. We helped them find the Camp office, and we spoke with kelly o'hara, the Park Ranger on duty. after giving us information about the Canyon and reassuring Mom about the bright angel Trail, Ranger o'hara asked if we were from the south. I guess our accents are more noticeable than i had thought...

Since I know that you, as my english Professor, will be asking for this later, Maybe you could look over my Outline for the Annual "what I did this summer" paper.

  I. Memorial day pool Visit

  A. sunburn

   1. Second degree burns

sincerely yours,

Leigh Harper

PUNCTUATION

As with capitalization, **punctuation** can mean the difference between writing that is polished and professional or amateurish and sloppy. A brief run-down of the major punctuation rules follows:

COMMAS

Rule 1. **Commas separate *independent clauses* (groups of words that form a coherent sentence) only when they are joined by a *conjunction* (words like *and, but, or, nor, for, yet, so*).**

  Example: Jesse ran to the gas station, but he forgot his money.

  Example: Renatta works at a copier center, and she has to stand up most of the time.

Rule 2. Commas are used to set nonrestrictive elements off from the rest of the sentence. Nonrestrictive elements are clauses, appositives, and phrases that are not essential to the meaning of the words they modify. Restrictive elements, on the other hand, are essential to the meaning of the words they modify and are *not* set off by commas.

> **Example: Nonrestrictive** - The three adventurers involved in the rescue, *who were not afraid of risking their lives*, jumped into the pit to save their friend.

> **Example: Restrictive** - The adventurers *who were not afraid of risking their lives* jumped into the pit to save their friend.

Rule 3. Commas usually follow an introductory word, phrase, clause, or expression.

> **Example:** *Besides*, the child was only six years old.

> **Example:** *When I drive home from school*, I go right by your house.

Rule 4. Commas are normally used to separate items in a series of three or more words, clauses, or phrases. However, modern English usage now allows for the optional use of a comma before "and" with items in a series. A comma before "and" is required if the meaning is unclear.

> **Example:** Tim, Amanda, and Satisha are all on phone restriction.

> **Example:** Tacos, tamales and fajitas are my favorite foods.

Practice 9: Punctuation with Commas

On your own paper, write a *C* if each sentence in the following paragraph is correctly punctuated. Revise the sentence if the sentence is incorrectly punctuated.

(1) In the book *The Outsiders*, S.E. Hinton makes the point that Ponyboy is becoming a better person, despite the environment in which he grows up. (2) Ponyboy who has a rough life makes the transition from childhood to adulthood because of the relationship he has with his brothers, the hardships he encounters, and the advice of his loved ones.

(3) Ponyboy is left to decide his future, and he tries very hard to act like an adult in the process. (4) It is difficult to bear when other kids who are wealthier make comments about the advantages they have. (5) In the end, he realizes he will face many problems in life but he can get through them with friends and family helping him.

Rule 5. Commas are used to set off added comments or information. Transitional expressions such as conjunctive adverbs are also set off with commas.

> **Example:** My records, however, indicate that he paid his taxes every year.

> **Example:** Lyla, as we know, was out of the house when the fire started.

Rule 6. **Commas are used to set off direct address, tag questions, interjections, and opposing elements.**

Direct Address Example: Carla, what is on the agenda today?

Tag Question Example: We're not going in there, are we?

Interjection Example: We drove across Tennessee, surprisingly, in one day.

Opposing Elements Example: Rene was supportive, not critical, toward the project.

Rule 7. **Commas are used before and after quotations. Commas are not used when the quotation is a question, an interjection, an indirect quotation, or when the quotation includes the word *that*.**

Example: "Go at once," Gene commanded, "and see what is causing that commotion."

Example: The lawyer says that the trial system is fair.

Example: People who say "so long" are using an expression.

Rule 8. **Commas are *not* used after a quotation when the quotation is an exclamatory statement or a question.**

Example: "What are you doing here?" asked the baker.

Practice 10: Punctuation with Commas

Read the following passage. On your own paper, write a *C* if the sentence is correctly punctuated, or revise the sentence if it is incorrectly punctuated.

(1) We've never had a family pet, before. (2) Bringing home a new puppy last weekend, therefore, turned our lives upside down! (3) "I think we should get a doggy door?" my brother ventured.

(4) "It might be a good idea Mike," my dad replied.

(5) We watched the hyperactive rascal run around the kitchen and all of a sudden disappear into the broom closet. (6) A loud crash signaled that he had knocked over the cleaning supplies.

(7) My mom rolled her eyes and said, "I think the regular door is fine. (8) I'd like to see his coming and going controlled by us not him."

Rule 4. **Commas are used between the date and year as well as after the year. Do not use a comma between a month and year.**

Example: On December 3, 1995, Lupe got her wish.

Example: We went camping in May 2002.

Rule 5. Commas are used after the street address or PO Box, city, and state in addresses. If the zip code is included, do not place a comma between the state and the zip code. If a city and state are given in a sentence or city and name of a country, commas go after the city and another after the state or country.

Greg Durham has lived at 627 Grant Rd., Atlanta, GA, for three years.

> **Example:** The senior class is going to London, England, this summer.

QUOTATION MARKS

Rule 1. Use quotation marks (") to signify a direct quotation.

> **Example:** "Poor old tree!" said Dave, pointing to a crooked and gnarled oak standing by itself at the edge of a field.

Rule 2. Periods and commas always go inside the quotation marks. Exclamation points and question marks go inside if they're part of the quoted material. Colons and semicolons go outside the quotation marks. Quotes within quotes use single quotation marks.

> **Example:** "Here we go again," Keisha said.

> **Example:** "What's the matter?" Lisa asked.

Rule 3. Use quotation marks (") to signify a short work of literature or a speech. Also, use single quotation marks (') when the title of any short work is inside a person's quotation.

> **Example:** Martin Luther King's speech, "I Have a Dream," had a wide impact.

> **Example:** "Have you read the story, 'The Lady or the Tiger'?" Holly asked.

Rule 4. Do *not* use quotation marks for indirect quotations, because they do *not* contain someone's exact words. Conjunctions like *that, if, who, what,* and *why* often introduce indirect quotations.

> **Example:** Jane said that she didn't want to go to the mall.

Practice 11: Punctuation with Quotation Marks

Read the following passage. On your own paper, revise sentences as needed by adding or changing quotation marks as you rewrite them on the blank lines. Write *C* on the line if the sentence is correct.

(1) The word *kudos* comes from the Greek noun *kydos* and means "praise and honor" (Oxford English Dictionary). (2) Kudos is a mass noun and, like *acclaim, renown* and *prestige*, it takes a singular verb:

(3) In *The Last Secrets*, John Buchan writes "... they had acquired much kudos among the pilgrims."

(4) "We showered kudos on Milo for his excellent report on 'Young Goodman Brown.'"

(5) "Why would you say that"? Roseanne asked. "I think they deserve kudos for doing it."

(6) The dictionary says that "someone always tries to prune the -s off kudos to create a single kudo," but this is incorrect. (7) Instead, one can ask, How would the word *prestige* be used here?

COLONS

Rule 1.   **Use a colon to introduce a list, series, quotation, or formal statement.**

   Example: At some time in your life, you will ask the question: Why do I exist?

Rule 2.   **Use a colon before a second independent clause which restates or explains the first clause.**

   Example: The singer had a great voice: every tone that she sang was in tune with the music.

Rule 3.   **Use a colon to separate hours and minutes when telling time.**

   Example: It is 2:38 PM.

SEMI-COLONS

Rule 1.   **Semi-colons separate independent clauses that are *not* joined by a conjunction. Usually, semicolons are used in place of periods when the two independent clauses are closely related.**

   Example: The saleswoman sold two houses; she was very happy that day.

Rule 2.   **Semi-colons separate independent clauses that are joined by sentence interrupters (for instance, nevertheless, besides, moreover, instead, besides, and so on.).**

   Example: The people were panicking in the streets; nevertheless, the ambulance was able to move through the crowds.

Rule 3. Semi-colons are sometimes used to split independent clauses when there are several commas inside the clauses.

   Example: Mr. Howard, a writer, announced his new horror, mystery, and science fiction series; yet the books, oddly enough, had not been written.

Rule 4.   **Semi-colons are used if a colon precedes items in a series and if commas are part of the items.**

   Example: These athletes were all participating in the national competition: Judy Dawes, a world class diver; Joe Chung, a champion weight lifter; and Sherry Whittaker, an Olympic gymnast.

Practice 12: Punctuation with Semi-colons

Read the following passage for the use of semicolons. Use your own paper and if the sentence is correctly punctuated, write *C*; if it is not, revise the sentence.

(1) Skydiving, scary yet exciting, is one of the most exhilarating experiences I've ever had. (2) I was, of course, extremely nervous as the plane took off and climbed, but the worst part, aside from the wide eyes and silence of my friends on board, was when the door was opened at 13,000 feet. (3) When it was my turn, I crawled to the open door and followed instructions: Grab hold of the wing strut and hang on tightly then count one, two, three, and let go. (4) I barely recall the sequence of events, but soon I was falling through the air, until my guide caught up to me and pulled the rip-cord. (5) Everything slowed down, and I was floating; taking in an incredible panorama and barely remembering to breathe. (6) Someone once said that people are crazy to jump out of a perfectly good plane, but I would do it again in a heartbeat!

END PUNCTUATION

End punctuation has only three very simple rules to remember:

Rule 1. A period comes after a complete statement.

 Example: There are many grammar rules to remember.

Rule 2. A question mark comes after any question.

 Example: When will this section end?

Rule 3. An exclamation point follows an emotional or forceful statement.

 Example: I can't take it anymore!

Practice 13: End Punctuation

Read the following passage. Write *C* if the sentence has correct end punctuation. If it is incorrectly punctuated, revise it on a separate sheet of paper.

(1) Imagine our surprise coming home to a flooded kitchen? (2) We called a plumber immediately, of course; (3) After shutting off the water, we cleaned up and moved out all the dishes, pots and pans, and utensils! (4) Now, with the kitchen being repaired, do you think we can remember where we put everything? (5) What a mess. (6) It's not much fun to have a disaster happen in the house, is it.

For more practice in English grammar, usage, and convention, please consult American Book Company's *Basics Made Easy: Grammar and Usage Review 2004.*

CHAPTER 7 SUMMARY

Sentences come in four different types

- **simple** sentences have only one independent clause.

- **compound** sentences are made from two or more simple sentences, joined either by a comma, semicolon, or conjunction. It may include two or more independent clauses.

- a **complex** sentence contains one independent clause and one or more dependent clauses.

- a **compound-complex** sentence contains one or more compound sentences and one or more complex sentences.

A sentence **fragment** is a collection of words that do not express a complete thought.

Run-on sentences occur when inadequate punctuation divides two complete sentences.

Comma splices occur when two independent clauses are joined with only a comma.

Parallel sentence structure means parts of a sentence with equal importance are expressed with equal emphasis.

Verbs must agree with their **subjects** in **tense** and be parallel with one another in a sentence.

Modifiers are phrases and clauses that help to clarify the meaning of a word.

- **misplaced** modifiers alter a word or phrase ambiguously.

- **dangling** modifiers come at the beginning of a sentence but do not modify its subject.

Capitalize the first word of a sentence, the first word of a direct quotation, and specific persons, places, or things.

Punctuation rules:

- **commas** separate independent clauses, restrictive phrases, direct address, before and after quotations, between the date and the year, and after the street address and PO Box in addresses.

- **quotation** marks signify a direct quotation and include punctuation marks inside them.

- **colons** separate series and independent clauses in a sentence and are used in timekeeping; **semicolons** split independent clauses that are joined by sentence interrupters or commas.

- **End punctuation** involves **periods** after complete statements, **questions marks** after any questions, and **exclamation points** after an emotional or forceful statement.

CHAPTER 7 REVIEW

1. A collection of words that do not express a complete thought is known as
   A. compound sentences   C. affixes
   B. complex sentences   D. fragments

2. _____ sentences have only one independent clause.
   A. Straightforward   C. Fragmentary
   B. Simple   D. Complicated

For questions 3–7, write *S* if the sentence is simple, *Cd* if the sentence is compound, *Cx* if the sentence is complex, and *CC* if the sentence is compound-complex.

3. After we finished dinner, we all went out to a movie, and we stopped at Brewster's for ice cream. _____

4. Natalie stayed up until 3 a.m. and still got up this morning to get to school. _____

5. She was only 20 years old when she graduated from college, her proud parents sitting in the front row. _____

6. The human body is very resilient, but when pushed to extremes for too long a period, it will let you know. _____

7. Antarctica would be the smallest continent if you counted only the actual land. _____

For questions 8 – 12, tell whether each question is a sentence, run-on, or sentence fragment. If the example is a run-on or a sentence fragment, rewrite it to make it into a proper sentence. If it is correct, write C next to the sentence.

8. The jungle was unusually quiet.

9. People moved quickly there was no time to stop.

10. With one inning left and bases loaded.

11. They hiked the mountain they saw a squirrel.

12. The schools closed because of the blizzard, so we played Nintendo.

For questions 13 – 17, write a *C* next to the sentence if the subject and the underlined present tense verb agree. Correct the verb in the present tense if it does not agree with the subject.

13. Because of a death in the family, Jeff Rainier <u>is</u> not available for appointments.

14. Steve, in addition to Mike, <u>check</u> all the locks in the building every night.

15. Neither Nathan nor his brother <u>walk</u> to school.

16. We accountants <u>calculates</u> the taxes owed by various companies.

17. The congregation <u>rise</u> up singing when the preacher walks to the pulpit.

18. The following sentence contains a misplaced modifier:

    The tourists were safe from the piranhas in the raft.

Which of the following is the correct form of the sentence?

    A.   The tourists in the piranhas were safe from the raft.
    B.   The tourists in the raft were safe from the piranhas.
    C.   From the piranhas, the tourists were safe in the raft.
    D.   The piranhas were safe from the tourists in the raft.

19. The following sentence contains a dangling modifier:

    After a few years of playing music, medicine became his chosen course of study.

Which of the following is the correct form of the sentence?

    A.   Medicine became his chosen course of study after a few years of playing music.
    B.   While playing music, medicine became his chosen course of study.
    C.   After he played music for a few years, medicine became his chosen course of study.
    D.   He played music a few years after medicine became his chosen course of study.

For questions 20 – 22, add a colon where necessary in each sentence:

20. Shakespeare stated the problem best "To be or not to be. That is the question."

21. Theresa was a great swimmer her body barely made a splash when she dived.

22. These three remained on the list Anne Richards, Kelly Joyce, and Fred Wilson.

For questions 23 – 27, choose which choice from among those given contains an error in capitalization. If there is no error, choose _D_:

23.
    A.   Quebec is a canadian
    B.   province located north
    C.   of the U.S. border.
    D.   No mistakes.

24.
    A.   Jack Means has lived
    B.   at 267 Stanton ave.
    C.   for most of his life.
    D.   No mistakes.

25.

    A.   The student asked, "how

    B.   many times did Columbus

    C.   travel to the New World?"

    D.   No mistakes.

26.

    A.   Mr. Tucker has been

    B.   the President of Southern

    C.   Airlines for many years.

    D.   No mistakes.

27.

    A.   Mr. Krenshaw, a renowned journalist,

    B.   was seated next to Deacon Powers

    C.   at the funeral.

    D.   No mistakes.

For questions 28 – 30, circle the letter that contains an error in punctuation within the line. If there are no errors, choose *D*:

28.

    A.   The woman asked,

    B.   "Are you sure there aren't

    C.   any bathrooms on this floor?"

    D.   No mistakes.

29.

    A.   Did Jan take Dave, Kenneth,

    B.   Stephanie, and Courtney

    C.   with her to the concert.

    D.   No mistakes.

30.

    A.   Teri and Mark went to the park;

    B.   roller-blades in hand,

    C.   to skate in a race.

    D.   No mistakes.

Chapter 8
Speaking, Listening & Viewing

This chapter addresses the following performance standards:

Standards	ELA9LSV1, ELA9LSV2

English and the Language Arts are more than just reading and writing. The skills you need for effective and clear communication also include speaking, listening, and viewing information. Because these activities must be done "live" — in person, in the presence of others — only live practice will give you the proper skills needed. Just the same, there are some strategies to help your presentation, viewing and listening skills become more effective.

The information needed for assignments or tests is often heard rather than read. When you listen to a lecture, for example, you take notes to help prepare. Being able to listen well is critical for following directions, knowing policy and procedures, and staying on top of the latest events.

Speaking, like writing, is a way to convey information to others and can serve the same purpose as compositions: to inform, persuade, or entertain. You may be required to give an oral report in class, to present to a club or organization, or give testimony in a court proceeding.

SPEAKING

After your research (and written composition) is finished, you should carefully organize it in a way that lends itself to **good public speaking**. As with the composition, you should always consider your audience. Will they be interested in your subject, or will they be reluctant to listen? Other factors to keep in mind include:

- Where will the presentation take place?

- What equipment will be available?

- Who will be in the audience: classmates, adults, club members?

In deciding how to present your information, you should consider the type of information you are working with and your audience. If the information is complex, with a great deal of numbers and statistics, you may want to include a graph or chart detailing the data. A simple search engine sweep on the Internet will provide any number of presentation ideas on almost every subject.

DETERMINE YOUR PURPOSE

One of the most important elements to consider when writing and reading is **purpose**. The same is true for oral presentations. Knowing your purpose is the first step toward a successful presentation. Like compositions, oral presentations can have any of the following purposes or a combination of two or more:

Inform	An **informative or descriptive speech** presents a new subject or new information about a familiar subject. You can use some of the same types of supporting detail you would in an expository composition, such as concrete examples, vivid description, and instructions (if applicable). **Example:** "How Whale Sonar Works"
Persuade	A **persuasive speech** is meant to change attitudes or behavior of the audience or to convince them of your point of view. **Example:** "Our Community's Public Library Needs to Expand"
Entertain	Often incorporating narrative presentation, **speeches that entertain** often also have another purpose, such as informing or persuading. **Example:** "A Funny Thing Happened to Me on the Way to the Monster Truck Rally"

Your specific purpose might be determined for you as an assignment. In addition to informational and persuasive speeches, you might have to deliver a narrative or descriptive monologue, respond verbally to literature you read, or use interview techniques to gather information. Remember to use credible sources and choose your resources wisely.

CRAFTING THE ORAL PRESENTATION

After choosing a topic and purpose, begin putting together an **outline** that provides the major points you will discuss and any key words or phrases to remember. Using an outline gives you the opportunity to maintain eye contact with your audience, which is a great way to connect with them and keep their interest.

Much like a composition, a well-developed **oral presentation** needs a clear beginning, middle and end. The points you make also need to be supported.

Types of Supporting Evidence	Techniques to Capture Audience Attention
facts, statistics	tell a brief, related narrative
authoritative or expert opinions	cite surprising or little known facts
appropriate examples	utilize humor, if appropriate
definitions	use a relevant and interesting quote
logic	incorporate audiovisual aids

There are a number of ways to organize a speech, and your outline will organize your points according to the one you choose. Here are examples of different ways in which to organize and present your information.

A **topical presentation** outline has a list of the main ideas to present, with transitions and key words and phrases included. It works especially well for expository topics.

Example: Cinema of the 1980s

I. Resurgence of Studio Control

II. Rise of the Multiplex

    A. Shopping malls

    1. More malls, more theatres

III. Advent of Video Cassette Recorders

Chronological organizations are organized along a timeline and work well for narrative presentations. These can also be especially helpful in presenting information in a limited amount of time.

A **cause-effect focus** can be very effective for persuasive speeches. The outline can show the problem or cause first, followed by the solution or effect.

Comparison-contrast organization is useful for both informative and persuasive presentations. The outline can focus on the topics being compared and contrasted, either point-by-point or one side at a time.

No matter how you organize, you should spend time practicing your presentation, going over it several times and making sure you:

- remember all your information
- have the right tone of voice
- use appropriate language and terminology
- complete your presentation in the time allotted

More help and detailed examples of outlines can be found online, either at http://www.nsknet.or.jp/~peterr-s/public_speaking/detailoutline.html or http://en.wikipedia.org/wiki/outline.

ANALYZE YOUR AUDIENCE

Sometimes, you will know your **audience** ahead of time, as when you are scheduled to speak in front of your class. Other times, you may not know exactly who will be in a given audience, but you can make assumptions based on why people would choose to be part of it. For example, if you will be speaking to your school's PTSA, you can assume the audience will be made up of teachers, parents, and some students.

The kinds of things you can anticipate about your audience include: who will be there, what kind of language and tone will be appropriate for them, how they might react to what you will say, and what questions or opposing ideas they might have.

A great deal of how you prepare your presentation will come from how interested your audience may be in your topic or how much they will agree with your point of view. Sometimes you can anticipate this. Other times, you will need to adjust for unanticipated reactions.

> **receptive** audience (interested or agrees with your view): focus on *new points*, *conclusions* and *recommendations*.
>
> **skeptical** audience (not as interested or disagrees with your view): focus on *importance of topic* and *logical arguments*.

Some other factors to consider include:

- Will people be seated or standing?
- Will there be someone to help you?
- If it's a large room, is there a public address system?
- Is there any noise in the room from nearby activities?
- If using any audiovisual aids for your presentation, will the equipment be available, or do you need to bring it?
- Is the lighting appropriate for whatever you need to show?

KEEPING YOUR AUDIENCE INTERESTED

A simple way to gauge your audience's interest is to look at **body language**: the way people sit or stand, the way they hold their head, look you in the eye or down at their shoes communicates a lot about how a person feels. Knowing how to identify and interpret these forms of non-verbal communication will help you decide whether what you are saying is reaching your audience.

Signs your Audience is *Not* Interested

Foot slightly kicking or swinging, fidgeting

Checking the time

Head in hand, looking down at the floor

Frequent yawning

Eyes closed, snoring

Not asking questions at the end of presentation

Signs your Audience *is* Interested

Tilted head

Direct eye contact

Sitting relatively still

Asking questions at the end of presentation

Pleasing everyone is impossible. There may be a few people in your audience who display signs of boredom no matter how lively your presentation is. However, if the majority of your audience is yawning and fidgeting, you may want to consider telling a joke, or get them to participate in your presentation by asking their opinion on the subject.

Practice 1:   Audience Interest

Finish the sentences below by choosing the correct ending from the choices provided:

1. You are giving a presentation on "Teenage Driving and Fatal Accidents." You know your class-mates are interested in what you are saying because

    A.   they are speechless at the end of your presentation.

    B.   they look you directly in the eye.

    C.   they close their eyes.

    D.   they look out the window at passing cars.

2. During your presentation, you notice most of the audience is either looking at the floor or looking at the clock on the wall. Based on this, you know your audience is

    A.   excited about the topic you're discussing.

    B.   waiting to ask questions when you're through.

    C.   bored and uninterested in your presentation.

    D.   tired from too much homework.

3. After concluding your presentation called "The Last Days of Recess," you know your classmates are interested because they

    A.   ask a lot of questions.

    B.   leave the room as fast as possible.

    C.   ask the teacher if listening to your presentation is worth extra credit.

    D.   laugh as they walk past you.

EMPHASIZING YOUR DELIVERY: VOICE AND BODY LANGUAGE

Although *what* you say during your presentation is important, *how* you say it can make the difference between a great presentation and a mediocre one. Just as body language informs you about your audience, your own body communicates a message to your audience. Your **posture**, your **facial expressions** and your **gestures** are all important factors to keep in mind.

VOICE

SPEAK LOUD ENOUGH TO BE HEARD

The audience needs to hear you from every area in the room, not just the front row. Don't worry about being too loud. Practice your speech at home or in the area you will be speaking and have a friend listen from different places in the room.

VARY YOUR PITCH

Pitch is the highness or lowness of your voice. Sticking with one pitch — called a *monotone* — can make your presentation tedious for your audience. Be sure to vary your pitch to communicate emotion or meaning through your voice.

RATE

Rate refers to the speed at which you speak. Many nervous speakers tend to rush through their presentation, barely stopping for breath. This makes it difficult for listeners to understand what you're saying. Likewise, going too slow can lead to boredom. Try to balance the rate of your speech: not too slow and not too fast.

IT'S OKAY TO PAUSE

Pause to let your audience know when there's a change in thought or when you want to let something "sink in" to their thoughts.

PRACTICE ENUNCIATING (PRONOUNCING) WORDS

Mark words that are difficult to pronounce. Look them up in the dictionary and learn how to pronounce them correctly. Practice repeating these words until they feel natural and you can say them with confidence, without stumbling or repeating yourself. Avoid mumbling or slurring your words.

BODY LANGUAGE

KEEPING UP APPEARANCES

A **neat and tidy appearance** adds to your credibility as a speaker. Your attire should be appropriate for the setting.

BE CONFIDENT

Although it's important to keep audience in mind, don't worry about them *too* much. Concentrate on what you need to say. Take a couple of deep breaths to calm yourself before beginning. Then, walk calmly up to where you give your presentation. Do not rush; instead, take the time to arrange any notes or visual aids.

GESTURES

Use **gestures** that feel natural, not forced. Do not keep your hands stiffly at your sides or stuffed into your pockets. Relax while delivering your speech, and enjoy yourself while you show off the results of your research. If you are enthusiastic about a particular subject, your gestures become more animated. Try to avoid a nervous thabit such as fidgeting with hair. Do not slouch! Good posture communicates confidence more than any other body language.

MAKE EYE CONTACT

You probably heard the advice to "look people in the eye" while growing up. Studies have shown that people who make **direct eye contact** are viewed as more credible than people who do not. Look around at your audience and make brief eye contact with a few of them. Do not concentrate on one person. Practice your speech in front of a mirror or before friends or family, letting your eyes focus on each member.

GRAPHIC AIDS

Graphic aids include **tables**, **graphs**, **pie charts**, and **maps**.

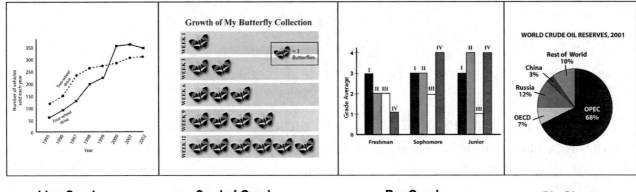

| Line Graph | Symbol Graph | Bar Graph | Pie Chart |

Tables are a concise way to present large quantities of data. They allow the audience to have the facts and statistics of your presentation at a glance.

Graphs convey a large amount of information in a small space. There are three primary kinds of graphs:

- A **line graph** usually presents a trend or prevailing pattern across a length of time. With a line graph, it's important to read both the vertical and horizontal headings.

- A **bar graph** is helpful for showing amounts arranged according to various criteria. Audiences can see the extent to which something happened at a quick glance.

- A **symbol graph** is less common than the other two, but can still be helpful for representing the differences between specific types of data.

Pie charts are used to show the various parts of a greater whole. They are helpful in showing the difference in opinion on a given issue or the varieties that comprise a larger whole. Pie charts suffer from the disadvantage of being hard to read and to display subtle, more diverse quantities of information.

Maps are charts that detail part or the whole of the earth. Maps can be useful in showing the geographic location or setting of a given event or trend.

Graphic aids are useful for giving the audience something to fix their attention on while you speak, and they illuminate your evidence. Indeed, maps, tables, and charts carry by their very appearance a kind of authenticity and authority, which you can use to impress an audience.

Practice 2: Graphic Aids

Go through a history, geography or science textbook, finding examples of maps, tables, and charts. Do you find information easier to read on one than the others? Why or why not? Share your findings with a classmate, teacher, or mentor.

ELECTRONIC AIDS

Only in recent years have electronic display systems become widespread in the corporate and business worlds. However, they are becoming more prevalent all the time, and as you enter the professional workforce, you are certain to encounter them eventually. The most common forms of electronic presentation are **PowerPoint™ slide slows**, **video presentations**, and **Internet Web sites**.

- **PowerPoint™** is a form of presentation software developed by Microsoft Corporation. The format of its presentation is similar to old-fashioned slide shows, with one image replacing another at a speed controlled by the presenter. While newer versions offer animation, enhanced graphics, and easier use, critics charge that PowerPoint™ software allows users to rely too much on graphics and not enough on evidence when making their presentations.

- **Video** presentations have become increasingly popular since the mid-990s, when production tools became available to a wider market. Video productions usually resemble television news programs, interviews, or movie segments. They can entertain or amuse an audience, and be very persuasive for those reasons, but like PowerPoint, video can promote "style over substance" presentation over evidence.

- **Web sites** are pages on the Internet specifically designed to accompany a presentation. The information is available to the audience before, during and after the time the argument is given. Audience members can log on to the page and access information directly. Web sites benefit the user in that they allow easy access to the information. Drawbacks include the time involved in building a site and the cost of maintaining its domain and granting Internet access to the entire audience.

GET READY TO DEFEND YOUR POSITION

Audience members will likely have questions at the end of your presentation (if questions are allowed in the presentation format), and some may even disagree with your point or with some of the information used. Be prepared to *politely* answer their questions or debate your points.

- Listen to questions carefully and reiterate the relevant information from your presentation.

- Don't appear condescending or arrogant; appearing gracious by answering questions or debating points will make a good impression on the rest of the audience.

- Don't assume the other person is wrong and you're right: arrogance will also isolate you from your audience.

- Don't shout when debating points, and *don't lose your cool*. The facts in a well-researched piece speak for themselves.

Practice 3: Delivering your Speech

1. During your class presentation on "Increasing Recycling at Sunshine High School," you can best relate your excitement about the subject by

   A.   shaking your head emphatically.

   B.   pounding on the podium or desk.

   C.   speaking clearly and appearing enthused.

   D.   making wild circular gestures with your arms.

2. To make sure the audience hears you and understands your presentation, you should

   A.   speak quickly and softly.

   B.   use a monotone pitch.

   C.   repeat hard to understand words.

   D.   speak loudly and enunciate clearly.

3. When delivering your presentation, it is important to

   A.   research.

   B.   ask your instructor what the topic is.

   C.   sit with your legs crossed.

   D.   make eye contact with members of the audience.

4. If you're nervous while you give your speech, you should

   A.   breathe deeply and try to relax.

   B.   ask to go to the bathroom.

   C.   sit on the edge of your chair.

   D.   shout your presentation at the top of your lungs.

5. Which one of the following is *not* important to a successful speech?

   A.   a neat and tidy appearance

   B.   speaking clearly and loudly

   C.   making sure the audience likes you

   D.   varying your pitch

Practice 4:   Giving A Speech

Prepare and deliver a five-minute oral presentation on a topic of your choice, using the strategies and guidelines detailed in this chapter. Work with your teacher or fellow classmates and practice in front of friends or family members before making your final presentation.

LISTENING

When listening to a teacher, fellow student or other speaker, the criteria for listening is much the same as for speaking, except *you* are the judge. Listen carefully to the information presented, evaluating it as you would a written composition. Often times, the weaknesses in an argument are communicated through the presentation itself. When watching a speech or presentation, consider:

- the presentation's language and clarity of delivery
- the speaker's knowledge of the subject
- the presentation's argument: its authority, appeals to emotion or bias, logic, and tone.
- the speaker's delivery: his voice, tone, pitch, gestures, and comfort speaking.

Don't hesitate to ask questions after a presentation, or *politely* disagree with the information presented. If you're unclear about a point or need a better explanation of a key word or other information, asking for elaboration will give the speaker the opportunity to further the entire audience's understanding. It will also point out any weaknesses in his familiarity with the subject. Questions not only benefit you. They benefit the entire audience as well.

Practice 5: Listening

Attend a speech, presentation or press conference at your school, in your hometown, or on television. Evaluate it for its delivery, its effectiveness in delivering information, and the speaker's ability to convincingly communicate ideas. Was the presentation one you felt effective in reaching its audience? Why or why not?

VIEWING INFORMATION

Viewing information includes more than passively watching a speech, presentation, or event on television or film. It involves an active mental engagement with the material, in much the same way as active reading was described in Chapter Four.

When viewing films or other forms of media, you should have your own mental criterion to evaluate the effectiveness of the material. The criterion standards may be your own, but they should incorporate the ideas of active reading and the listening guidelines discussed in this chapter as well.

Sample criteria might include any and all of the questions listed in the chart below. The chart may also be adapted to develop powerful listening skills, as well:

- Did the presentation clearly address the topic, with good evidence and description of unfamiliar ideas or vocabulary?
- Did the presentation genuinely contribute to the knowledge or beliefs of the audience?
- Did the presentation maintain positive interest, feeling, and amount of attention from the audience?
- Did the presentation contain powerful, vivid speech that the audience would appreciate?
- Was the presentation delivered in a convincing, articulate manner?

Practice 6: Evaluating A Presentation

As with Practice 5, evaluate a film or other electronic presentation for the criteria above. You might wish to pick a controversial movie of recent years, such as *Fahrenheit 911*, *The Da Vinci Code*, or *The Passion of the Christ* on which to base your evaluation. Discuss your results with someone with whose opinion you might not necessarily agree. How do the criteria affect your opinions? If you wish to completely avoid controversy, you can also choose to evaluate a television sitcom, a documentary, or a family film.

CHAPTER 8 SUMMARY

Any presentation is usually crafted to fill one of three purposes: to **inform**, to **educate**, or to **entertain**.

Crafting an **oral presentation** involves using an argument based on *facts*, *expert opinions*, *examples*, *definitions*, and *logic*.

Create **outlines** to organize your speech, along the lines of **topical presentations**, **chronological outlines**, **cause-effect outlines**, and **comparison-contrast outlines.**

A **receptive audience** is interested or agrees with your viewpoint. A **skeptical audience** is not interested or disagrees with your viewpoint.

Signs your audience *is* interested include: tilted head; direct eye contact; sitting relatively still; asking questions at the end of your presentation.

Signs your audience is *not* interested include: foot slightly kicking or swinging; fidgeting; checking the time; head in hand; looking down at the floor; frequent yawning; eyes closed; snoring; not asking questions at the end of presentation.

Effective **voice** and **body language** skills include:

- speaking loud enough to be heard
- varying your pitch
- varying your rate of speech: do not go too slow or too fast
- using pauses to provoke thought or give emphasis
- clearly enunciating words; practicing repeating difficult words
- dressing and grooming appropriately for the setting
- standing up straight and avoiding nervous gestures such as toying with your hair
- using natural, not forced, gestures
- maintaining eye contact with your audience

Graphic aids include **tables, graphs, pie charts**, and **maps**. Electronic aids include **PowerPoint, video presentations**, and Internet **Web sites**.

Defending your position involves calmly and accurately drawing the audience's attention to the presentation, reiterating important points and information.

Listening skills include evaluating a presentation using the same criteria involved in making a presentation. The effectiveness of a presentation depends largely on the speaker's ability to clearly and convincingly share information with his or her audience.

Viewing skills involve both the skills of speaking and the skills of listening. When viewing an electronic presentation, such as a film or other means of communication, formulating criteria to judge its effectiveness will help you determine the value and strength of the presentation.

CHAPTER 8 REVIEW

1. Signs your audience is interested in your presentation include

   A. looking down at the floor and fidgeting.
   B. looking you directly in the eye.
   C. listening to headphones while you talk.
   D. running for the exits when you finish.

2. Which of the following is **not** a consideration when preparing to deliver your presentation?

   A. where the presentation will take place
   B. what equipment will be available
   C. if your speech is given in the morning or afternoon.
   D. who will be in the audience

3. During your presentation on "Promoting Study Abroad Programs," you can best convey your belief in the topic by

   A. standing stiffly with your hands clenched at your sides.
   B. using a slide show with pictures of Europe.
   C. emphasizing important words and using natural gestures.
   D. telling humorous anecdotes about traveling.

4. If you are nervous during your presentation, it is highly unlikely that

   A. your audience will notice.
   B. your presentation will be successful.
   C. you'll forget what your speech is about.
   D. the audience will run screaming from the room.

5. One of the nonverbal signals you can give to keep your audience interested is

   A. maintain eye contact.
   B. look at one member of the audience intently.
   C. speak rapidly and at a clear volume.
   D. use words no one understands to keep them guessing.

6. A _____ focus can be very effective for persuasive speeches.

   A. chronological
   B. cause-effect
   C. comparison-contrast
   D. descriptive

7. When delivering your presentation, a monotone pitch is most often

   A. interesting and engaging.
   B. tedious and boring.
   C. animated and humorous.
   D. calming and soothing.

8. The first step to creating an effective speech is to

   A. speak clearly and concisely.

   B. use creative visual aids.

   C. consider how many people will be in the audience.

   D. know your purpose.

9. When speaking of oral communications, *pitch* is best described as

   A. the level of audience interest.

   C. the highness or lowness of the voice.

   B. the speed at which the speaker talks.

   D. either fast, slow, or curveball.

10. A _____ typically presents a trend or pattern across a length of time.

   A. line graph

   C. pie chart

   B. bar graph

   D. PowerPoint presentation

11. One disadvantage to video presentations is

   A. bad acting.

   B. expensive costs.

   C. tendency to put style over strength of evidence.

   D. good acting.

12. PowerPoint is similar to which traditional type of presentation?

   A. filmstrip

   C. overhead projector

   B. slide show

   D. finger puppet shows

13. When dealing with a _____ audience, it's best to focus on the importance of topic and logical arguments.

   A. receptive

   C. close-minded

   B. tired

   D. apathetic

14. _____ involves careful attention to the information and speaker style in a presentation.

   A. Audience awareness

   C. Speaking

   B. Listening

   D. PowerPoint

15. Which of the following is *not* considered a purpose for giving a presentation?

   A. to inform

   C. to confuse the audience

   B. to entertain

   D. to persuade

Georgia 9th Grade Literature & Composition Post-Test One

The purpose of this post-test is to measure your progress in reading comprehension, grammar and critical thinking. This test is based on the **Georgia Performance Standards** and adheres to the sample question format provided by the Georgia Department of Education.

General Directions:

1   Read all directions carefully.

2   Read each question or sample. Then choose the best answer.

3   Choose only one answer for each question. If you change an answer, be sure to erase your original answer completely.

4   After taking the test, you or your instructor should score it using the answer key that accompanies this book. Then review and practice for the reading comprehension and critical thinking skills tested on the EOCT.

Read the following passage. Then answer the questions that follow it:

Cherokee Indians' Removal to Oklahoma

We wish to remain on the land of our fathers. We have a perfect and original right to claim this, without interruption or molestation. The treaties with us…guarantee our residence, and our privileges, and secure us against intruders. Our only request is that these treaties may be fulfilled, and these laws executed.

But if we are compelled to leave our country, we see nothing but ruin before us. The country west of the Arkansas territory is unknown to us. From what we can learn of it, we have no good news in its favor. All the inviting parts of it, as we believe are preoccupied by various Indian nations, to which it has been assigned. They would regard us as intruders, and look upon us with the evil eye. The far greater part of the region is, beyond all controversy, badly supplied with wood and water; and no Indian tribe can live as agriculturalists without these articles. All our neighbors, in case of our removal, though crowded into our near vicinity, would speak a language totally different from ours, and practice different customs. The original possessors of that region are now wandering savages, lurking for prey in the neighborhood. They have always been at war, and would be easily tempted to turn their arms against peaceful emigrants… It contains neither the scenes of our childhood, nor the graves of our fathers…

Shall we be compelled by a civilized and Christian people, with whom we have lived in a perfect peace for the last forty years, and for whom we have willingly bled in war, to bid a final adieu to our homes, our farms, our streams and our beautiful forests? No. We are still firm. We intend still to cling, with our chosen affection, to the land which gave us birth, and which, every day of our lives, brings to us new and stronger ties of attachment. We appeal to the judge of all the earth, who will finally award us justice, and to the good sense of the American people, whether we are intruders upon the land of others. Our consciences bear us witness that we are the invaders of no man's rights — we have robbed no man of his territory — we have usurped no man's authority, nor have we deprived anyone of his unalienable privileges. How then shall we indirectly confess the right of another people to our land by leaving it forever? On the soil which contains the ashes of our beloved men we wish to live — on this soil we wish to die.

– from a Council of the Cherokee Nation to the people of the United States, 1830

1   What concerns did the Cherokee raise about the land they were being forced to move to?   9RL2

   A   There was no grass for their animals to graze on.

   B   There were hostile bands of Indians rampaging the countryside.

   C   It lacked sufficient resources for them to farm and grow food.

   D   The water was polluted.

2   What was the basic argument the Cherokee made for being allowed to stay where they were and *not* move?   9W1

   A   They had invaded nobody's rights, so why should their rights be invaded.

   B   They owned the land already, so should not have to move.

   C   The land was not fit for anyone but them to live on.

   D   Their ancestors had guaranteed them the land forever.

3 What does the phrase "indirectly confess the right to another people to our land" most probably mean? ^{9RL1}

A By moving, they would be admitting that they could not maintain the land.

B By confessing it was not their land, they would be shamed.

C By admitting it was not their land, they would be seen as thieves.

D Giving their land to another people would be admitting it was not truly their land.

4 What type of argument does the writer present in making his case for staying? ^{9W1}

A He uses statistics and examples to make his point.

B He appeals to the sentiment or good nature of the reader.

C He uses legal language to prove his argument.

D He dismisses the argument as unimportant.

5 Who is most likely the author's audience? ^{9W1}

A the president of France

B the Indian nation

C the military leader sent to force the Cherokee to move

D the war chief of the neighboring tribe

6 What evidence does the author give that in the new place, his people will not be welcome? ^{9RL1}

A It is already occupied by other Indian nations, some at war already, and with most having different customs and languages than the Cherokee.

B He says that the people living there have ravaged the land and made it unfit to live on by any newcomers.

C He details how the land is unfit for farming and incapable of maintaining a good supply of food.

D He exaggerates the difficulty of moving his entire nation of people such a long distance.

7 What does the term *usurped* near the end of paragraph three most closely mean in this passage? ^{9RC3}

A sugary, slimy

B stolen or taken away

C slippery to the touch

D humiliated, put down

Read the following passage. Then answer the questions that follow it:

College Decisions: Living at Home vs. Living Away

1 When a young person begins to make a decision about which college to attend, there are many factors to consider. Students today find that one of the first decisions they are faced with is the question of whether they want to stay at home and commute to a local college — if one is nearby and offers the courses a student is interested in — or live away from home in a dormitory or apartment. There are several pros and cons for each choice. Students should think carefully about their personality, finances, and family situations when deciding which option is more suitable to them.

2 The cost of housing is very often the primary consideration. If you live at home and commute, you will not pay rent and food costs like you would if you lived in an apartment or dormitory.If you will be paying your own college fees or using student loans, this can be an appreciable amount of money saved.

Although many students help out their family by paying room and board, probably it will not be as expensive as living away from home.

3 Likewise, transportation is an important consideration. If you choose to commute, you need either public transportation, a vehicle of your own, or a dependable arrangement for getting to and from campus. However, if you have to have your own vehicle, you may want to calculate to see if driving is cheaper or a better use of money than living on campus and using the school transportation system. Purchasing and maintaining a vehicle may be as expensive as living on campus in the long run.

4 While living on your own gives you a great amount of freedom and helps you learn to be independent, living at home has the advantage of being familiar and providing structure, allowing you to better focus on your studies. Many students living on their own for the first time find they are overwhelmed by their new freedom and the responsibilities that go along with it. Still, while you may give up some independence choosing to live at home, commuting does require extra preparation and proper organization. You can't run back to your house across town for books or other forgotten items; you have to plan ahead for what you will need on campus each day.

5 Your individual family situation could also play an important part in the decision. Are you needed at home to help out with family responsibilities, a family business, elderly grandparents, or younger siblings? Do you need to stay at home because your family depends on you? I had to weigh these things against living on campus when I was deciding on how to handle college, and it was not an easy choice for me. However, if other arrangements can be made, being away from those commitments should be beneficial by allowing you to concentrate more on your studies.

8 **Which side of the argument does the author most likely fall on?** 9W1

A living at home, but taking public transportation

B living in a dormitory on campus

C living at home and commuting

D choosing a college in another city

9 **In paragraph two, the word *appreciable* most likely means** RL5, 9RC3

A very little.

B outrageous.

C something appreciated.

D considerable or substantial.

10 **The main idea of the passage is** 9RL1

A there are many considerations when deciding on a college.

B college can be very expensive, and expenses should be calculated down to the penny.

C each person has his own reasons for staying at home and commuting to college.

D the newfound freedom of heading off to college can be very exciting.

11 **What happens in the final paragraph that is inconsistent with the rest of the passage?** 9W4

A The author switches into first person, changing the point of view of the writing.

B The author becomes cynical toward going to college.

C The author tries to strongly persuade the reader toward his viewpoint.

D The author moves into third person.

12 **A one-sentence summary of paragraph three might read:** 9W2

A When deciding on how to commute, students must factor in whether they want to use their own car or someone else's.

B When choosing how to get to and from college, a person needs to consider whether it is more cost-effective to stay home and commute or to live on campus and get around without a car.

C To get around the campus, many people choose the school's transportation instead of their own.

D In order to make a sound decision on commuting, one has to factor in the time it takes to get from home to campus versus the time it might take to go from the dorm to class.

13 How might living on your own for the first time be "overwhelming"?   9RL1

A With so much going on, you may not be able to juggle your classes.

B Your studies may be too difficult for you at first.

C The freedom may cause some students to not properly budget their study time.

D Freedom from responsibilities at home may cause you to get homesick.

Read the following passage. Then answer the questions that follow it:

A New Way to Give Birth?

1 Where is the safest place for a mother to give birth to her baby? You may think a hospital, but the facts show that the mother's own home is just as safe — if not safer — when a trained midwife attends the birth. This may seem like a strange idea, but for millennia women gave birth at home; only in recent centuries have they come to natal term in hospitals. Age-old wisdom and modern science are coming together to show that for a woman with a healthy pregnancy, her own home is the safest birthplace because she is in a familiar environment, surrounded by loved ones and free from standardized hospital policies.

2 Pregnant women must feel safe and comfortable, or they will have interrupted labor. This fact is recognized in the animal world but often neglected in regard to human mothers. For example, when a doe feels labor coming on, she seeks out a secure and protected place to give birth. If she detects a predator approaching, her contractions will stop, so that she can run away and find another safe spot. Once settled in, her labor will resume. In a similar way, many women progress well in their labor at home, but when they arrive at the hospital their labor slows down. Sometimes, the hospital even sends the woman home, where her contractions will resume normal progression. The disruption and anxiety of the trip to the hospital can cause a woman's labor to slow or halt. If she remains in the safety and comfort of her home throughout labor and delivery, her birth experience will probably follow a more natural and rhythmic pattern.

3 A more important factor in the woman's feeling of safety and comfort is the presence of loving and supportive friends and family. This may seem like a nice extra that has little biological effect on the birthing process, but there are significant differences between births of women with and without help. The comforting presence of a friend or family member leads to diminished desire or need for anesthetic drugs and fewer surgical procedures known in medical terminology as "Cesarean" sections. Many hospitals still place limitations on who can be with the mother while she is giving birth. There is also little space in one hospital room. At home, friends and family are welcome to come and go as the mother chooses, not as the hospital dictates.

4 The number of people allowed to be with the mother is just one restriction hospital policies place on birthing mothers. Freedom from these restrictive policies is probably the best part of giving birth at home. Hospitals require birthing mothers to eat nothing more than ice chips during labor, so that the mother's stomach is empty in case she needs general anesthesia for an emergency Cesarean. This deliberate starvation causes the mother to lose the energy she needs to deliver the baby, which in turn increases the need for a Cesarean section. Furthermore, hospitals require women to lie down in bed for electronic monitoring of the baby. This electronic vigilance allows fewer nurses to be on staff and

provides insurance companies with a record of the baby's health. However, it prevents the mother from walking—a natural way of using motion and gravity to facilitate the birthing process. Finally, hospitals routinely use drugs which severely affect the unborn or newborn child, causing the mother to be less able to enter contractions or usethe Lamaze method. These practices can benefit some women, but when they are empirically applied to all women across the board, they can make labor more strenuous. Under the care of a midwife at home, a woman has more flexibility with procedures that aid her unique birth.

5 For women who are experiencing medical problems in the birth process, hospitals provide the necessary interventions to save lives. However, these interventions are unnecessary for a normal, healthy birth. In this case, a woman can have a wonderful birth experience with loved ones nurturing her in her own home and with a knowledgeable midwife attending to her needs.

14 **The use of the term "age old wisdom" refers to**   9RC3

A   common knowledge that ordinary people have used for centuries.

B   the latest gossip.

C   ignorance and superstition.

D   previous beliefs about midwifery.

15 **In paragraph four, the author describes hospitals as being**   9W1, 9 RL1

A   costly and crowded.

B   sterile and professional.

C   warm and compassionate.

D   cold and impersonal.

16 **The passage serves mainly to**   9RL1

A   inform readers about the dangers of midwifery.

B   argue that hospitals are unclean places for childbirth.

C   discuss the history of childbirth practices.

D   argue for natural childbirth performed at home.

17 **Cesarean sections most likely involve**   9RC3

A   midwives.

B   complicated medical procedures.

C   painful labor techniques.

D   doctors working with midwives.

18 **Which of the following, if true, would undermine the author's argument about the virtues of natural childbirth at home?**   9W1

A   Births in hospitals are less susceptible to infection or complications.

B   More infants die in hospitals than at home.

C   People go to hospitals to die.

D   Doctors do not like children.

19 **The author mentions contractions and Lamaze in order to**   9W1

A   give examples of natural childbirth techniques.

B   support the worth of a Cesarean section.

C   prove her theories about birth in the wild.

D   discredit doctors.

Read the following passage. Then answer the questions that follow it:

As President Kennedy once implied: knowledge and peace seem to be ideals best looked for somewhere over the rainbow or beyond. Knowledge found here on earth often takes the form of learning new devious technologies to destroy and corrupt social fabrics and societies. Advantages in physics in the 1940s were turned to mass destruction by the atomic bomb. Peace on this earth is so fleeting and rare that even in utopias no peace could last. What turns knowledge to the evil side and twists yearnings for peace into power struggles? Human nature may be that volatile flash point. Looking for knowledge and peace must then be found in places so alien that human nature may be transcended.

Human nature is an inquisitive beast, always grasping at the mysterious and misunderstood. Albert Einstein, the gentle scientist who pondered the cosmos in his woolen socks, supported the construction of the atomic bomb until, realizing the mistake of unleashing such power, asked President Truman not to use nuclear weapons against Japan. But in wartime the temptation of such power was irresistible, and Truman ordered the nuclear attacks on Hiroshima and Nagasaki. Again, human nature struggled to combat fears — the fear of defeat, the fear of losing millions more men in war — by creating something more terrifying than anything else before it, using newfound language.

Utopias have risen and fallen throughout the span of history in almost all countries. Utopias are defined as unworldly places of perfect peace on earth. None of them have survived for more than a few decades — most collapsing quickly under the weight of rivalry, jealousy and the seductions of power. Even in our schools where the ideal is to have a peaceful coexistence of peer groups, we always have human nature to contend with. The book *Lord of the Flies* is a good example of a paradise being lost to the struggle for power. Spaceship crews are also selected for their good natures and "playing well with others." I guess when your life depends on getting along, it's a totally different thing than losing TV time.

Knowledge and peace have been looked for throughout the ages and found in micro-seconds and then lost again. President Kennedy may have been right, saying that knowledge and peace are out there to be discovered — but it may be in an alternate universe or on a celestial plane where human nature may be transformed that knowledge and peace will be truly found.

20 Which of the following *best* describes the author's attitude about utopias?　9RL1

   A He thinks they are noble but doomed to failure.

   B He thinks they are a waste of time and money.

   C He wishes they weren't so popular.

   D He thinks they only exist on other planets.

21 Based on the selection, what does *inquisitive* mean?　9RL5

   A strong   **C** curious

   B uncivilized   **D** angry

22 What statement *best* explains why the author includes this sentence at the beginning of the passage?　9W3

> As President Kennedy once implied: knowledge and peace seem to be ideals best looked for somewhere over the rainbow or beyond.

   A to show how even great men have unrealistic expectations

   B to use a quote from someone famous to back up his point

   C to point out the weakness in Kennedy's argument

   D to discuss the basic nature of peace and knowledge

23 What does the phrase "the seductions of power" refer to in paragraph three?   9RL5

   A adult entertainment on television

   B the ways people use power to ignore others

   C people who flirt with others to get their way

   D the beguiling lure of political influence

24 What conflict is most closely related to the theme of this selection?   9RL2

   A man vs. nature

   B man vs. himself

   C man vs. society

   D man vs. man

25 How should the following sentence from the passage be punctuated?   9C1

> As President Kennedy once implied: knowledge and peace seem to be ideals best looked for somewhere over the rainbow or beyond.

   A As President Kennedy once implied, knowledge and peace seem to be ideals best looked for somewhere over the rainbow or beyond.

   B As President Kennedy once implied; knowledge and peace seem to be ideals best looked for somewhere over the rainbow or beyond.

   C As President Kennedy once implied, knowledge and peace seem to be ideals best looked for somewhere over the rainbow or beyond?

   D As President Kennedy once implied; "knowledge and peace seem to be ideals best looked for somewhere over the rainbow or beyond."

Read the following passage. Then answer the questions that follow it:

A Formal Night Out

I don't often go to events that require formal attire. Jeans are much more comfortable. But tonight my dad and I are in suits, and my mom is in her best dress. We are near the High Museum to listen to the Atlanta Symphony. I usually spend Friday nights with my friends at the school football game. But for a couple of friday nights each year, somehow, this concert hall is just as much fun. The audience is so proper that they almost appear snobbish. But soon the grand array of musicians on the stage fills the hall with magnificent sound. Then the audience becomes the warmest, most inspired group of people you can imagine. Everyone should experience the symphony at least a few times in their lives they would see how much fun it can be.

26 Which of the following sentences expresses a *fact*?   9W1

   A Jeans are much more comfortable.

   B But for a couple of Friday nights each year, somehow this concert hall is just as much fun.

   C I don't often go to events that require formal attire.

   D Everyone should experience the symphony at least a few times in their lives.

27 Which of the following sentences presents an *opinion*?   9W1

   A But tonight my dad and I are in suits, and my mom is in her best dress.

   B I usually spend Friday nights with my friends at the school football game.

   C We are near the High Museum, to listen to the Atlanta Symphony.

   D Then the audience becomes the warmest, most inspired group of people you can imagine.

28 What change should be made to the following sentence from the passage? 9C2

> But for a couple of friday nights each year, somehow, this concert hall is just as much fun.

A   change *year,* to *year;*
B   change *But* to *But,*
C   change *friday* to *Friday*
D   change *concert hall* to *Concert Hall*

29 Which of the following is a run-on sentence? 9C2

A   Everyone should experience the symphony at least a few times in their lives they would see how much fun it can be.
B   But tonight my dad and I are in suits, and my mom is in her best dress.
C   I don't often go to events that require formal attire.
D   Then the audience becomes the warmest, most inspired group of people you can imagine.

30 Which of the following would be the *best* addition to strengthen the author's argument? 9W4

A   pointing out that going to the symphony can help you make friends
B   specific examples of songs and music performed
C   a list of musicians' names
D   specific examples of how trips to the symphony have improved his quality of life.

Read the following poem. Then answer the questions that follow it:

No more be grieved at that which thou hast done:
Roses have thorns, and silver fountains mud;
Clouds and eclipses stain both moon and sun,
And loathsome canker lives in sweetest bud.
All men make faults, and even I in this,
Authorizing thy trespass with compare,
Myself corrupting, salving thy amiss,
Excusing thy sins more than thy sins are;
For to thy sensual fault I bring in sense--
Thy adverse party is thy advocate--
And 'gainst myself a lawful plea commence:
Such civil war is in my love and hate
That I an accessory needs must be
To that sweet thief which sourly robs from me.

– William Shakespeare

31 The passage is an example of a(n) 9RL1

A   epic.   C   ballad.
B   sonnet.   D   haiku.

32 What does the poet mean by "roses have thorns, and shining fountains mud?" 9RL1, 9RL4

A   Nothing's perfect.
B   He would ruin anything if it would please his love.
C   He doesn't think they're beautiful enough.
D   His love deserves better.

33 The poet's intended audience for this passage is *most* likely 9W1, 9W2

A   a friend or relative.
B   an audience of like-minded poets.
C   someone for whom he feels deep affection.
D   a complete stranger.

34 The term *civil war* as used in line twelve most likely means 9RL5, 9RC3

A   a fight between two sides.
B   the war between the states.
C   the poet struggling with his own faults.
D   all of the above.

35 The poet uses all of the following *except*

   9RL1

A rhythm.   **C** imagery.

B rhyme.   **D** fallacies.

Read the following passage. Then answer the questions that follow it:

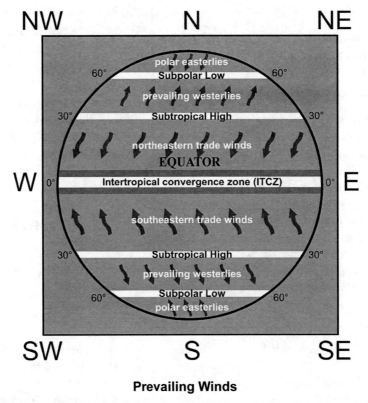

Prevailing Winds

The globe can be divided into six belts by latitude. In each of these belts, there are winds that blow most often. These are called the "prevailing winds" of that latitudinal belt. These belts are marked by their distance — in degrees — from the equator. For instance, one belt extends from the equator — which is 0 degrees — to 30 degrees north of the equator.

If you were to look closely at the bands of prevailing winds around the world, you will see a pattern in the directions these winds take. If you start at the equator and go north, you will notice that in the first belt, the winds blow from upper right to lower left (or, from northeast to southwest). In the next band to the north, the winds reverse, blowing from southwest to northeast. In the top band, which includes the North Pole, the winds again reverse direction.

Now, if you look at the wind belts from the equator going south, the same reversals occur. This time, however, they start with winds that blow from southeast to northwest.

Winds are named for the direction from which they come. For instance, if winds are called northeastern winds, or "north easterlies," it means that the winds are traveling *from* the northeast.

Between 30° north and 30° south of the equator, the prevailing winds are called trade winds. Above the equator they are the Northeast Trade Winds, and below the equator they are the Southeast Trade Winds. If you understand what causes the trade winds, you will understand the basic causes of all prevailing winds.

As has been stated, the trade winds occur near the equator. As the hottest latitude on earth, the equator produces very warm air. Warm air rises and expands. At the equator, the air rises and expands, moving away from the equator. As it flows away from the equator, it cools down. Cool air sinks. Now we have a warm area near the equator, from which the air is leaving, and a cool area about 30° away from the equator, in which there is a lot of cool air. Air always moves from cool to warm. That is why the cooled winds blow back to the equator from the cooler zones around 30° north and 30° south of the equator. This movement of air is the trade winds.

Why do the Northeast Trades travel back to the equator from the northeast, moving southwest, and not directly due south towards the intertropical convergence zone? The reason why the prevailing winds do not travel directly north and south is because they are not only influenced by the heat and coolness of the planet; they are also influenced by the motion of the planet. The earth is spinning around, and this makes the winds move in diagonal directions of the compass. The force that the earth's spinning has on prevailing winds is called the *Coriolis* force.

36 **The prefix *inter-* in the word *intertropical* makes the word mean_____.** 9RL5

   A within the tropics

   B above the tropics

   C below the tropics

   D between the tropics

37 **In which direction do the trade winds south of the equator blow?** 9RL1

   A northeast to southwest

   B southeast to northwest

   C northwest to southeast

   D southwest to northeast

38 **Winds that blow from the southeast to the northwest are known as _____.** 9RC3

   A easterlies

   B westerlies

   C South Eastern Trade Winds

   D north westerlies

39 **The author presents the ideas in this selection mainly by** 9W1

   A generalizing and giving examples.

   B developing an idea by presenting facts.

   C using a series of events to illustrate a point.

   D presenting an idea with personal opinions.

40 **What happens as air moves away from the equator?** 9RL1

   A It rises.   **C** It expands.

   B It cools.   **D** It warms.

41 **Which statement from the selection best supports the main idea?** 9RL1

   A "The trade winds occur near the poles."

   B "The equator is the hottest latitude on Earth."

   C "Winds are seldom influenced by the motion of the planet."

   D "Warm air rises and expands."

42 **Winds blow in all of the following directions *except*** 9RC4

   A southeast to northwest.

   B southwest to northeast.

   C northwest to southeast.

   D northwest to southwest.

Read the following passage. Then answer the questions that follow it:

Sibling Rivalry

Chez Beouf Malaise. A mother, father, daughter, and son are seated around a table, next to a window with a view of the ocean. They are celebrating their son's first day of high school.

Hank: Hey Mom and Dad, thanks for taking me out for dinner. High school isn't really that big a deal.

Father: You're welcome Hank. We're just proud to see you working so hard. We know school doesn't come easily for you.

Jessica: [*rolling her eyes*] Yeah. It wasn't a big deal to me because I'm at the top of my class, but you're doing OK. [*flashes him a forced smile*]

Hank: Thanks Jesse. [*faking a smile back at her*] You know, it's really too bad you don't have more friends. But, I guess you like spending time with yourself.

Mother: [*firmly*] Kids. Try to act like you like one another for one evening.

Jessica: [*whining*] I was trying, but he can't take a compliment.

Hank: Not when it's a put down at the same time.

Father: Jesse, quit insulting your brother. Hank, try to be nicer to your sister, you may actually miss her when she leaves for college next week.

Hank: I won't miss having the bathroom to myself.

Jessica: Yeah, and I won't miss my privacy!

Mother: [*angry*] Children! Can't we have just one night without you two at each others' throats? This is supposed to be a celebration.

Jessica: [*sarcastically*] Yeah, a celebration since the wonder boy is going to high school.

Father: Yes, a celebration of his hard work. I think he deserves it. Don't you?

Jessica: I think you guys give him everything he "deserves." What about me? Don't I deserve anything?

[*Just then, the waiter arrives with dinner. The family stops conversation until he's finished serving them.*]

Mother: Jessica, what is this all about? We've celebrated your accomplishments too. I don't understand where all this anger is coming from.

Jessica: [*quietly*] Never mind. Let's get on with the celebration.

Father: No, not never mind. What's going on?

Jessica: Hank does the most ordinary things, and you guys jump for joy. I get straight A's, letter on the debate team, get into three of the best colleges, and do volunteer work besides. You let him get away with so much. It's just not fair.

Hank: [*annoyed*] Here we go again. Whine, whine, whine. Poor Jesse has so much responsibility! Why does everything always have to be about you?

43 The passage can best be described as_____. 9RL1

A drama   C memoir

B poetry   D allegory

44 The passage serves mainly to 9RL1

A depict a feuding brother and sister interacting with their parents.

B show how people can get along with one another.

C portray the climax of an epic family drama.

D relate in real time how families interact.

45 Father explaining that "we know school doesn't come easily" for Hank lets the reader infer that 9RL1

A Hank isn't as smart or as driven as his sister Jessica.

B Hank has flunked out of other high schools.

C both Hank and Jessica have severe learning disabilities.

D high school isn't easy on anyone, let alone the little brothers of smart young women.

46 Based on the context of the passage, the cliche *at each others' throats* could be replaced with which of the following? 9RL5

A getting along so well

B viciously arguing and fighting

C bothering your father and I

D sitting around avoiding your chores

47 Read the following sentence from the passage: 9W4

> I get straight A's, letter on the debate team, get into three of the best colleges, and do volunteer work besides.

How could this sentence be rewritten to reduce wordiness?

A I did great in school, I got into the best colleges, and I also do volunteer work.

B I get straight A's, letter on the debate team, get into three of the best colleges, and do volunteer work besides.

C I made good grades, performed very well on the debate team, and also performed volunteer services.

D I got bad grades, but I was on the debate team and I helped read to the blind.

48 Which of the following sentences from the passage contains a comma splice? 9C1

A You know, it's really too bad you don't have more friends.

B But, I guess you like spending time with yourself.

C Hank, try to be nicer to your sister, you may actually miss her when she leaves for college next week.

D I was trying, but he can't take a compliment.

49 Based on the passage, we can most logically predict that 9RL1

A Hank and Jessica will continue to fight their whole lives.

B they will make up and enjoy their dinner.

C Father will beat them both severely for ruining his dinner.

D Hank and Jessica's rivalry will continue at least until Jessica leaves for college.

SECTION II

Read the following passage. Then answer the questions that follow it:

Family Time

1   The steam from the bread pan scorched Selena's face as she took it from the oven. She wiped her face with an apron after carefully setting the bread down. The day would not go well with her if she dropped the bread. Selena's mother had already scolded her for ruining a batch of cookies. It had been her fault, but how could she not go chasing after the late autumn butterfly? It would have brought her such luck to catch it today. She knew that butterflies are a symbol of this holiday season, The Days of the Dead. That is because caterpillars wrap themselves up as if dead, and then come to life again in glorious new colors and in new butterfly bodies, able to fly. Selena had not moved fast enough and could only watch as this butterfly disappeared into the trees; then, she suddenly remembered the cookies.

2   "A busy day like this needs to be broken a little," her mother had said kindly after seeing the regret on Selena's face over the burned and cracked cookies. "But let's spare the food from breaking and burning. It is hard enough to keep the babies from taking bites out of all the loaves!"

3   Such words from her mother made Selena feel more a part of getting ready for her favorite celebration. The kids at school didn't understand how a celebration called the Days of the Dead, Los Dias De Los Muertos, could be joyful and fun.

4   "Well," Selena thought to herself as she buried a toy skeleton into the next loaf of bread she would bake, "for us this is just the best time of the year."

5   Selena wished that the drive to the countryside where her great-grandparents had settled after arriving from Mexico and where her grandparents still lived, was not so far away. It was really hard to ride for hours smelling the pan de muerto, the special bread of this celebration of the dead, without being able to take even a nibble. It was also difficult to ride knowing that the cookies and chocolates shaped as skulls, coffins, and skeletons were wrapped up so she could not sneak one out along the way to the grave sites. Besides the enticing aroma from the delicacies, there were miniature silver bells and religious ornaments adorning the baskets full of food which teased her hunger as they made inviting, jingling come-to-supper sounds. Once her family reached the cemetery though, there would be feasting and storytelling and cleaning of the graves to be done. Selena and her family would also place bouquets of fresh yellow mari-golds and golden chrysanthemums at the headstones, as well as some of the favorite foods of the departed.

6.   Selena knew people who thought the idea of picnicking at a graveyard was disrespect-ful. She had explained to them it was done to include the members of the family who had passed on. It was a celebration of the people in the final stage of this life. It was also a celebration of the dead. Also it was a celebration of the people beginning a new stage of this life, the children. The children would continue to gather in the memory of the ones who had lived before them until it was time for them to join the departed, marking the eternal circle of the family. To be sure, some families in cities had to cre-ate an altar, an ofrendas, in their homes to decorate and celebrate around, but Selena was glad that her family could celebrate the days together out underneath the pale November sky.

7   As her parents pulled into the cemetery parking lot, Selena heard her name being called. She saw seven of her cousins racing over. They grabbed her by the arms and pulled her to the far side of the gates with them. They wanted her to see the calacas (skeleton doll) collection they had made. As she was the eldest cousin, she was to judge each of the handmade dolls for her cousins.

Selena could not decide which was the most clever: was it the skeleton bride holding flowers, the skeleton cowboy holding a lariat, or the skeleton poet holding a book? As she thought about it, her cousins handed her one last calacas to add to the group.

8. "This is the cleverest calacas ever!" Selena announced with a merry smile lighting her eyes. She gently held up the doll, a small skeleton child holding a tiny butterfly net with a bright orange butterfly inside.

50 **What is the author's purpose in having a butterfly at the beginning and at the end of Selena's story?**   9RL1, 9RL2

A to bring luck to Selena and her attempts at baking

B to prove that Selena and her family live in a remote location

C to symbolize the story's theme of birth and death

D to foreshadow the arrival of butterflies on the fresh flowers set at the headstones.

51 **Which statement best supports the idea that the culture represented in this story values every member of the family?**   9RL3

A The children would continue to gather in the memory of those who had lived before them until it was time for them to join the departed, marking the eternal circle of the family.

B As she was the eldest cousin, she was to judge each of the handmade dolls for her cousins.

C Selena wished that the drive to the country-side where her great-grandparents had settled after arriving from Mexico, and where her grandparents still lived, wasn't so far.

D Once her family reached the cemetery though, there would be feasting and story-telling and cleaning of the graves to be done.

52 **What is ironic about the story?**   9RL1

A Selena gets to judge the handmade dolls.

B Many people consider the tradition Selena and her family celebrate morbid, but it really is a happy time.

C The butterfly is seen more than once that day.

D Selena doesn't enjoy the holiday but pretends she does so she doesn't upset her mother.

53 **Which of the following *best* explains the author's purpose in writing the passage?**   9RL1

A to persuade   **C** to entertain

B to instruct   **D** to cause doubt

54 **Read these sentences from the passage:**   9W4

"It was a celebration of the people in the final stage of this life. It was also a celebration of the dead. Also it was a celebration of the people beginning a new stage of this life, the children."

What is the *best* way to combine the sentences above into one?

A It was a celebration of not only the people in the final stage of this life, but also of the dead and of the children, who are the people beginning a new stage of this life.

B The people in the final stage of this life, the dead, and the children, the people beginning a new stage of this life, are who it was a celebration of.

C It was a celebration because of the people in the final stage of this life, the dead, and because of the people who are beginning a new stage in this life, the children.

D It was a celebration of the people in the final stage of this life, the dead, and a celebration of the people beginning a new stage of this life, the children.

55 Read this sentence from the passage: 9RL1

> "The kids at school don't understand how a celebration called the Days of the Dead, Los Dias De Los Muertos, could be joyful and fun."

Joyful is to _____ as *angry* is to *mad*.

A sad

B worried

C happy

D thoughtful

56 Read these lines from paragraph 5: 9RL5

> "Besides the enticing aroma from the delicacies, there were miniature silver bells and religious ornaments adorning the baskets full of food which teased her hunger as they made inviting, jingling come-to-supper sounds."

Which dictionary definition of the word *teased* best applies to its use in these lines?

A tempt or entice

B comb against the grain

C pull or pick apart

D irritate by making fun of

57 The story is told in which point of view? 9RL1

A first person

B second person

C third person limited

D third person omniscient

Read the following passage. Then answer the questions that follow it:

"To Peel Potatoes"

excerpted from *Peace Corps: The Great Adventure*, by John P. Deever

"Life's too short to peel potatoes," a woman in the supermarket announced, putting a box of instant mashed potatoes in her cart. When I overheard her, I nearly exploded.

Having recently returned from my Peace Corps stint in the Ukraine, I tend to get defensive about the potato in all its forms: sliced, scalloped, diced, chopped, grated, or julienned; then boiled, browned, french-fried, slow-fried, mashed, baked, or twice-baked —with a dollop of butter or sour cream, yes, thank you.

A large portion of my time in the Ukraine was spent preparing what was, in the winter, nearly the only vegetable available. Minutes and hours added up to days spent handling potatoes. I sized up the biggest, healthiest spuds in the market and bought buckets full, then hauled them home over icy sidewalks.

Winter evenings, when it got dark at four p.m., I scrubbed my potatoes thoroughly under the icy tap — we had no hot water — until my hands were numb. Though I like the rough, sour peel and prefer potatoes skin-on, Chernobyl radiation lingered in the local soil, so we were advised to strip off the skins. I peeled and peeled, pulling the dull knife toward my thumb as Svetlana Adamovna had taught me, and brown-flecked stripe after stripe dropped off to reveal a golden tuber beneath. Finally I sliced them with a "plop" into boiling water or a hot frying pan. My potatoes, my kartopli, sizzled and cooked through, warming up my tiny kitchen in the dormitory until the windows clouded over with steam.

Very often my Ukrainian friends and I peeled and cooked potatoes together, either in my kitchen or in Tanya's or Misha's or Luda's, all the while laughing and talking and learning from each other. Preparing potatoes became for me a happy prelude to food and, when shared with others, an interactive ritual giving wider scope and breadth to my life.

But how could I explain that feeling to the woman in a grocery store in the United States? I wanted to say, "On the contrary, life's too short for instant anything."

Back home, I'm pressed by all the "instant" things to do. In the Ukraine, accomplishing two simple objectives in one day — like successfully phoning Kiev from the post office and finding a store with milk—satisfied me pretty well. I taught my classes, worked on other projects, and tried to stay happy and healthy along the way. Now it takes an hour of fast driving to get to work, as opposed to twelve minutes of leisurely walking. I spend hours fiddling with my computer to send "instant" e-mail. Talking to three people at once during a phone call is efficient—not an accident of Soviet technology. With so much time-saving, I ought to have hours and hours to peel potatoes. Somehow I don't.

What I wish I'd said to the woman in the supermarket is this: "Life's too short to be shortened by speeding it up."

But I wasn't able to formulate that thought so quickly. Instead, I went to the frozen food section and stared at the microwave dinners for a while, eventually coming to the sad, heavy realization that the Szechuan chicken looked delicious—even if it didn't come with potatoes.

58 **What does the author seem to miss most about the Ukraine, even with all of its difficulties?**   9RL3

  A   the grocery markets

  B   the slower pace

  C   the friends he made

  D   peeling potatoes

59 **As the title of the passage states, it is about potatoes on the surface, but what is the underlying theme?**   9RL2

  A   Life is too short to peel potatoes.

  B   There's never enough time to shop.

  C   Take time to enjoy even small tasks.

  D   Potatoes can be prepared in many ways.

60 **What point of view is used to tell this story, and why was it chosen?**   9RL1

  A   It is presented in second person, as if the reader were actually there.

  B   It is related in third person, so we can get to know all the characters equally.

  C   It is told in first person, as the author is relating his own personal experience.

  D   It is written in third person, which allows the facts to be presented objectively.

61 **The author writes, "Preparing potatoes became for me a happy prelude to food." A *prelude* is**   9RL5

  A   an event leading up to something else.

  B   a substitute for anything that is not in season.

  C   something served alongside a main dish.

  D   a difficult task rewarded by something pleasant.

62 The tone that the author uses to talk about this topic is   9W1

A humorous.   C dreadful.

B disinterested.   D sincere.

63 The author begins the passage with the story of the woman in the supermarket in order to   9RL3

A show how American attitudes are superior to Eastern European attitudes.

B show how stupid people in the supermarket are.

C give a vignette about Eastern Europe.

D dramatize differences in attitudes between America and Eastern Europe.

64 How should the following sentence be correctly punctuated?   9C2

> What I wish I'd said to the woman in the supermarket is this, "Life's too short to be shortened by speeding it up."

A What I wish I'd said to the woman in the supermarket is this: "Life's too short to be shortened by speeding it up."

B What I wish I'd said to the woman in the supermarket is this; "Life's too short to be shortened by speeding it up."

C What I wish I'd said to the woman in the supermarket is this. "Life's too short to be shortened by speeding it up."

D What I wish I'd said to the woman in the supermarket is this: Life's too short to be shortened by speeding it up.

Read the following passage. Then answer the questions that follow it:

A French Revolution

1   The Battle of Yorktown, which took place in October of 1781, was the turning point in the American Revolutionary War. It was also the battle that involved the greatest amount of help from the French. In fact, of the four major leaders on the side of the Americans during the Battle of Yorktown, three were French. General George Washington was the fourth. The French certainly influenced the outcome of the Battle of Yorktown, and the army that fought against the British was a Franco-American army. However, some of the French soldiers were not happy about helping the Americans.

2.   The battle would not have taken place as it did had it not been for a French military leader, Admiral Rochambeau. When he met with Washington in 1781, Washington was about to attack New York to win it back from the British. However, Rochambeau convinced Washington that it would be wiser to go south to Yorktown. He had heard from another French general, Lafayette, that the British general Cornwallis had taken Yorktown. Because of this news, Rochambeau advised Washington to deal with Cornwallis and forget the British in New York for the time being. Washington took Rochambeau's advice, and the two of them, along with their troops, marched south.

3   Meanwhile, Rochambeau notified yet another French officer, Admiral Françoise de Grasse, to sail into Chesapeake Bay, near Yorktown, and to confront the British naval vessels that were there. De Grasse did so and defeated the British fleet. As a result, Cornwallis had no naval back-up to help him hold Yorktown.

4.   After that, de Grasse's men, Rochambeau's men, and Lafayette's men all joined with Washington's forces in laying siege to Yorktown, surrounding Cornwallis' men and starving them for 21 days.

5 On September 19, 1781, Cornwallis surrendered to the French and American forces. As a result of this defeat, the British government began to realize that winning the war against the American colonists would be next to impossible. Because of this realization, the prime minister of Great Britain immediately resigned. This resignation led to the end of the American Revolutionary war.

6. The help of the French, who had long admired the revolutionary spirit of the American colonists, made a crucial difference in the course of the war for American freedom.

65 We can infer from reading the passage that the author 9RC4

A dislikes the French people.

B is pro-American.

C doesn't think much of French leaders.

D is pro-French.

66 Which of the following is an *opinion*, not a *fact*? 9W1

A On September 19, 1781, Cornwallis surrendered to the French and American forces.

B Washington marched south with his troops toward Cornwallis.

C The Battle of Yorktown was the only turning point in the American Revolution.

D Cornwallis had taken Yorktown.

67 What is the main idea of the passage? 9RL1

A It is best to get advice from other military leaders when fighting a war.

B Many of the American officers in the Revolutionary War were inferior.

C Much of the fighting in the Revolutionary War took place near New York.

D The French did a great deal to help the United States in the Revolution.

68 Why was going to Yorktown a better idea than attacking New York? 9RL3

A Cornwallis was there and needed to be defeated first.

B The British were easier to defeat than Cornwallis.

C Getting to Yorktown would be easier than getting to New York.

D Cornwallis was in New York and would be difficult to defeat.

69 The term *Franco-American* most likely refers to 9RC3

A the French being first in helping the Americans.

B a mixture of French and Americans.

C the French being better than the Americans.

D a tasty lunchtime pasta.

70 What reason is given for the French helping the Americans? 9RL1

A The French admired the Americans' spirit.

B The French realized the Americans had poor information.

C The French leaders felt superior to the Americans.

D The Americans pleaded for help from the French.

71 Which sentence below from the passage actually weakens the author's argument for the French's involvement in helping the Americans? 9W1

A "As a result, Cornwallis had no naval backup to help him hold Yorktown."

B "However, some of the French soldiers were not happy about helping the Americans."

C "Because of this realization, the prime minister of Great Britain immediately resigned."

D "However, Rochambeau convinced Washington that it would be wiser to go south to Yorktown."

72 Considering strictly the events outlined in the passage, what was the most valuable assistance the French provided the colonists? 9RL1

A leadership and important information

B their expertise in fighting naval battles

C their large, experienced army

D clothing and much-needed weapons

Read the following passage. Then answer the questions that follow it:

For centuries, the southern giant petrel, a large, long-living bird, has been reviled as a bird full of disgusting habits. Living on the remote islands and coastlines of the ocean surrounding Antarctica, these creatures are able to live in the world's harshest ocean and usually die of old age! They can fly thousands of miles in search of food with relative ease. Their lives as chicks, adults and parents, and their future are pretty interesting.

Stormy petrel
(about 5½ in. long)

These petrels begin their lives as eggs, incubated for many weeks under their mother. Finally, they hatch. These chicks grow. They immediately demand large quantities of food. When times are tough and the food carrion, squid, and krill are scarce, both the mother and the father are known to fly far from their coastal or island roosts in search of food. Usually, the parents alternate the guarding of the chicks. However, they are occasionally both required to search for food. While the parents are gone, these hatchlings are vulnerable to attacks from predators. Actually, they are not that vulnerable. A young petrel can take care of him or herself by shooting out disgusting vomit up to six feet away! When the parents return with food for the youngsters, which they have stored in their own body by swallowing, they regurgitate the food as a way of creating a kind of baby food for their children.

73 **The passage focuses mostly on**   9RL1
    A   global warming.
    B   the Southern Ocean.
    C   the petrel's eating habits.
    D   lifespan of the petrel species.

74 **Read the thesis statement from the report:**   9W4

> Their lives as chicks, adults and parents, and their future are pretty interesting.

Which of these thesis statements is *more effective* than the one above?

    A   What is fascinating about these birds is their lives as chicks, adults, and parents and even their future as a part of the ecosystem.

    B   Examining their lives as chicks, their lives as adults and parents, and their futures as part of a complex ecosystem provides a new perspective of the importance of this "dirty" creature.

    C   You might start to have a new perspective on this "dirty" creature if you examine its life as a chick, as an adult and parent, and its future as part of a complex ecosystem.

    D   The southern giant petrel is pretty interesting.

75 Read the following sentences from the selection: 9W4

> "These chicks grow. They immediately demand large quantities of food."

What is the *best* way to combine these lines?

A These chicks grow, and they immediately demand large quantities of food.

B These chicks grow, yet they immediately demand large quantities of food.

C These chicks grow, but they immediately demand large quantities of food.

D These chicks grow, or they immediately demand large quantities of food.

76 Read the following sentence from the passage: 9C2

> "When times are tough and the food carrion, squid, and krill, are scarce both the mother and the father are known to fly far from their coastal or island roosts in search of food."

What is the correct way to punctuate this sentence?

A When times are tough, and the food carrion, squid, and krill are scarce, both the mother and the father are known to fly far from their coastal or island roosts in search of food.

B When times are tough and the food carrion, squid, and krill are scarce: both the mother and the father are known to fly far from their coastal or island roosts in search of food.

C When times are tough and the food, carrion squid and krill are scarce; both the mother and the father are known to fly far from their coastal or island roosts in search of food.

D When times are tough and the food, carrion, squid, and krill are scarce, both the mother and the father are known to fly far from their coastal or island roosts in search of food.

Read the following passage. Then answer the questions that follow it:

Northern Lights Head South?

The southern sky has a unique beauty to it. The darkness of space is filled with the perfume of honeysuckle, the glow of lightning bugs, and moonlight through the pines. Only one other spectacle would make a southerner leave the porch fan, or the air conditioning, to go outside for a look. That spectacle would be a sky filled with glorious northern lights. No need to wait for this to happen; the lights had been showing up sporadically in southern states for the last couple of months. We all know how hot southern nights can get.

How and why has this occurred? The northern lights are more formally known as the Aurora Borealis. They usually occur in a range from the earth's magnetic poles. This range is about 1,200 miles. In this range, the lights can be seen most any night, but outside that range they can be seen only once in a blue moon or once in a stormy sun. The time for magnetic storms on the sun has been at an eleven-year cycle peak. The solar magnetic storms, also known as sunspots, have been pretty strong in the last two months. Even cell phone service and Internet connections were disrupted around the globe at that time. That was the dark side of the storms. The positive or light side of the storms was, literally, a display of northern lights in the southern states. So if you are a sky watcher you will not have to go to the frozen North to view the majesty of this natural wonder — at least until the sun's storms have abated for another eleven years.

77 Read this sentence from the passage: 9C1

> "No need to wait for this to happen; the lights <u>had been showing</u> up sporadically in southern states for the last couple of months."

What is the correct way to write the underlined verb in the sentence?

A has been showing

B have been showing

C has been shown

D no change

78 Which of these sentences from the passage *best* reveals the author's attitude about the southern sky?   9W2

A The southern sky has a unique beauty to it.

B The darkness of space is filled with the perfume of honeysuckle, the glow of lightning bugs, and moonlight through the pines.

C Only one other spectacle would make a southerner leave the porch fan, or the air conditioning, to go outside for a look. That spectacle would be a sky filled with glorious northern lights.

D That spectacle would be a sky filled with glorious northern lights.

79 Choose the sentence in which *accept* or *except* are used correctly.   9C1

A Everyone <u>accept</u> me saw the northern lights.

B I love rainy nights, <u>except</u> when it is cold out.

C She <u>excepted</u> my invitation to sit outside and look for the northern lights.

D During the storm, everyone went inside <u>accept</u> for Kathy.

80 Below are some sources that were used in writing the passage. Which source probably gave the *best* information about the Northern Lights being viewed in the south?   9W3

A personal experience

B interviews with people who have seen the lights

C encyclopedia articles about the lights

D recent news footage about the lights

Georgia 9th Grade Literature & Composition Post-Test Two

The purpose of this post-test is to measure your progress in reading comprehension, grammar, and critical thinking. This test is based on the **Georgia Performance Standards** and adheres to the sample question format provided by the Georgia Department of Education.

General Directions:

1   Read all directions carefully.

2   Read each question or sample. Then choose the best answer.

3   Choose only one answer for each question. If you change an answer, be sure to erase your original answer completely.

4   After taking the test, you or your instructor should score it using the answer key that accompanies this book. Then review and practice for the reading comprehension and critical thinking skills tested on the EOCT.

Read the following passage. Then answer the questions that follow:

My Family's Special Holiday Treats

When holidays are approaching, one of the traditions that many families enjoy is the baking and cooking of various holiday treats. In every country and every culture, there are special foods associated with various holidays and celebrations. Many holidays are centered around religious celebrations. Other holidays are specific to a particular country. Americans really enjoy the celebration of Independence Day — the 4th of July — but in England, it's just another day.

In my family, the 4th of July is a day for an all-day picnic with family and friends. A backyard cookout or barbecue is a great way to celebrate. Most of the foods are not exclusive to the holiday; we like to eat hot dogs, hamburgers, and the usual picnic trimmings all year long. My family though, has a special tradition — we make homemade ice cream. It is usually the only time during the year that we do that.

In the Christian culture, Christmas is probably the biggest holiday of the year. It is a time that my family and friends gather and enjoy each other's company along with some special foods that we only eat during the holidays. Each of my aunts and cousins seems to have a specialty! Eggnog is popular with the grown ups and usually only seen at Christmas. Certain types of cookies and desserts are only made during Christmastime as a special treat for the family parties. The best Christmas cookies are the rolled sugar cookies that are cut out with shaped cutters and decorated with colored frostings and sugar decorations. Some people prefer the elaborate cakes and desserts that cooks will spend lots of time on.

One of my favorite aunts makes fudge and other candy that is out of this world. It is really delicious, but a little goes a long way. Another of my aunts is Greek, so she makes stuffed grape leaves and baklava, items that I only see at Christmas. My older brother is now the grill king of the family. No matter what the weather, he is outside basting and turning until he has perfectly barbecued ribs. And I can't forget Uncle John he is the master of pies. No one in any family anywhere can match his delicious pies. No one else in our family would even think of baking a pie for a family party; that is strictly his domain.

I'll bet your family has traditions, too, and I'm guessing that some of them include holiday food!

1 Which of the following sentences is an *opinion*? 9W1

    A   In every country and every culture, there are special foods associated with various holidays and celebrations.

    B   Americans really enjoy the celebration of Independence Day — the 4th of July — but in England, it's just another day.

    C   In the Christian culture, Christmas is probably the biggest holiday of the year.

    D   No one in any family anywhere can match his delicious pies.

2 Which of the following sentences is a *fact*? 9W1

    A   One of my favorite aunts makes fudge and other candy that is out of this world.

    B   Some people prefer the elaborate cakes and desserts that cooks will spend lots of time on.

    C   The best Christmas cookies are the rolled sugar cookies that are cut out with shaped cutters and decorated with colored frostings and sugar decorations.

    D   No matter what the weather, he is outside basting and turning until he has perfectly barbecued ribs.

3 The passage is designed to

9RL1

    A give information about family get-togethers.

    B brag about the author's family's skill at cooking.

    C invite others to join the author's family.

    D explain family get-togethers and why they're important to the author.

4 If the author added more to this section, it would *most likely*

9W3

    A offer more descriptions of holiday foods.

    B explain different holidays around the world.

    C debate the virtues of the world's religions.

    D offer insight into how the author's family gets along.

5 Based on the information in the passage, you can tell that the author

9RL1

    A treats other religions' holidays with suspicion.

    B wants to believe in other ways of thinking.

    C avoids spending holidays with his family.

    D takes pride in her family's cooking skills.

6 Read the following sentence from the passage:

9C2

> And I can't forget Uncle John he is the master of pies.

A better way to punctuate this sentence would be:

    A And I can't forget Uncle John; he is the master of pies.

    B And I can't forget Uncle John, he is the master of pies.

    C And I can't forget Uncle John; yet he is the master of pies.

    D And I can't forget uncle John; he is the master of pies.

7 Which of the following sentences contains a *cliche*?

9C1

    A In the Christian culture, Christmas is probably the biggest holiday of the year.

    B One of my favorite aunts makes fudge and other candy that is out of this world.

    C A backyard cookout or barbecue is a great way to celebrate.

    D In my family, the 4th of July is a day for an all-day picnic with family and friends.

Read the following passage. Then answer the questions that follow it:

Galveston

1 The island of Galveston has a long and colorful history. Galveston is a barrier island off the coast of Texas in the Gulf of Mexico. Its history is cluttered with shipwrecks, buccaneers, outlaws, cannibals, and explorers. Some of the remarkable characters that have shaped the history of Galveston include the Karankawa Indians, the Spanish explorer Alvar Nunez Cabeza de Vaca, and the swashbuckling pirate Jean Lafitte.

2 In the 1400s and 1500s, the island was inhabited by natives known as the Karankawa Indians. In Texas, the Karankawa were known for being cannibals. This label, however, is sometimes misunderstood. The Karankawa were a tribe of hunters and fishers. They lived in the coastal area of Texas between Galveston and Corpus Christi. They fished in the shallow waters along the coast and used longbows to hunt. The longbows were as long as the Indians were tall. And the Karankawa were a tall people: many were over six feet tall.

3   It is true that the Karankawa were known to practice cannibalism, but it was not for food. It was for superstitious reasons. The Indians believed it was a way of gaining power over enemies. A few eyewitness records of the Kawankawa still exist. One account, by Alice Oliver, describes the Indians as a tolerant people who taught her some of their language when she was a child in the 1830s.

4. The Karankawa may have gotten their fierce reputation from the Europeans. These Europeans often tried to kidnap Indians and sell them as slaves. In those days, the slave trade was a large part of the world economy. In their travels as part of this economy, Europeans spread diseases which killed thousands of Indians. They also fought the Indians for their lands. For these reasons, the Kanakawa, like many natives, were unfriendly towards Europeans.

5   One European landed on the island of the Karankawa without a slave ship or any other form of threat to the natives. His name was Alvar Nunez Cabeza de Vaca. He came to the island as a starving survivor of a shipwreck. De Vaca was a famous Spanish explorer. He had sailed from Spain and was out to claim territory for his king and his country. While he was in the Gulf of Mexico in 1528, a hurricane washed him onto the shores of Galveston Island.

6   The Kanakawa Indians were generally friendly to de Vaca. He lived among them for four years, treating them with due respect. De Vaca learned about the Indians' way of life. He was able to understand them and communicate with them.

7. In 1532, de Vaca left Galveston Island and traveled across Texas in search of his fellow countrymen. He found some of them, but the meeting was a shock for his fellow Spaniards. After four years with the Indians, de Vaca looked more like an Indian than a Spaniard. De Vaca wrote of this meeting that the Spaniards he met "just stood staring for a long time."

8   De Vaca was a writer. In his day, many explorers of the "New World" kept written records of their travels. De Vaca's writings were important for two reasons. First, even today they give us a close-up look at the land and people of North America in the 1500s. The second reason is even more unique to de Vaca. At the time when de Vaca was exploring, European nations were trying to claim as much of the world as they could. Any native people that they met in their quest were considered to be obstacles. These natives were most often conquered, murdered, or enslaved. De Vaca, however, had come to know the natives as people. He was appalled by the way Europeans treated the natives. He wanted to let people know about these injustices.

9   When de Vaca returned to Spain in 1537, he wrote in graphic detail of the abuses that Europeans were inflicting upon the native people of the New World. His written accounts of cruelty, torture, and murder make a shocking story. They enlightened many Europeans who then called for a better policy towards the natives. Alvar Nunez Cabeaza de Vaca was one of America's first human rights champions.

10 About 300 years after de Vaca left Galveston, the island was adopted by another colorful personality. In 1817, the "gentleman pirate," Jean Lafitte, came out of no certain origin and arrived on the island. He hoped to set up a base of operation in the Gulf and continue his work of smuggling illegal cargo.

11. At the time, Texas was fighting for independence from Spain. Jean Lafitte did not become involved in the war. He considered himself a businessman, not a soldier. His shipmates were mostly criminals, and his business often involved illegal activity; but Lafitte's manner was, for the most part, refined. Many people found the handsome "privateer" intriguing. Lafitte set up a small village on the island. There were huts for his pirate friends, places of business, and a red brick mansion built for himself. There was a lot of pirated wealth in the village and constant parties as well.

12 The island people welcomed Lafitte because of the money, but were uneasy about his friends. On a fall night in 1820, a U.S. government ship threatened Lafitte with death if he did not leave the island. The next morning, the village was in ashes and Lafitte and his band had vanished. There is no record of what happened to Lafitte after that time, but he probably did not retire as a boot maker somewhere. Chances are that he joined the many nameless high seas buccaneers that prowled the Gulf of Mexico in the 1800s.

13 History still recalls the name of Jean Lafitte, as well as de Vaca and the Karankawa Indians as some of the more captivating chapters in the story of Texas. Today, Galveston's people and cultures are as diverse as ever. This "port of entry" for many immigrants to the United States continues to be a source of stories, legends, and vibrant history.

8 As used in paragraph three, *tolerant* most nearly means_____.   9RL5

A accepting   C forgiving
B enduring   D generous

9 Paragraph 9 is important in this selection because it helps the reader understand   9RL1

A when de Vaca returned to Spain.
B the type of person de Vaca was.
C how de Vaca viewed the native people.
D why de Vaca's writing was important.

10 The native people welcomed Jean Lafitte mainly because   9RL1

A he was a gentleman.
B he was handsome.
C he was wealthy.
D he built a village on the island.

11 The main reason the Karankawa Indians accepted de Vaca was because   9RL1

A he wrote stories about them.
B he treated them with respect.
C he taught them how to communicate.
D he looked more like an Indian than a Spaniard.

12 Which statement from the selection is an *opinion*?   9W1

A Galveston is a barrier island off the coast of Texas.
B The Karankawa may have earned their fierce reputation from Europeans.
C Jean Lafitte had a colorful personality.
D De Vaca traveled across Texas in 1532.

13 The author probably wrote this selection to   9W3

A persuade the reader to visit Galveston.
B describe the early explorers of Galveston.
C provide background information about Galveston.
D entertain the reader with a story about the people of modern-day Galveston.

14 From the information about the Karankawa provided in this selection, the reader can conclude that   9RL1

A they were hostile toward newcomers.
B they were distrustful of the Europeans.
C they were involved in illegal activities.
D they were unable to communicate with others.

Read the following passage. Then answer the questions that follow it:

1 Though not as popular among history enthusiasts as its "sequel" in the 1940s, the First World War, also known as World War I and (ironically) The War to End All Wars, played just as much an impact on modern civilization. The war began on June 28, 1914, when an obscure Austrian noble named Archduke Francis Ferdinand (heir to the throne of Austria-Hungary) was visiting Sarajevo, the capital of his empire's province of Bosnia. Gavrilo Princep, a Serbian nationalist who wanted Bosnia to be part of Serbia, shot the Archduke and his wife after they left a parade route and became lost. Austria-Hungary accused its neighbor, Serbia, of plotting to kill the Archduke and threatened war. Russia, which was allied with Serbia, threatened war with Austria-Hungary. Germany supported Austria-Hungary, and France mobilized its forces to help Russia.

2 By that August, Germany and Austria-Hungary were at war with France and Russia. Crucial to Germany's strategy was the conquering of neutral Belgium and crippling France. When Germany attacked Belgium, Great Britain entered the war on the side of France and Russia, forming the military alliance known as the Triple Entente. Germany attacked France, coming within sight of Paris until the French stopped their advance at the hideously destructive Battle of the Marne. For their next tactic, the French dug trenches as defensive positions, a technique theorized sixty years earlier but not put into common practice. The Germans did the same and soon lines of opposing trenches stretched from Switzerland to the North Sea, creating long gashes in the earth that teemed with men and equipment but also bred germs and disease.

3 Over the next three years each side's army hunkered down, digging in and constantly fortifying their trenches. In between lay the notorious "No Man's Land:" — a stretch of blighted earth lain with landmines, barbed wire, and other booby traps. When each side introduced machine guns and poison gas, the war turned especially deadly. Firing bullets in uncannily rapid succession, soldiers used machine guns to shoot massive amounts of ammunition at the enemy in a short amount of time, increasing efficiency a thousand fold. Deadly canisters of mustard gas, first used by the Germans, killed or disabled soldiers instantly. Artillery shells carried the gas to the enemy. As the artillery exploded, gas would engulf the soldiers, liquifying their internal organs and leaving them struggling for breath. Often the gas destroyed the soldiers' lungs, causing them to fill with fluid, literally drowning from the inside out. Soldiers died by the hundreds of thousands. In the Battle of Verdun, which lasted six months in 1916, 330,000 men died on the French and British side. Some 330,000 men died on the German side.

4 Another important development in the war was the use of the airplane. In 1909, Wilbur and Orville Wright built the first functioning airplane. By World War I, the warring powers on the Western Front used over 400 aircraft. At the beginning of the war, nations used these planes primarily for scouting and reconnaissance. By the end of the conflict, countries equipped airplanes with machine guns that could fire through an aircraft's propeller and attack enemy aircraft.

5 From the war's outset, the people of the United States took the position of neutrality. President Woodrow Wilson — who campaigned for reelection in 1916 on the slogan "He Kept Us Out of War" — urged Americans to resist the propaganda coming from both sides. However, many events and factors pushed the United States towards declaring war against Germany. For example, numerous business interests were tied to Great Britain, as they supplied the nation with weapons and other supplies. Corporations were eager for a war effort also, because the nation was in a period of high unemployment. With a war, employment and productivity would increase. Moreover, wealthy bankers such as J. P. Morgan had loaned millions of dollars to Great Britain as it fought Germany. The banking elite had a vested interest in seeing Great Britain win the war and repay the loans with interest. Still, the United States watched the war from a distance, only involving itself once a German submarine sank the American-laden passenger ship *Lusitania* in May 1917.

15 The word *outset* in paragraph five most probably means_____. 9RL5

    A cause of

    B beginning

    C end

    D viewpoint

16 The description of the effects of mustard gas in lines 61 – 66 serve(s) to 9W1

    A demonstrate the hostility the war produced.

    B incite the reader to hate Germans.

    C show how warfare in World War One was cruel and painful.

    D relate one soldier's experiences.

17 The first paragraph serves primarily to 9RL1

    A complain that people don't know enough about WWI.

    B assert that more wars like WWI are inevitable.

    C assert that WWI remains important and explain its start.

    D explain that the events in the essay happened a long time ago.

18 The author's assertion about the wealthy bankers in paragraph five would be most weakened if 9W4

    A Britain didn't want to repay their loans.

    B the debts were paid by private citizens.

    C America also owed money to Britain.

    D Germany and Austria-Hungary also owed America money.

19 The author uses the phrase "a stretch of blighted earth lain with landmines, barbed wire, and other booby traps" in paragraph three to depict 9W1

    A how deadly the two armies' weapons had become.

    B that no one wanted to fight for the land.

    C why America wouldn't enter the war.

    D the land as uninhabitable.

20 According to the fifth paragraph, we can infer that the people of the United States prior to the sinking of the *Lusitania* were 9RL1

    A uninterested in the war.

    B passionate to go to war.

    C ready to believe anything the president told them.

    D interested in but slow to take sides in a European war.

Read the following passage. Then answer the questions that follow it:

Shop 'Til They Drop

1 Each year, Americans in increasing numbers flock to malls for entertainment, procurement of needed items, a break in the schedule, or whatever reason will suffice for the day. The average American spends over 6 hours shopping every week. Many people today consider shopping as a recreational activity. Over 90 percent of teenage girls consider store-hopping a favorite activity. Money seems to be of little consequence. Clothing items produced literally for pennies entice shoppers with hefty $100 price tags. Yet Americans are in more debt and have fewer savings today than ever before.

2   The pressure to dress in the latest fashions and to consume the latest products fuels a fire unknown to most who do not live according to those pressures, and that fire is a plight to laborers in developing countries around the world, who produce the clothes Americans buy. It is the conditions of people in dozens of countries like Indonesia, China, and Vietnam, who work from morning Over 90 percent of teenage girls until night for wages insufficient to feed their families. It is the economic framework which facilitates impoverished countries to produce the goods which will sustain exceptionally high profits for businesses in developed countries.

3   Efforts have been made by international companies to mitigate the exploitation rampant in countries which have "sweatshop" working conditions. In 1997, the Clinton administration announced a new code of conduct for businesses with international product sources. This initiative, in agreement with business leaders, non-government agencies, church leaders, and human rights groups, called for a voluntary adherence to business practices which would limit child labor, control the length of the work week, and ensure that minimum wage was paid to all workers.

4   While the agreement was a step in a positive direction it remains a voluntary policy. In some cases children under 15 can be put to work, and workers can work as many as 60 hours per week, as long as the worker "volunteers" to work the overtime. When the regular 48 hours of work each week fail to pay enough to subsist on, it is likely that the worker will have little choice but to "volunteer" to work several more hours at a paltry 12 to 60 cents per hour.

21   **The author's *tone* can be best described as**   9W2

   A   condescending   **C**   hopeful

   B   ironic   **D**   disapproving

22   **The statement in paragraph 1 that "over 90 percent of teenage girls consider store-hopping a favorite activity" supports the idea that**   9W2

   A   Americans spend an average of 6 hours a week shopping.

   B   Americans commonly think of shopping as a recreational activity.

   C   Americans are more in debt today than ever before.

   D   money does not seem to be an issue for many American shoppers.

23   **The author's attitude in this passage is that**   9W2

   A   sweatshops are harmful for both developing countries and for Americans.

   B   initiatives against sweatshops that are not definitive and enforceable are useless.

   C   the use of sweatshops benefits the economies of the countries they exist in.

   D   the demand for new fashions feeds the economies of developing countries.

24 How could the following sentence best be written to improve clarity and reduce wordiness? 9W4

> Efforts have been made by international companies to mitigate the exploitation rampant in countries which have "sweatshop" working conditions.

   A   International companies have made efforts to reduce exploitation in sweatshop countries.

   B   Efforts were made by international companies to mitigate the exploitation rampant in countries which have "sweatshop" working conditions.

   C   Efforts have been made by international companies to mitigate the exploitation rampant in countries which have "sweatshop" working conditions.

   D   International companies want to mitigate the exploitation in countries with "sweatshop" working conditions.

25 What change should be made to correct the following sentence? 9C2

> While the agreement was a step in a positive direction it remains a voluntary policy.

   A   change *direction* to *direction,*
   B   change *was* to *is*
   C   change *it* to *they*
   D   change *policy* to *Policy*

Read the following passage. Then answer the questions that follow it:

KISS: Keep It Simple and Separate

1   America is the land of free speech and the pursuit of happiness and the free pursuit of knowledge. To answer a question regarding the role of government in the teaching of science, you have to define the overall role of a democratic government, of science, and of religion in our lives. I think government has to take care of people physically; science is meant to find knowledge; religion gives you freedom of faith. None of them need to get mixed up with the others.

2   It would be awful if government, including school boards which are elected, decided to make all the teachers in its schools become members of, say, the Methodist church. History has shown that this sort of government interference with people's religions turns out poorly. For instance, look at how Afghani women were killed by the Taliban for not wearing religious scarves! OK, that example is pretty brutal, but hey, it shows what can happen.

3   Now, science is the pursuit of knowledge. In order to be proven, that knowledge has to be tested in the same way as all scientific knowledge. Science shouldn't be used to promote beliefs—unless those beliefs can hold up to the same tests that science is. Think about it: in the early 20th century, white supremacists tried to use science to prove that non-white peoples were genetically inferior. It turned out to be full of holes, of course, but we shouldn't use science that way.

4   Finally, science teachers should be respected. As professionals. They know their stuff. Better than members of school boards, unless they are all biologists. My cousin is on a school board, and he was an English major. Therefore, government should listen to science teachers. Instead of telling them what to teach. And if science teachers feel it is against their principles, they shouldn't have to do it. Just as a pharmacist should be allowed to follow their consciences when dispensing medicines, science teachers should, too.

26   **Which of the following best describes the author's opinion about government and religion?**   9W1

    A   He dislikes them both.

    B   He favors keeping them separate.

    C   He wants them both abolished.

    D   There is not information to make a firm decision.

27   **Based on the passage, what does the word *dispensing* mean?**   9RL5

    A   to deal out in portions

    B   to follow their own faith

    C   to listen to governments

    D   to insist on what teachers teach in schools

28   **What does the phrase "full of holes" refer to in paragraph three?**   9RC3

    A   sciences that wanted to marry religion and government

    B   all sciences practiced by white supremacists

    C   sciences which did not back up religion

    D   sciences meant to teach white superiority

29   **Which conflict is *most closely* related to the theme of this passage?**   9RL2

    A   science versus government

    B   schools versus churches

    C   religion versus government

    D   religion versus religion

30   **How should the following two sentences from the passage *best* be combined?**   9W4

> Therefore, government should listen to science teachers. Instead of telling them what to teach.

    A   Therefore, government should listen to science teachers, instead of telling them what to teach.

    B   Therefore, government should listen to science teachers: instead of telling them what to teach.

    C   Therefore, government should listen to science teachers; instead, of telling them what to teach.

    D   Therefore; government should listen to science teachers, instead of telling them what to teach.

Read the following passage. Then answer the questions that follow it:

Tschubukov: Oh, don't beat about the bush, my dear fellow. Tell me!

Lomov: Immediately—in a moment. Here it is, then: I have come to ask for the hand of your daughter, Natalia Stepanovna.

Tschubukov: Angel! Ivan Vassiliyitch! Say that once again! I didn't quite hear it!

Lomov: I have the honor to beg—

Tschubukov: My dear, dear man! I am so happy that everything is so—everything! I have wanted this to happen for so long. It has been my dearest wish! And I have always loved you, my dear fellow, as my own son! May God give you his blessings and his grace and—I always wanted it to happen. But why am I standing here like a block head? I am completely dumbfounded with pleasure, completely dumbfounded. My whole being—I'll call Natalia—

Lomov: Dear Stepan Stepanovitch, what do you think? May I hope for Natalia Stepanovna's acceptance?

Tschubukov: Really! A fine boy like you—and you think she won't accept on the minute? Lovesick as a cat and all that—!

Lomov: I'm cold. My whole body is trembling as though I was going to take my examination! But the chief thing is to settle matters! If a person meditates too much, or hesitates, or talks about it, waits for an ideal or for true love, he never gets it. Brrr! It's cold! Natalia is an excellent housekeeper, not at all bad looking, well educated—what more could I ask? I'm so excited my ears are roaring!

- excerpted from "A Marriage Proposal," by Anton Chekhov

31 By reading the passage, we can infer that the complete work is a_____.   9RL1

   A drama

   B comedy

   C autobiography

   D memoir

32 Which of the following *best* explains the author's purpose?   9RL1

   A to entertain

   B to inform

   C to persuade

   D to instruct

33 By reading the passage, we can infer that Lomov's request to marry Natalia is ironic because   9RL1

   A he is actually her distant cousin.

   B he doesn't truly love her.

   C Tschubukov loves her more than he.

   D Tschubukov wants Natalia for himself.

34 The cliche "don't beat around the bush," as used in the passage, means   9RC3

   A "get to the point."

   B "get lost."

   C "don't raise your voice."

   D "look me in the eye when you speak."

35 The passage uses all of the following *except*_____.   9RL1

   A verbal irony

   B dialogue

   C suspense

   D flashback

Read the following passage. Then answer the questions that follow it:

Buck O'Neil

1 John Jordan "Buck" O'Neil was a first baseman and manager in baseball's Negro leagues during the thirties, forties and fifties. He is best known for his playing career with the Kansas City Monarchs of the Negro leagues and as a coach and scout for the Chicago Cubs and Kansas City Royals in the major leagues.

2 O'Neil was born Nov. 13, 1911, in Carrabelle, Florida. Due to racial segregation, he was denied the opportunity to attend high school in Sarasota, Florida, or play baseball in the major leagues. He began his baseball career with the Memphis Red Sox of the Negro leagues in 1937 and was traded to the Monarchs the following year. A tour of duty in the Navy during World War II briefly interrupted his playing career.

3 In the Negro leagues, O'Neil amassed a career batting average of .288, including four .300-plus seasons at the plate. In 1946, the first baseman led the Negro League in hitting with a .353 average and followed that in 1947 with a career best .358 mark. He posted averages of .345 and .330 in 1940 and 1949, respectively.

4 In 1948, he took over as manager of the Monarchs and guided the team to league titles in 1951, 1953, and 1955. He played in four East-West All-Star games and two Negro League World Series during his playing days.

5 O'Neil also joined the legendary Satchel Paige as a teammate during the height of the Negro League barnstorming days of the 1930s and 1940s. This was a period when teams of Negro all-stars would travel the countryside playing town teams, college teams, and teams of major leaguers to earn extra money and gain exposure for the Negro leagues.

6 O'Neil left the Monarchs following the 1955 season, and in 1956, became a scout for the Chicago Cubs. In 1962, the Cubs hired him as a coach, making him the first black coach in Major League Baseball history. As a scout, he signed Hall of Fame outfielder Lou Brock to his first pro contract.

7 He is sometimes credited with having signed future Cubs' Hall of Fame second baseman Ernie Banks to his first pro contract, but, in fact, only signed him to his first MLB contract. Banks had actually been scouted and signed to the Monarchs by Cool Papa Bell, manager of the Monarchs' barnstorming "B" team, in 1949. Banks played for the Monarchs in 1950 and briefly in 1953 when O'Neil was his manager.

8 O'Neil has worked as a Kansas City Royals scout since 1988 and was named Major League Baseball's "Midwest Scout of the Year" in 1998.

9 O'Neil gained national prominence during the late 1990s with his poignant and compelling narration of Negro League history as part of Ken Burns' PBS documentary on baseball. He has since been the subject of countless national interviews, including appearances on *Late Night with David Letterman* and the *Late, Late Show with Tom Snyder*.

10 Today, Buck O'Neil serves as honorary Board Chairman of the Negro Leagues Baseball Museum (NLBM) in Kansas City, Missouri. He was a member of the 18-member Baseball Hall of Fame Veterans Committee from 1981 to 2000 and was instrumental in the induction of eight Negro League players during that time.

11 O'Neil was a candidate in 2006 for induction into Major League Baseball's Hall of Fame in a special vote for Negro League players, managers, and executives. However, he did not receive the necessary nine votes for induction from the 12-member committee.

12 O'Neil commented after hearing that he had not been elected to the Hall at age 94.

13 "God's been good to me," he told about 200 well wishers who had gathered to celebrate but instead stood hushed and solemn. "They didn't think Buck was good enough to be in the Hall of Fame. That's the way they thought about it, and that's the way it is, so we're going to live with that.

14 "Now, if I'm a Hall of Famer for you, that's all right with me. Just keep loving old Buck. Don't weep for Buck. No, man, be happy, be thankful."

36 **The *theme* of the passage can best be summarized by which of the following?** 9RL2

- **A** O'Neil personifies what is wrong with baseball today.
- **B** O'Neil deserves to be in the Hall of Fame.
- **C** O'Neil is a great ambassador of good will and a good family man.
- **D** Baseball is better off with people like Buck O'Neil representing it.

37 **The last two paragraphs tell us what about O'Neil's outlook on life and his character?** 9RL1

- **A** He is bitter about not being let into the Hall of Fame.
- **B** He feels his life is not yet complete.
- **C** He is a positive man, who doesn't let things get him down.
- **D** He is a happy man, but would be happier if allowed into the Hall of Fame.

38 **The author's purpose in writing the passage is most likely** 9RL1

- **A** to introduce an interesting person.
- **B** to inform the reader of an injustice in the world.
- **C** to persuade the reader to be active in a cause.
- **D** to relate an adventure.

39 **Which paragraph in the passage is unnecessary in detailing the key points of O'Neil's life?** 9W4

- **A** paragraph 11, about his current life
- **B** paragraph 3, about his baseball statistics
- **C** paragraph 14, the last paragraph
- **D** paragraph 7, about the signing of Ernie Banks

40 **What can the reader infer from O'Neil's experiences about baseball in the first half of the 20th century?** 9RC4

- **A** Negro league players were better than major league players.
- **B** Baseball was not very popular during that time.
- **C** Baseball did not allow Negroes to play in the major leagues.
- **D** Most of the baseball teams were in the Midwest.

41 **The word *poignant*, as used in paragraph nine, most closely means** 9RL5

- **A** interesting and exciting.
- **B** troublesome.
- **C** touching and memorable.
- **D** shocking, hard to believe.

42 **The story of O'Neil is told from the point of view of** 9RL1

- **A** a narrator.
- **B** O'Neil himself.
- **C** first person.
- **D** second person.

43 **The author of this selection is likely a** 9W1

- **A** former player.
- **B** baseball historian.
- **C** friend of O'Neil's.
- **D** fiction writer.

SECTION II

Read the following poem. Then answer the questions that follow it:

The World Is Too Much with Us
by William Wordsworth

The world is too much with us; late and soon,
Getting and spending, we lay waste our powers;
Little we see in Nature that is ours;
We have given our hearts away, a sordid boon!
This Sea that bares her bosom to the moon,
The winds that will be howling at all hours,
And are up-gathered now like sleeping flowers,
For this, for everything, we are out of tune;
It moves us not.--Great God! I'd rather be
A Pagan suckled in a creed outworn;
So might I, standing on this pleasant lea,
Have glimpses that would make me less forlorn;
Have sight of Proteus rising from the sea;
Or hear old Triton blow his wreathed horn.

44 **The poem uses all of the following except_____.**   9RL1

  A   rhythm

  B   rhyme

  C   imagery

  D   verbal irony

45 **The phrase "the winds that will be howling at all hours" is an example of _____.**   9RL1

  A   irony

  B   cliche

  C   imagery

  D   theme

46 **By reading the poem, we can infer that Proteus and Triton are**   9RL1

  A   friends of the poet.

  B   elements of nature.

  C   symbols of the future.

  D   pagan deities.

47 **The poet expressing "Great God" is an example of _____.**   9RL1

  A   invocation

  B   epithet

  C   lyric

  D   imagery

48 **As used in the passage, *sordid* most likely means_____.**   9RL5

  A   cheap

  B   sacred

  C   important

  D   poetic

Read the following passage. Then answer the questions that follow it:

I'd saved for months but the best passage I could afford went only so far as the supply station above Meroe Patera, a dilapidated wagon-wheel model from two hundred years ago that was, incredibly, still in use. Stepping off the liner and through its airlock was like walking back in time: the scrubbed air might as well have twinkled with the dust that floated in real sunlight back home.

Commuter shuttles, the ticket agent back home had promised me, left for the surface very two hours. A terminal at the farthest end of one spoke told me the schedule had been cut back to twice daily, even going so far as to blame the economic troubles on the system-wide recession. I went back to the station's central hub, and the ring of calling booths at its center. At one time the area might've looked like an urban plaza or seaside park. Now the plastic flower boxes were empty, and the trees had dropped dead leaves to the ceramic floor.

Of all the old names, only Halbursham still had a listed number. He broke out in a grin as his face came on the screen.

"Well, well," he said laughing. "How you been, Johnny?"

5   His smile faded when I told him where I was. "You're really in orbit?"

I poked at the screen. On his end, it would look like I was trying to tap his forehead. "I can't really explain right now," I said. "This thing's expensive."

"Of course." He glanced at something off to one side. "There's a cargo truck coming up in a bit. I'll set you up to hitch a ride."

Two hours later the truck's pilot strapped me into a rear cockpit couch and fired the maneuvering jets. The station fell away from us, the craft rotating towards the murky red and blue swirls of Mars. As we turned, I remembered my childhood fear of elevators and closed my eyes, dreading the sensation of waiting for a halt that never comes. At the end of the drop, I would imagine landing on springs, or steel cables above me pulling taut. So I wasn't paying attention as we descended towards the dark soil of the Elysium Plain.

Halbursham waited for me on the runway, fatter since I'd been gone and with deep rings around his eyes smudged with red dust.

10   We hugged just like old friends. "What have you been doing with yourself?" he asked.

"I'm a security analyst back on Earth," I said, trying to sound proud of myself. "At the space museum in New New Orleans."

"I know what you're doing here," he said. "You've come back for Kyla, haven't you?"

I looked away. There were rain clouds above the volcanic rills to the east. "The court's agreed to a hearing."

"The hell with them," he said. "How did you persuade her mother?"

15   It had taken months to even get my ex-wife to respond to my letters. "She wouldn't pass this up."

Halbursham led me to the motor pool and put a key fob in my hand. "Follow the old railroad, out to the Syrtis valleys," he said. "You can't miss her husband's place."

When I tried to thank him, he walked off. "Best of luck to you, John." he said.

I called Lyssa from the phone inside the dirty spaceport. Her new husband answered the phone.

"She took Kyla out for a walk," he said before I'd spoken. His face had the pinkish hue that is a kind of tan there, and his hair was neatly combed despite the winds. "They'll be back within the half-hour."

20 I told him I'd be stopping by before heading on to a hotel in Kennedy City.

"You're welcome to stay with us," he said calmly. "You've come a long way, and it's stupid to run back and forth after that."

The kindness made me think before speaking. "Thanks just the same."

Halbursham insisted on loaning me a jeep, a fairly new model with tires threaded like a screw. At the gates, a throng of squatters milled about, their shoulders stooped and their backs hunched, almost certainly from working off their emigration passage in some ore foundry under one of the mountains. Entire families stood or huddled against the fence, some not taking their eyes off the sky to notice the jeep coming within inches of running them down. They were still looking up as I turned onto the highway, hypnotized by their own hopes of escape floating out in the ruddy sky.

49 In paragraph one, *dilapidated* most nearly means_____.   9RL5

  A   brand-new.
  B   innocent.
  C   rundown.
  D   poorly built.

50 In paragraph eight, the description of elevators serves to   9RL1

  A   provide a real-world comparison to an interplanetary landing.
  B   show that the narrator doesn't want to crash.
  C   remind us the narrator is on another planet.
  D   foreshadow that Mars is a happy place.

51 The author's main point in describing the space station is to show that   9RL1

  A   the future will be an exciting time.
  B   not everyone wants to explore Mars.
  C   Mars is a very hostile planet.
  D   not everything in the future will always be brand new.

52 The description of Lyssa's new husband in paragraph 19 includes what literary device?   9RL1

  A   verbal irony
  B   imagery
  C   situational irony
  D   epithet

53 It can be inferred that since leaving Mars, the narrator   9RL3

  A   has gotten rich.
  B   has kept close ties with old friends and family.
  C   wants to stay on Earth.
  D   has struggled with money and a new career.

54 The phrase "shoulders stooped" in paragraph 23 infers that   9RL5

  A   people feel optimistic about getting on a spaceship.
  B   they hurry to get out of the narrator's way.
  C   they've had to endure hard labor since coming to Mars.
  D   no one wants to leave Mars.

55 In paragraph 20, *hypnotized* most nearly means_____.   9RL5

  A   distracted
  B   focused
  C   preoccupied
  D   uncaring

56 From the information provided in the passage, all of the following can be inferred about the Martian colonies *except* 9RL1

A   people came to Mars wanting a better life.

B   the colonies were once in better economic shape.

C   life on Mars is hard and uncompromising.

D   conditions will eventually get better.

57 The tone of the passage can best be described as 9RL1

A   happy and enthused.

B   cynical and bitter.

C   remorseful and sad.

D   angry and spiteful.

Read the following passage. Then answer the questions that follow it:

The Two Tigers of the East

1   It is amazing how the Japanese have retained their cultural heritage while simultaneously integrating many parts of Western culture. One of the most popular adaptations is the style of dress. Many Japanese today wear "western" style clothing such as business suits, active wear, jeans and T-shirts. Traditional clothing is now often only reserved for special occasions.

2   Many Japanese also have adopted western furnishings into their homes. It is not unusual to have a completely westernized home with only one traditional Japanese room. Western influences can be seen throughout Japanese culture, such as fast-food restaurants, music, and the movies.

3   The Japanese also have more time to devote to leisure. Surveys show that spending time with family, friends, home improvement, shopping, and gardening form the mainstream of leisure, together with sports and travel. The number of Japanese making overseas trips has increased notably in recent years. Domestic travel, picnics, hiking and cultural events rank high among favorite activities.

4   Japan is a land with a vibrant and fascinating history, with varied culture, traditions and customs that are hundreds of years old. Still, segments of its society and economy are as new as the microchips in a personal computer.

5   India, meanwhile, is the seventh largest country in the world with a population of nearly one billion people. Only China contains more people. It is a land of deserts, plains, jungles, and mountains. The people speak about 180 different languages and come from many different races and religious backgrounds.

6   Many Indian customs have remained the same for hundreds of years, even though many social and scientific advances have also occurred. For example, cows, which are sacred to many practicing Hindus, are allowed to roam freely in modern business districts. Factory workers may wear traditional costumes on the job. In rural areas, girls take care of younger brothers and sisters at home while their brothers go off to school.

7   For hundreds of years, India was a land of mystery, wealth, and adventure. Columbus thought he was in India when he discovers America. Other European explorers later found India and its famous jewels, rugs, silks and spices. When the British entered India in the late 1700s, they governed many parts of the country. They built roads, telephone systems, and railroads and established a system of education still in place today. Under Gandhi, India achieved independence from Great Britain in 1947. One year later, he was assassinated. Today, India exists as an independent, democratic republic.

58 How could the following sentence be written to reduce wordiness? 9C1

> "Western influences can be seen throughout Japanese culture, such as fast-food restaurants, music, and the movies.

A Western influences, fast-food restaurants, music, and movies, can be seen throughout Japanese culture.

B Western influences, such as fast-food restaurants, music, and movies, can be seen throughout Japanese culture.

C Western influence such as fast-food restaurants and music and movies can be seen throughout Japanese culture.

D Fine as is

59 Which is an example of *irony* found in the passage? 9RL1

A The Japanese also have more time to devote to leisure.

B Segments of Japanese society are as new as the microchips in a personal computer.

C One of the most popular adaptations is their style of dress.

D Traditional clothing is now often only reserved for special occasions.

60 In paragraph six, the term *hindus* probably most closely refers to 9RC3

A factory workers in India.

B people who speak several different languages.

C religious people in India.

D European explorers who discovered India.

61 The passage is most likely written from the perspective of 9RL1

A a person who has visited both countries.

B a travel agent.

C a Hindu.

D a resident of that country.

62 The passage is written in a(n) _____ style and voice 9W1

A objective   C cultural

B biased   D historical

63 What change should be made to the following sentence? 9C1

> Columbus thought he was in India when he discovers America.

A change **discovers** to **discovered**

B change **America** to **United States**

C change **Columbus** to **columbus**

D change **India** to **india**

Read the following passage. Then answer the questions that follow it:

History's Losers: Maryland in the Civil War

1 By the beginning of the 1860s, the secessionist and abolitionist crises throughout the states and territories had come to a boiling point. A number of causes urged voices in the South towards secession, but at their heart was the issue of slavery. Despite his assertions to the contrary, leaders in the Southern states believed Abraham Lincoln would challenge the two-century old practice, which would mean a crippling loss of cheap (albeit unethically-gained) labor. For Lincoln, maintaining the union of states was more important than any other concern, including his personal dislike of the institution of slavery. The Southern states were also angered by the fact that Northern states did not always comply with the Fugitive Slave Clause of the Constitution, which promised that runaway slaves would be returned to their owners and were not free simply because they moved to a free state. The *Dred Scott v*

Sanford decision, in which the Supreme Court stated that former slaves in free states did not have legal standing because they were not citizens, dealt a powerful blow to abolitionists but did not end the controversy. Northerners were unhappy with the decision because it overturned the free-soil movement that attempted to build a slavery free land in the West. Other issues played a role as well. Northerners wanted tariffs on manufactured goods to protect their industries, but Southerners opposed tariffs because they wanted cheaper manufactured goods and did not want to endanger the lucrative trade relations they had with Britain.

2 As tensions rose on both sides of the Mason-Dixon line, the country armed itself and braced for what almost everyone understood to be inevitable. On December 20, 1860, South Carolina decided to secede from the Union. Six other states followed suit by February 1861. Four more would withdraw from the Union when the war began at Bull Run, Virginia on July 21, 1861. This would bring the total number of secessionist states to eleven, enough to outweigh the Union in size if not population and industrial development; enough to become a credible nation in its own right if not checked, one that would almost certainly side against a reduced United States and with its trade-hungry European rivals

3 As the battle lines were drawn, Maryland was split between the North and the South. Maryland was a slave state but did not rely on plantation agriculture to nearly the degree the Deep South did. Evidence taken from the memoirs of Maryland slaves, most notably the great abolitionist and orator Frederick Douglass, suggests that, compared to their brethren farther south, slaves in relatively industrialized Maryland were treated more humanely and given educations and comforts uncommon among slaves in the Cotton Belt of the Deep South. Nevertheless, Maryland bore the weight of both sides of the crisis: owning slaves and wanting to abolish slavery once and for all. Economically, Maryland's wealth was hinged upon its port city, Baltimore; the state was beholden to the industrial centers of the north — most notably Pennsylvania, New York, and Massachusetts — for export of goods, and trembled before the possibility of separation from its northern client-states. Continued slavery and secession would mean losing the markets of those states' cities, devastating its economy.

4 Four slave states remained on the side of the Union (Missouri, Kentucky, Delaware, and Maryland), but Southern sympathizers were common in these states and routinely pressured their governments for secession. To the Union, the secession of Maryland represented a threat to Union border security. If Maryland joined the Confederacy, Washington, DC would find itself surrounded by Confederate territory. Concerned that Confederate sympathizers might succeed in swaying Maryland into the Confederate camp, President Lincoln declared martial law in Maryland and suspended the right of *habeas corpus*, which guarantees a person cannot be imprisoned without being brought before a judge. The president then jailed the strongest supporters of the Confederacy. As a result, Maryland backed down and its legislature voted to remain in the Union. The suspension would not be lifted until the end of the Civil War, four years later.

64 As used in paragraph one, *institution* most nearly means   9RL5

A   a formal place of learning.

B   a mental asylum.

C   a correctional facility.

D   a long-standing practice.

65 The author indicates that the end of the free soil movement and tariffs were   9RL2

A   reasons the South wanted to secede from the North.

B   important reasons for Europe to boycott the South.

C   reasons the North wanted to avoid a war.

D   reasons the North wanted a war with the South.

66 The term *tensions* in paragraph 2 refers to the   9RL5

   A feeling of unease had by one side of the secessionist debate.

   B heated disagreements between North and South.

   C strain to fit everyone in a limited land space.

   D potential consequences of secession.

67 The author cites the Dred Scott Decision in the first paragraph in order to   9RL3

   A describe a particular event in the months leading to the war.

   B show how laws about slaves were already in place.

   C demonstrate how the South ignored laws passed in the North.

   D show the effects of the abolitionist cause.

68 The third paragraph presents a(n)   )3   9W1

   A overview of conditions in Maryland.

   B list of reasons for Maryland to secede.

   C list of sources.

   D introductory aside.

69 In paragraph 3, the phrase *relatively industrialized* indicates that   9RC4

   A there were few industries in Maryland.

   B there were more industries in the South than Maryland.

   C the industries of North and South were related.

   D Maryland was more industrialized than the Southern states.

70 The phrase "hinged upon… Baltimore," within the context of paragraphs three and four, indicates that   9RC3

   A Maryland's economy depended on the prosperity of Baltimore.

   B Baltimore was the only interchange for goods into the South.

   C the North would occupy Baltimore if war broke out.

   D the South wanted to invade Baltimore

71 The emphasis on secession and abolitionism in the passage can be described as   9RL2

   A uninterested and uncaring.

   B enthused and involved.

   C open-minded and hopeful.

   D objective and interested.

72 In paragraph four, "the Confederate camp" is understood to mean   9RC4

   A all the states and people in favor of secession.

   B anyone outside Maryland.

   C everyone in the South.

   D where Robert E. Lee slept.

Read the following poem. Then answer the questions that follow it:

We Wear the Mask

We wear the mask that grins and lies,

It hides our cheeks and shades our eyes,–

This debt we pay to human guile;

With torn and bleeding hearts we smile,

And mouth with myriad subtleties.

Why should the world be over-wise,

In counting all our tears and sighs?

Nay, let them only see us, while

We wear the mask.

We smile, but O great Christ, our cries

To thee from tortured souls arise.

We sing, but oh the clay is vile

Beneath our feet, and long the mile;

But let the world dream otherwise,

We wear the mask!

           - Paul Laurence Dunbar

73 What is this poem mainly about? 9RL2

   A the ways people hide their true feelings from one another

   B how to talk to someone who is upset and trying to hide his or her feelings

   C masks worn on stage during dramas

   D the hardships of humankind

74 The mask described in the poem can be seen as a metaphor for _____. 9RL4

   A crying

   B telling lies

   C hiding emotions

   D praying

75 Why do we "wear a mask"? 9RL1

   A to keep others from seeing our true selves

   B to protect our skin from UV rays

   C to disguise the often bad nature of human-kind

   D to seem more intelligent

Read the following passage. Then answer the questions that follow it:

Mauna Kea Observatory

On the top of an extinct volcano on the Big Island of the state of Hawaii, there is a wonderland for astron-omers. The world's largest astronomical observatory is perched there on the highest point in Hawaii. The very modern scientists who work there share the mountain with ancient sacred grounds of the native islanders.

Mauna Kea is a tall mountain. The summit is 13,796 feet above sea level, but the base of the mountain sits about 35,000 feet below on the floor of the Pacific Ocean. The top of the mountain is so high that even in the tropical location of Hawaii the daytime summer temperature reaches only about 60 degrees F, but can also drop below 32 degrees! Large amounts of snow sometimes fall. The upper elevations often keep some snow year round.

The Mauna Kea Observatory site boasts many telescopes. There is a total of 13 telescopes from 11 countries. In 1968, the University of Hawaii built the first telescope, and university officials also own a second telescope at the observatory. The other telescopes are jointly owned by various universities and countries.

The summit is above 40% of Earth's atmosphere, and it has one of the highest proportions of clear nights, about 300 out of 365, of any location in the world. Mauna Kea is considered to have better conditions for observing than any other developed site. The atmosphere is extremely dry, which is important for the mea-surements scientists are taking.

76 The student probably included the information about the temperatures on the observatory in order to   9W1

A   help the reader realize there are places similar to the observatory all over the world.

B   help the reader realize how drastic the elevation of the observatory is.

C   help the reader identify with the employees at the observatory.

D   entice the reader to visit the observatory.

77 Read the thesis statement from the passage: 9W1

Mauna Kea is a tall mountain.

Which of these thesis statements is more effective than the one above?

A   For many reasons Mauna Kea is a fascinating place.

B   If you get a change, visit Mauna Kea.

C   Mauna Kea, which means "white mountain" in the Hawaiian language, is the tallest mountain in Hawaii.

D   Mauna Kea means "white mountain" in Hawaiian.

78 Read the following sentences: 9W4

"Large amounts of snow sometimes fall. The upper elevations often keep some snow year-round."

What is the *best* way to combine these sentences?

A   "Large amounts of snow sometimes fall, and the upper elevations often keep some snow year-round."

B   "Large amounts of snow sometimes fall, but the upper elevations often keep some snow year-round."

C   "Large amounts of snow sometimes fall, or the upper eleations often keep some snow year-round."

D   "Large amounts of snow sometimes fall, yet the upper elevations often keep some snow year-round."

79 Read this sentence from the passage: 9C1

"The top of the mountain is so high that even in the tropical location of Hawaii the daytime temperature reaches only about 60 degrees F, but it can also drop below 32 degrees!"

What is the correct way to write the underlined part of the sentence?

A   reached   C   have reached

B   had reached   D   no change

80 Which of these shows the correct way to combine the following sentences using a semicolon?   9C2

"The Mauna Kea Observatory site boasts many telescopes. There is a total of 13 telescopes from 11 countries."

A   The Mauna Kea Observatory site boasts many telescopes there is a total of 13 telescopes; from 11 countries.

B   The Mauna Kea Observatory site boasts many telescopes; there is a total of 13 telescopes from 11 countries.

C   The Mauna Kea Observatory site boasts many telescopes; there are a total of 13 telescopes from 11 countries.

D   The Mauna Kea Observatory site boasts; many telescopes there is a total of 13 telescopes from 11 countries.

Appendix
Games and Activities

VOCABULARY (WORD MEANING)

Here are some suggestions for vocabulary games and activities:

1. **Pop Poetry.** Cut out new words, phrases, and accompanying pictures from newspaper and magazine ads, articles, or catalogues. Enlarge the words if they are too small. Make poems or collages by gluing them together on construction paper or poster board. Explain the meanings of the new words and the theme or message of the poem or collage.

2. **Crossword Puzzles.** Locate crossword puzzles in magazines, newspapers, books, or Websites. Working in pairs, students guess at the letters that fit the horizontal and vertical boxes. Looking up some words in the dictionary may be necessary to encourage vocabulary development.

    If you want to learn content-specific vocabulary words, *Crossword Magic* (HLS Duplication, Inc.), a computer software program, takes lists of words and clues and automatically creates a crossword puzzle.

3. **Test Creator Software.** Teachers and students can create their own vocabulary or comprehension tests. This program creates multiple-choice and true/false questions for any subject. Hints and feedback can also be included with the tests. In addition, tests show student scores and track time on tasks. *Test Creator Software* can also be used for classroom presentations and demonstrations with features such as spotlight, magnify, zoom, underline, edit, create sounds, and more. You can download a free demo disk at www.americanbookcompany.com. To place an order, contact American Book Company toll free at 1-888-264-5877.

4. **Shopping Trip.** Students sit in a circle of 5 – 6 persons. In a class, several circles would be formed. The leader starts the chain by saying, "Today, I'm shopping for a short story for dinner. I'll need some ingredients like a plot. A plot is a series of events leading to a climax and resolution." The next student says, "The leader is going to buy a plot, and I am going to buy a character. A character is.. . " Continue around the circle until all of the ingredients are identified and defined. Then the leader can ask, "Who remembers what anyone bought?" Students can volunteer answers such as, "remember that Ben bought some conflicts."

Variation. For variation, students can shop for types of clothing, parts of a car, house, etc. For example, the leader could say, "I'm dressing up for my poem, so I'm going shopping for a verse. A verse is…."

5. **Word Game.** Each week students bring two words and their definitions to class. Students can choose these words from newspapers, magazines, books, television, etc. Weed out duplicate words. In the following week, students can either take a quiz by defining the words, using them in sentences, or taking a multiple-choice test. Students can also form teams with the teacher asking questions and providing prizes for the best scores.

6. **Semantic Map.** A semantic map is a visual aid that helps you understand how words are related to each other. You write a word or concept in a circle in the center of a page. Then you draw branches out of the center of the circle with related words in circles at the end of these branches. You can work in pairs or in groups. For example, the word collaborate relates to the words cooperate, team, communicate, etc. The root word *super* relates to such words as superior, supersede, superstar, etc.

READING COMPREHENSION

Here are some suggested games and activities:

1. **Prereading.** Before reading an article or story, preview the title, the first paragraph, first sentences of each of the other paragraphs, the last paragraph, and any illustrations. Then write down and discuss what you already know about the article or story. This prereading activity helps improve comprehension.

2. **5 Ws and H.** After you preread or skim a selection, you can increase your comprehension by developing questions based on the 5 Ws and H. The 5 Ws stand for *who, what, when, where,* and *why.* The H refers to *how* something happened or was done. After prereading, you should write down questions about the selection based on the 5 W's and H. After reading the selection, you then answer these questions, rereading the text as needed to confirm your answers.

3. **K-W-L.** With K-W-L, you can improve your comprehension of many types of literature. It involves activities you can do before and after you read. **K** stands for what you already *know* about the article. **W** refers to what you *want* to know about the article. **L** stands for *what* you learned from the article. Discussing and writing down your K-W-L thoughts will help you remember what you read.

4. **Think-Alouds.** With think-alouds, you talk to yourself and ask questions while reading a selection. In this way, you can think about and understand the ideas better. You can also form thoughts and questions and write them down as you are reading. As a result, you are starting to learn and retain what you are reading.

5. **Semantic Map.** In format, a semantic map for comprehension is similar to the one you learned about under Vocabulary (Word Meaning). Since it represents ideas visually, it can help you remember what you have read. To summarize what you have learned in a reading selection, create a semantic map of the main ideas and supporting details in the article. Then use it for recalling and reviewing what you have read.

6. **Split-Half Sheets.** With a split-half sheet, you can review the main ideas and facts in a reading selection. Fold a sheet of paper in half lengthwise. On the left side of the sheet, write the questions you wrote based on the 5 Ws and H and K-W-L. On the right side of the sheet, write the answers to each question in your own words. Review the reading selection to check your answers. Then fold back the answer side of the sheet so you cannot see the answers. Then read the questions only and answer as many you can. Place a check besides the questions you got right, and review the ones you missed until you can answer them correctly.

7. **Make Your Own Tests.** You will read more effectively if you make your own tests. After you complete a reading selection, work in a small group to develop practice tests based on the reading. You can develop true/false statements, multiple-choice questions, short answer, or essay questions. The teacher will collect the best test questions and include them in a comprehensive test on the reading selection.

ANALYSIS OF LITERATURE

Here are some suggested games and activities:

1. **A Book a Day.** Reading books often is one of the best ways to develop an understanding and appreciation for literature. The teacher and/or the students choose a book to read in one day. They rip the book apart into sections of 1-2 chapters. Students then divide into groups of two or four. They read their section, take notes on the key ideas, and discuss what they read. Then each group draws pictures and words based on the characters, setting, and events in the section. Finally, the teacher reviews the entire book with the class with each group explaining their section of the book with the pictures and words.

2. **Poetry Gallery.** The teacher posts ten to twenty short to medium-length poems around the room. As the students enter the classroom, they are told to take out their notebooks and walk through the poetry gallery. As they read each poem, they would decide on the one they like the best and the one they dislike the most. They would copy these poems into their notebooks and answer these questions:

   What did you like or dislike about the poem? Describe what is happening in the poem. List a few examples of figurative language. Is there a theme or message the poem is trying to convey? Does this poem have any special meaning for your life? Why? With whom would you share this poem? Why?

3. **Anticipation Guide.** The teacher distributes a handout with a short excerpt from a work of literature. The author's name and the title of the work are omitted. The teacher or a student reads the selection aloud while the students follow along from the handout. For ten to fifteen minutes, the students write their impressions of the author and the work. They should include what we can learn about the author's values and beliefs from the selection. Students then share their impressions with the class. The teacher shares the name of the author and his/her background and the title of the work with the class. Students reread the selection and discuss if their impressions changed as a result of the additional information.

Variation. Students can read the same selection or a new selection and write their impressions of the aesthetic qualities of the work. These qualities include style, diction, figurative language, plot, character, tone, theme, and impact on the reader. They share their impressions, and the teacher then provides additional information about the aesthetic qualities of the work.

4. **Class Newspaper.** This project can help you understand the setting, historical background, author's values and beliefs, and the various cultural influences on a work of literature. For example, after reading *The Outsiders*, students would create a daily city newspaper from the early 1960s. The articles would contain eyewitness accounts of events in the book as well as ads, town announcements, editorials, and other parts of a newspaper from that time. Students work together in groups to revise their articles and create a compete newspaper edition.

   Variation. Instead of a newspaper, students can create an early 1960's radio or television news show and include features and television commercials from that time. Students could also try a talk show format. The teacher and students can choose other works of literature for these types of projects as well.

5. **Point of View.** After reading a work of literature, students write a brief description of the narrator and explain how the story reflects his/her perspective of the characters and events. Identify also the point of view. Students then retell the story from another character's point of view. How does this new perspective change the story? Is it an advantage or disadvantage?

6. **Concept Cards.** You can use concept cards to help you retain key ideas, facts, and definitions about literature. Concept cards are usually 3×5 or 5×8 index cards. On the front of the card, write the concept or term you are learning. On the back of the card, write a definition with an example from literature. Review these cards to reinforce your understanding of literary analysis. You can also use concept cards to test your comprehension of fiction or nonfiction. Write a question on the front of the card and the answer on the back of the card. Then quiz yourself on the information you are trying to learn.

222